Judgement Day

Deeds That Light the Way

OMAR SULEIMAN

KUBE PUBLISHING

In association with

YAQEEN™
INSTITUTE FOR ISLAMIC RESEARCH

Judgement Day:
Deeds That Light the Way

First published in England by
Kube Publishing Ltd
Markfield Conference Centre
Ratby Lane, Markfield
Leicestershire, LE67 9SY
United Kingdom
Tel: +44 (0) 1530 249230

Website: www.kubepublishing.com
Email: info@kubepublishing.com

Cataloguing-in-Publication Data is available from the
British Library.

ISBN 978-1-84774-197-4 Casebound
eISBN 978-1-84774-198-1 Ebook

Proofreading and editing: Wordsmiths
Cover design, Arabic calligraphy and typesetting: Jannah Haque
Printed by: IMAK Ofset, Turkey.

Transliteration Guide

A brief guide to some of the letters and symbols used in the Arabic transliteration in this book.

th	ث	*ḥ*	ح	*dh*	ذ
ṣ	ص	*ḍ*	ض	*ṭ*	ط
ẓ	ظ	ʿ	ع	ʾ	ء

ā	ـَا ـا آ	*ī*	ـِي	*ū*	ـُو

ﷺ May the peace and blessings of Allah be upon him.	عَزَّ وَجَلَّ Glorified and Majestic (is He).	رَضِيَ ٱللَّهُ عَنْهُ May Allah be pleased with him.
رَضِيَ ٱللَّهُ عَنْهَا May Allah be pleased with her.	رَضِيَ ٱللَّهُ عَنْهُمَا May Allah be pleased with them both.	عَلَيْهِ ٱلسَّلَامُ May peace be upon him.
عَلَيْهَا ٱلسَّلَامُ May peace be upon her.	عَلَيْهِمَا ٱلسَّلَامُ May peace be upon them both.	

Contents

Introduction

There is an inevitable and undeniable truth that, one predetermined day, we will die and depart from this world. But this naturally leads to the existential question of what will occur in the next domain. Regarding the nature of the worldly and otherworldly realities, ʿAlī ibn Abī Ṭālib ﵁ has stated:

اِرْتَحَلَتِ الدُنيَا مُدْبِرَةً وَارْتَحَلَتِ الآخِرَةُ مُقْبِلَةً، وَلِكُلٍّ وَاحِدَةٍ مِنْهَا بَنُونَ،
فَكُونُوا مِنْ أَبْنَاءِ الآخِرَةِ، وَلَا تَكُونُوا مِنْ أَبْنَاءِ الدُنيَا،
فإنَّ اليَوْمَ عَمَلٌ وَلَا حِسَابَ، وَغدًا حسَابٌ وَلَا عَمَل.

"The life of this world is fast departing, while the life of the Hereafter is fast approaching, with every one of them having their own children. Thus, opt to be the children of the Hereafter, and not of this world. For in the present state there are deeds without any reckoning, but in the case of tomorrow there will be a reckoning without deeds."

Even the most marginal amount of good done in the Earth will be accepted and rewarded by Allah ﷻ in the other world, provided it is done with a sincere heart. But in the Hereafter, having every ounce of gold in one's possession will not confer on one the slightest benefit. From the moment one rises from one's burial place and assumes one's spot in the assembly of resurrected humans, all dynamics change.

In the otherworldly plane, one will be subject to a number of trials and tribulations: one's official records will be weighed in the *Mīzān* (Scales) and one will be required to cross the *Ṣirāṭ* (Bridge-Over-Hell). In all these circumstances, the true saviour will be one's own virtuous deeds: they will physically appear and protect one from the heat of the Last Day by producing beneficial shade, illuminating one's path so that one may navigate through the pitch-black darkness that engulfs one, and even testify on one's behalf in the presence of the Lord of the worlds ﷻ. In sum, one's virtuous deeds will be the decisive factor in ensuring that one becomes an inhabitant of Paradise. Instead of constantly speculating and postulating when the Day of Judgement will occur, the Muslim should devote his energies to performing good deeds so that he may be assisted in the trials that he will face in the other world.

فَأَمَّا مَن ثَقُلَتْ مَوَٰزِينُهُۥ فَهُوَ فِى عِيشَةٍ رَّاضِيَةٍ

"So as for those whose scales are heavy with good deeds, they will be in a life of bliss."

AL-QĀRIʿAH, 6–7

1

After One Dies

As a thought experiment, I would like you to perceive yourself as being a parent in relation to your deeds. You bring them into being, nurture them, and facilitate their development while anticipating a variety of subsequent gains and benefits. The only difference between children and deeds is that while the former are tangible and concrete beings, the latter are abstract entities. But just as an ageing parent wishes to obtain benefits from his or her children in this world, one also hopes to benefit from one's deeds in the Hereafter through obtaining eternal bliss and comfort. Keeping the latter points in mind, the key questions ultimately are: how many deeds we have nurtured and raised in this temporal world? And in what state shall we find them in the next world?

The great ascetic Ḥātim al-Aṣamm ﷺ once shared the following poignant observation:

إِنِّي نَظَرْتُ إِلَى الخَلْقِ فَرَأَيْتُ كُلَّ وَاحِدٍ يُحِبُّ مَحْبُوبًا فَإِذَا ذَهَبَ إِلَى القَبْرِ فَارَقَهُ مَحْبُوبُهُ، فَجَعَلْتُ الحَسَنَاتِ مَحْبُوبِي فَإِذَا دَخَلْتُ القَبْرَ دَخَلَتْ مَعِي.

"I pondered over the state of humankind and found that everyone confers his or her love upon someone. But once he or she passes away, the beloved object turns away from him or her. Thus, I decided to make my virtuous deeds the object of my love, so that when I enter my grave, they will accompany me."

Likewise, the Prophet ﷺ said:

يَتْبَعُ المَيِّتَ ثَلَاثَةٌ: أَهْلُهُ وَمَالُهُ وَعَمَلُهُ؛ فَيَرْجِعُ أَهْلُهُ وَمَالُهُ وَيَبْقَى عَمَلُهُ.

"Three things follow the deceased person to his grave: his family, wealth, and deeds. After the burial is completed, his family and wealth turn back and depart from the grave, while his collection of deeds will follow him and become his sole companion."

The beautiful lesson encapsulated in the aforementioned *ḥadīth* is reiterated in the following verse of the Qur'ān:

يَوْمَ لَا يَنفَعُ مَالٌ وَلَا بَنُونَ.

"...the Day when neither wealth nor children will be of any benefit."[1]

[1] *Al-Shu'arā'*, 88.

The moment one enters the realm of the otherworld, the sole source of comfort and acceptable form of currency will be one's good deeds. In a narration, the Prophet ﷺ is reported to have once asked his Companions:

هَلْ تَدْرُونَ فِيمَا أُنْزِلَتْ فَإِنَّ لَهُ مَعِيشَةً ضَنكًا وَنَحْشُرُهُۥ يَوْمَ ٱلْقِيَـٰمَةِ أَعْمَىٰ.

"Do you know regarding whom the verse 'But whoever turns away from My Reminder will certainly have a miserable life, then We will raise them up blind on the Day of Judgement'[2] *was revealed?"*

In response, the Companions said: "Allah and His Messenger know best." The Prophet ﷺ then mentioned that this verse describes the constricted state and peril of the disbeliever when he enters his grave. He further elaborated on the horrors found in this realm by adding:

وَالَّذِي نَفْسِي بِيَدِهِ إِنَّهُ لَيُسَلَّطُ عَلَيْهِمْ تِسْعَةٌ وَتِسْعُونَ تِنِّينًا.

"By the One in Whose Hand is my soul, when they are placed in the grave, ninety-nine dragons will subdue them."

Furthermore, the Prophet ﷺ added that the plight of these disbelievers in the grave will be of the utmost severity, since every dragon will consist of seventy serpents, each of which has seven heads. Every one of these heads will be viciously stinging and maiming the disbelievers until they are resurrected on the Day of Judgement. But for the believer, his or her state of affairs during this testing time will be different, since it will

---

2 *Ṭāhā*, 124.

Good deeds,
such as fasting,
preservation of ties
of kinship and charity
will be ready to
intervene and protect
the believer in the
grave even before
the angels appear
to hold him or her
to account.

be the first time that his or her deeds—which represent his or her metaphysical children—will come to his or her aid. In fact, they will be ready to protect the believer even before the angels appear to hold him or her to account. In a beautiful and moving *ḥadīth*, the Prophet ﷺ stated that upon being placed in his or her burial place and hearing his or her family and loved ones depart, the believer will be all alone and subjected to the trial of the grave. At this moment, one can be exposed to the most severe form of punishment, as one is fully at the mercy of Allah's angels. But it is at this crucial juncture that one's prayer will appear and place itself between one's head and the angels, saying:

مَا قِبَلِي مَدْخَلٌ.

"You shall not find a way to pass through me."

The *ḥadīth* notes that, as the punishment attempts to envelop one from the right side, one's *ṣiyām* (fasting) will appear and intervene by protecting one from any subsequent punishment. Just like a guard, it will stand and shield one and say:

مَا قِبَلِي مَدْخَلٌ.

"You shall not find a way to pass through me."

One's *zakāt* will then present itself at one's left side and repeat the same words:

مَا قِبَلِي مَدْخَلٌ.

"You shall not find a way to pass through me."

To complete the protection process, one's *ṣadaqah* (voluntary charity), *ṣilat al-raḥim* (preservation of ties of kinship), and other virtuous deeds will stand before one's feet, and reiterate the same defiant words:

مَا قِبَلِي مَدْخَلٌ.

"You shall not find a way to pass through me."

At this juncture, the deceased person will be ordered to sit up, and he will willingly oblige. Then the Prophet ﷺ related that the following image will be produced before the person:

مَثُلَتْ لَهُ الشَّمْسُ وَقَدْ دَنَتْ لِلْغُرُوبِ

"The Sun will be made to appear before him while it is close to setting."

In other words, the person will be given the impression that the time of the Maghrib prayer is nearing. In such a setting, the believer's immediate reaction would be to prepare himself for the *ṣalāh* (prayer). In fact, whenever the mindful and God-conscious person awakens at a non-customary time or loses his or her bearings, he will immediately become apprehensive, wondering whether or not he or she had missed a prayer. This will in fact be the very reaction of the deceased believer, as he will plead with the angels and say:

دَعُونِي أُصَلِّي.

"Let me pray."

However, the angels will defer his appeal by first asking him a series of fundamental questions, which consist of the following:

مَنْ رَبُّكَ؟ مَا دِينُكَ؟ مَنْ نَبِيُّكَ؟

*"Who is your Lord? What is your religion?
Who is your Prophet?"*

First and foremost, the only way a person will be able to effectively identify his Lord ﷻ is if he or she consistently worshipped Him during his lifetime. Furthermore, a person will not be able to pinpoint his or her religion unless he actively practised it. Lastly, the deceased will not be able to know who Prophet Muhammad ﷺ was unless he loved him and followed his teachings. If all the aforementioned questions are answered correctly, a voice from the Heavens will issue the following proclamation:

صَدَقَ عَبْدِي.

"My slave has spoken the truth."

In another version of the *ḥadīth*, the Prophet ﷺ notes that while the angels may appear disconcerting at first sight, they will comfort the believer after he correctly answers the three questions by stating:

كُنَّا نَعْلَمُ أَنَّكَ تَقُولُ هَذَا.

"We knew that you would say all this."

With the believer's safety now secured, Allah ﷻ will give the angels the following set of commands:

أَفْرِشُوهُ مِنَ الْجَنَّةِ وَافْتَحُوا لَهُ بَابًا إِلَى الْجَنَّةِ وَأَلْبِسُوهُ مِنَ الْجَنَّةِ.

"Provide him the furnishings of Jannah, open a gate which will reach (and allow him to see his spot in) Jannah, and clothe him with the garments of Jannah."

After being adorned with the garments of *Jannah* and being provided a direct window to the infinite pleasures found in the next world, the occupier of the grave will ultimately find himself or herself in a blissful state. His or her grave will be expanded to a point beyond his or her perception or sight. In fact, despite still being in his or her grave, the deceased will have an early sense of the bounties and wonders that await him or her. While in this wonderful setting, the deceased person will be greeted by an unexpected visitor who has a beautiful face, wonderful fragrance, and delightful attire. The latter will then proceed to say:

أَبْشِرْ بِالَّذِي يَسُرَّكَ، هَذَا يَوْمُكَ الَّذِي كُنْتَ تُوعَدُ.

"I give you glad tidings of that which will make you pleased. For this is your day, which you were in fact promised with."

In the grave,
a righteous person will
be shown his or her final
place throughout the
morning and evening.
A metaphysical window
will be erected which
will show his or her final
destination: the eternal
realm of Paradise.

Amazed and puzzled by this statement, the deceased will interrogate the visitor and enquire:

مَنْ أَنْتَ؟ فَوَجْهُكَ الوَجْهُ يَجِيءُ بِالخَيْرِ.

"Who are you? For that face of yours can only belong to the one who bears good news."

The visitor will swiftly address the deceased person's query by stating:

أَنَا عَمَلُكَ الصَّالِحُ.

"I am your good deeds."

One can hardly imagine how one's deeds can become personified in this metaphysical realm. But our authentic religious sources explicitly indicate that whoever upholds the religious guidance imparted by Allah ﷻ and His Messenger ﷺ, then all his deeds—including his recitation of the Qur'ān, prayer, fasting, and charity—will manifest themselves as a single living person and expressly give good news to their doer. Thus, the beauty and utility of good deeds do not simply lie in their protective abilities, but they also include their status as bearers of good news. In other words, not only will one's deeds be personified, but they will also be one's greatest source of benefit and comfort.

There is a plethora of narrations which highlight the categories of people who will be protected from the punishment of the grave in absolute terms. These include the *shuhadā'* (martyrs) who die in the battlefield, as well as people who fall under the same ruling, such as the ones who die due to a terminal stomach illness. Individuals who die during a virtuous time—such as the day or night of Friday—will also receive a special and divine form of protection from the punishment of the grave. At the same time, however, there are particular sins and vices whose commission will lead to punishment in the grave. A person must avoid falling into such misdeeds. Such immoral transgressors include the consumers of *ribā* (interest), adulterers, slanderers, and the those who fail to observe the rules of *ṭahārah* (ritual purification) for their acts of worship. One should be aware of one's current moral status and mode of behaviour, since every deed will affect one's standing in the grave and on the Last Day.

In a beautiful *ḥadīth*, the Prophet ﷺ said that upon dying and being placed in his or her grave, a righteous person will be shown his or her final place throughout the morning and evening. A metaphysical window will be erected which will show his or her final destination: the eternal realm of *Jannah*. Likewise, if the person is one of the inhabitants of Hellfire, then he or she will be provided a window that will show his or her place in this eternal realm of damnation. Regardless of his or her final destination, he or she will be shown one more place: his or her point of disembarkation on Judgement Day. When the image of the latter is shown to him or her, it will be said:

هَذَا مَقْعَدُكَ الَّذِي تُبْعَثُ إِلَيْهِ يَوْمَ الْقِيَامَةِ.

"This is the location where you will be resurrected on the Day of Judgement."

For the believer, all these images will be a joyful experience. After all, his or her deeds are already accompanying and comforting him or her over there, while he or she is also adorned with beautiful garments from Paradise as well as being provided a window into the blissful realm. While being engulfed in such pleasures, this blessed person will invoke his Lord and say:

رَبِّ أَقِمِ السَّاعَةَ، رَبِّ أَقِمِ السَّاعَةَ ، رَبِّ أَقِمِ السَّاعَةَ.

"My Lord, let the Hour be now! My Lord, let the Hour be now! My Lord, let the Hour be now!"

فَأَمَّا مَن ثَقُلَتْ مَوَازِينُهُ فَهُوَ فِي عِيشَةٍ رَّاضِيَةٍ

"So as for those whose scales are heavy with good deeds, they will be in a life of bliss."

AL-QĀRIʿAH, 6–7

2

When the Trumpet Sounds

In essence, asking Allah ﷻ for a good ending necessitates aspiring to live a consistently good life in this ephemeral world and attaining a noble beginning in the Hereafter. In other words, the believer is not solely concerned with the current realm in which he or she is situated, but instead he or she is preoccupied with his or her spiritual standing vis-à-vis the Lord Who controls all planes of existence. The God-conscious person is determined to pass into and depart from this world in a manner that is pleasing to his or her Lord ﷻ. However, a person's plea for a faithful conclusion in his or her life must be sincerely articulated such that it corresponds to his or her current ethical behaviour.

The Prophet ﷺ once encountered a man who earnestly wished to die in the battlefield as a martyr. He ﷺ carefully listened to his wish, and then said:

إِنْ تَصْدُقِ اللّٰهَ يُصْدِقْكَ.

"If you are truthful to Allah, then He will be truthful to you."

In this regard, it is well known how fervently 'Umar ibn al-Khaṭṭāb ﷺ sought to die as a *shahīd* in the city of Madinah, despite such an outcome *prima facie* being counterintuitive, if not impossible. Yet, Allah ﷻ positively responded to 'Umar's supplication and facilitated his martyrdom, for he was stabbed while leading the Fajr prayer in the Prophet's mosque.

It would be a serious mistake to presume that these tales and accounts are simply a thing of the past. In actual fact, similar events and occurrences happened during modern history as well. For instance, it is related that the well-known Egyptian preacher Shaykh Kishk ﷺ regularly made the following *du'ā'* (supplication) while preaching from the *minbar* (pulpit):

اللَّهُمَّ أَحْيِنِي إِمَامًا وَأَمِتْنِي إِمَامًا وَاحْشُرْنِي وَأَنَا سَاجِدٌ بَيْنَ يَدَيْكَ يَا رَبَّ العَالَمِينَ.

"O Allah, permit me to live as an Imām, permit me to die as an Imām, and have me resurrected while I am in a state of sujūd (prostration) before You, O Lord of the worlds."

Amazingly, during one particular Friday prayer, Allah ﷻ granted his wish by having him die while he was in a state of *sujūd*, with his face on the ground. One can only imagine the immense blessings conferred on a person who awakens in the Hereafter while observing the *sujūd* or reciting words of *dhikr* (remembrance). At this juncture, another notable story may be cited. There was a man who was performing the *Ḥajj* rituals alongside the Prophet ﷺ, but in the midst of the process, he tragically fell off his mount while he was reciting the devotional formula known as the *talbiyah*, which consists of the following words:

لَبَّيْكَ اللَّهُمَّ لَبَّيْكَ.

"Here I am at Your service, O Allah, here I am at Your service."

Because he died while still being engaged in this act of worship, the Prophet ﷺ ordered the Companions not to terminate this man's sanctified state of *iḥrām*, adding that the man would be resurrected on the Last Day while chanting the *talbiyah*.

Keeping these stories in mind, it becomes evident that a person will be resurrected in line with the deed he or she was performing in the last moments of his or her life. Thus, every single one of us should ensure that we make our good deeds the prominent and dominant aspect of our daily lives. To build a home in Paradise, one must be aware that the building process begins in the temporal plane of this universe. In order to die in a blessed and pious state, one must make sure to live in that manner as well in all stages of one's life, since the last moments of one's existence in this world determine the quality of one's first moments in the other realm. These themes are reflected in the following verse of the Qur'ān:

وَنُفِخَ فِي الصُّورِ فَصَعِقَ مَنْ فِي السَّمَاوَاتِ وَمَنْ فِي الْأَرْضِ إِلَّا مَنْ شَاءَ اللَّهُ ۖ ثُمَّ نُفِخَ فِيهِ أُخْرَىٰ فَإِذَا هُمْ قِيَامٌ يَنْظُرُونَ.

"The Trumpet will be blown and all those in the Heavens and all those on the Earth will fall dead, except those Allah wills. Then it will be blown again and they will rise up at once, looking on."[3]

---

[3] *Al-Zumar*, 68.

As this verse clearly indicates, once the Trumpet is blown every human being will immediately arise, while carrying on with the same activities and undertakings they were performing immediately before they passed away. This same conclusion is reiterated in yet another verse, where Allah ﷻ states:

لَا يَحْزُنُهُمُ الْفَزَعُ الْأَكْبَرُ وَتَتَلَقَّاهُمُ الْمَلَائِكَةُ هَٰذَا يَوْمُكُمُ الَّذِي كُنتُمْ تُوعَدُونَ.

"The Supreme Horror will not disturb them, and the Angels will greet them, 'This is your Day, which you have been promised.'" [4]

If one carefully reflects on the above verse, one will notice that the angels are using, in their address, the very same words that were said to the inhabitants of the grave. This is not a coincidence, and instead reflects the continuity that exists between the occurrence of death in this world and resurrection in the Hereafter.

In this context, another topic which must be addressed is determining when one will encounter one's deeds in the next world. The Prophet ﷺ has provided a definitive answer to this question in an emotional and moving *ḥadīth*. In this report, the Prophet ﷺ mentions that once the ground splits asunder and one rises from one's grave, one will be almost immediately approached by a figure resembling an emaciated man, with the latter enquiring:

هَلْ تَعْرِفُنِي؟

"Do you know who I am?"

---

[4] *Al-Anbiyā'*, 103.

One will be, at that point, confused and admits one's ignorance of the interrogator's identity. The *ḥadīth* notes that the mysterious man will identify himself by stating:

أَنَا صَاحِبُكَ الْقُرْآنُ الَّذِي أَظْمَأْتُكَ فِي الْهَوَاجِرِ، وَأَسْهَرْتُ لَيْلَكَ، وَإِنَّ كُلَّ تَاجِرٍ مِنْ وَرَاءِ تِجَارَتِهِ، وَأَنْتَ الْيَوْمَ مِنْ وَرَاءِ كُلِّ تِجَارَةٍ، قَالَ: فَيُعْطَى الْمُلْكَ بِيَمِينِهِ، وَالْخُلْدَ بِشِمَالِهِ، وَيُوضَعُ عَلَى رَأْسِهِ تَاجُ الْوَقَارِ.

"'I am your companion, the Qur'ān, namely the one who used to keep you thirsty during the day and sleepless at night. Every trader out there in the world was in pursuit of his trade, but today you transcend all kinds of trade.' Dominion will be granted to his right hand, while eternal life will be conferred on his left. And the crown of dignity will be placed on his head."

This miraculous encounter will occur the moment one is resurrected from one's grave. There are further wonders that the companion of the Qur'ān will experience in the other world, but these will be discussed later. Regarding the proceedings of the Day of Judgement, Allah ﷻ states:

وَجَاءَتْ كُلُّ نَفْسٍ مَّعَهَا سَائِقٌ وَشَهِيدٌ.

"Each soul will come forth with an Angel to drive it and another to testify."[5]

The first angel will take the resurrected person to his or her place of accountability, while the second will proceed alongside him or her carrying his or her record of deeds. Every person

---

[5] *Qāf*, 21.

will be proceeding towards his or her Creator in a different fashion and pace. On this matter, the Prophet ﷺ said:

إِنَّكُمْ مَحْشُورُونَ رِجَالًا وَرُكْبَانًا وَتُجَرُّونَ عَلَى وُجُوهِكُمْ.

"You will all be resurrected, walking, riding, or dragged on your faces."

Furthermore, the Prophet ﷺ noted that for the case of the riders, there are a number of noteworthy variations. It may actually be the case that there are multiple individuals mounted on the same animal. But other animals will only be carrying a single rider; because of the nobility of this rider, he or she will be blessed with an animal to ride on. Furthermore, the Prophet ﷺ noted that the animals will differ in their quality, that is in terms of their pace and manoeuvrability. Not all animals will advance according to the same pace. The versatility and speed of the mount will be commensurate with the level of obedience and piety that the rider demonstrated to Allah ﷻ in the temporal world as manifested in his or her good deeds. This report of the Prophet ﷺ amazed the Companions, as they were surprised to be informed that there will be individuals in the Hereafter who will be trekking on their faces. In response, the Prophet indicated that it is Allah ﷻ alone Who decides such affairs by stating:

الَّذِي أَمْشَاهُمْ عَلَى أَرْجُلِهِمْ قَادِرٌ عَلَى أَنْ يُمْشِيَهُمْ عَلَى وُجُوهِهِمْ.

"The One Who made them walk on their feet is capable of making them walk on their faces."

The Prophet ﷺ also mentioned that on the Day of Judgement, all people will be gathered in a white and barren plane of land—as smooth and homogenous as a loaf of white bread—that will be devoid of any topographical markers or landmarks. In addition, there will be no trees or prominent structures that will provide them shade on that sweltering and scorching day. The Messenger of Allah ﷺ also noted that those gathered on this plane will be naked, barefoot, and uncircumcised, which strongly mirrors the way in which they were born. Their mobility will also be hampered, as they will be confined to the space where they were resurrected on. These revelations shocked the Prophet's wife ʿĀʾishah ﵂; the latter asked whether the people would be staring at each other in their nakedness. However, the Prophet said ﷺ:

لِكُلِّ امْرِئٍ مِنْهُمْ يَوْمَئِذٍ شَأْنٌ يُغْنِيهِ.

"Every person will be engulfed in their own affair that Day."

In other words, every human being will be concerned with his or her own trial and standing to the extent that he or she will not be bothered by his or her state of nakedness. The Prophet ﷺ then added that the sun will be at such a low altitude that it could be touched by the onlookers around them. Yet, in this same narration, he also noted how the spiritual and physical effects on those gathered will vary depending on their actions and moral standing. For instance, the Prophet ﷺ noted:

فَيَكُونُونَ فِي الْعَرَقِ بِقَدْرِ أَعْمَالِهِمْ.

"The elevation of their sweat will be in accordance with their deeds."

To build a home in Paradise, one must be aware that the building process begins in the temporal plane of this universe. In order to die in a blessed and pious state, one must make sure to live in that manner as well in all stages of one's life.

As the *ḥadīth* further elaborates, the sweat of some people will reach their ankles; for others it will reach their knees; while for some, it will reach up to their waist. And finally, some individuals will be fully engulfed by and immersed in their own sweat.

At this very moment, there will also be individuals who will be swallowed whole by earth. Such a punishment is meted out to people who unlawfully expropriated the land of others in this world. The Prophet ﷺ warned that the one who commits such a sin will be made to descend seven consecutive layers of land on the Day of Judgement. Additionally, there are other sins which will lower one's standing on that day both literally and figuratively. For instance, one who fails to pay *zakāt* on one's riches will be subject to a specific punishment, namely by having one's wealth heated and placed on one's body. Other sins that will increase the gravity of one's standing on that faithful day include consuming that which has been acquired through unlawful means. Conversely, the commission of good deeds will raise one's standing on the Day of Judgement both in literal and figurative terms. For instance, individuals who consistently spent their wealth and worldly earnings for the sake of Allah ﷻ will not only be protected from the intense heat and being swallowed by earth, but they will also be blessed with shade that will protect them from the intense sun rays. The Prophet ﷺ alluded to this fact when he said:

كُلُّ امْرِئٍ فِي ظِلِّ صَدَقَتِهِ حَتَّى يَفْصِلَ بَيْنَ النَّاسِ.

"Every person will be placed under the shade of their charity until Allah judges between the people."

Contrary to what some may understand from the above Prophetic saying, this narration is not actually alluding to the shade of Allah's Throne, since that is an eminent station conferred upon a limited number of outstanding individuals. Instead, this *ḥadīth* is applicable to virtually all Muslims, since it indicates how one's charity will turn into shade on the Day of Judgement, thereby protecting them from the heat and discomfort they will experience upon standing on the plane where all humanity will be gathered. Thus, the morally upright Muslim will arise on the Day of Judgement while being accompanied and comforted by the Qur'ān. In addition, his or her charity will also manifest in the form of a comforter and protector. This will lessen his or her burdens and allow them to overcome the trials and tests of a day that will be equal to 50,000 earthly years.

"So as for those whose scales are heavy with good deeds, they will be in a life of bliss."

AL-QĀRI'AH, 6–7

3

Attires of Honour or Humiliation

Besides simply serving the conventional function of covering one's body, clothing is also deemed to be a marker of one's socioeconomic status and social rank. There are even clothes which are assigned to specific classes and castes to distinguish them from others. Such discriminatory practices are undoubtedly problematic and employed to give the elite false notions of dominance and superiority. These types of despotic customs explain the motives and messages encapsulated in the popular saying, "Expensive clothing is a poor man's attempt to appear prosperous." As a result of such oppressive practices, Islam sought to create a relatively homogenous and egalitarian image of society, as manifested in the *Ḥajj* ceremony. This is best exemplified in the practice of *iḥrām*, whereby all the worshippers wear the same simple garments and stand before their Lord in one row. In a single voice, all these congregants call upon Allah ﷻ, Who alone is aware of each person's true moral rank and standing.

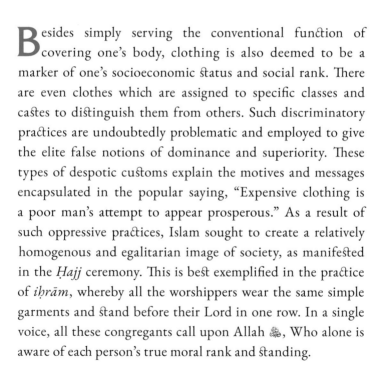

On the Day of Judgement, one's articles of clothing will be sewn and fashioned with one's righteous deeds and actions; one's deeds signify and represent garments of mercy and protection. This theme has been reiterated in several verses of the Qur'ān. For instance, Allah ﷻ uses the phrase *libās al-taqwā* (attire of piety), which denotes a spiritual form of covering that one attains by upholding the commandments of one's Creator. Likewise, in a powerful verse, Allah ﷻ issues the following imperative:

وَثِيَابَكَ فَطَهِّرْ.

"Purify your garments."[6]

According to numerous scholars, this ordinance's import is figurative, since it indicates one should purify one's deeds and undertakings. To this list of verses, one may also add the Qur'ānic passage in which Allah ﷻ metaphorically describes wives as being a garment, since they are a source of adornment, protection, and concealment for their husbands. The needles which one must use in this metaphysical sewing process for the other world consist of the current hours and days currently at one's disposal. Should one expend one's lifetime in this world doing virtuous acts, then one's efforts would culminate in the manifestation of a blessed garment in the Hereafter. As for the heedless and disobedient ones, then they will find themselves deprived of any garment or form of covering in the Hereafter. In this regard, Umm Salamah رضي الله عنها narrated that, on one particular night, she witnessed the

[6] *Al-Muddaththir*, 4.

Prophet ﷺ frequently stating:

كَمْ مِنْ كَاسِيَةٍ فِي الدُّنْيَا عَارِيَةٌ يَوْمَ القِيَامَةِ.

"How many people are well-dressed in this world, only for them to be completely naked on the Day of Judgement!"

In another sound *ḥadīth*, Abū Saʿīd al-Khudrī ؓ related that he heard the Messenger of Allah ﷺ state:

إِنَّ المَيِّتَ يُبْعَثُ فِي ثِيَابِهِ الَّتِي يَمُوتُ فِيهَا.

"The deceased will be resurrected in the same garments he passed away in."

This narration requires some reflection and pause, since it *prima facie* opposes the import of the widely reported and rigorously authentic *ḥadīth* which states that people will be resurrected on the Day of Judgement in a state of nakedness. Some scholars attempted to reconcile these two reports by stating that the deceased is first resurrected with the clothes they were wearing at the point of death, but they will be stripped of them shortly thereafter. Others noted that the reference to clothes in the latter report is an allusion to the *kafan* (shroud) put on the deceased after death, which also constitutes a distinguishing marker of the Muslim community. Other interpreters argue that the garments referred to in the report are one's deeds. Regardless of the exact meaning of the *ḥadīth*, there are numerous indicators which suggest that, as far as clothing in the Hereafter are concerned, priority will be given to the people of righteousness. More specifically, such a privilege is closely tied to being a person of honour, which is achieved through two things: (1) being characterised with personal piety, and (2) discharging the rights of one's brothers and sisters in Islam.

The Prophet ﷺ informed his Ummah that the first person to be dressed in the Hereafter will be none other than our father Ibrahim ﵇. The scholars have noted that he will not be simply conferred this status due to his honourable status and prayers for a divine rank, but due to the humiliation he had to undergo when emerging naked from the fire he was thrown in. Allah ﷻ will handsomely compensate him for the difficulties and discomfort he underwent by reversing the situation: instead of being naked in front of his people, on the Day of Judgement, Ibrahim ﵇ will be clothed and honoured with a special garment, while his community will remain exposed.

Unfortunately, there are people in this world who attempt to gain fame and prominence by donning ostentatious clothing in front of their communities. Regarding such people, the Prophet ﷺ has warned:

مَنْ لَبِسَ ثَوْبَ شُهْرَةٍ فِي الدُّنْيَا، أَلْبَسَهُ اللهُ ثوبَ مَذلَّةٍ يَوْمَ القِيَامَةِ.

"Whoever wears a pretentious garment in this world,
Allah will clothe them in a garment of humiliation
on the Day of Judgement."

In another narration, the Prophet ﷺ indicated the immense rewards conferred upon the one who leaves such ostentatious articles of clothing:

مَنْ تَرَكَ اللِّبَاسَ تَوَاضُعًا للهِ وَهُوَ يَقْدِرُ عَلَيْهِ، دَعَاهُ اللّٰهُ يَوْمَ القِيَامَةِ عَلَى رُؤُوسِ الخَلَائِقِ حَتَّى يُخَيِّرَهُ مِنْ أَيِّ حُلَلِ الإِيمَانِ شَاءَ يَلْبَسُهَا.

"Whoever gives up fine articles of clothing out of humility towards Allah while having the ability (to wear them), Allah will call him on the Day of Judgement in the presence of the entire creation and provide him the choice to wear any garment of faith he desires."

These reports may seem surprising at first glance since, *prima facie*, they suggest that wearing fine items of clothing is blameworthy, if not outright impermissible. Yet, by observing other reports, one knows that Allah ﷻ loves to see His slave show the blessings he has been bestowed in this world. Thus, these censorious *ḥadīths* are understood to refer to extravagant items of clothing that impinge on moral standards at the individual and societal levels. For instance, men are prohibited from wearing garments that are made of silk, for the Prophet ﷺ warned that the males who wear it in this world will be deprived of it in *Jannah*. Likewise, it is prohibited for individuals to wear forbiddingly expensive items of clothing in front of the poor and other underprivileged members of society who cannot afford them, as such doing so will break their spirits and ultimately disrupt the positive social bonds of the community. Lastly, it is always prohibited to wear a garment or dress with the intention of showing off. But if one wishes to wear a modestly valuable piece of clothing, it is permissible as long as one's intention is pure.

Beyond the blessing of the metaphysical garment, one's recitation of the Qur'ān and *ṣadaqah* (voluntary charity) will appear in the form of a supporting companion and shade respectively. The Qur'ān will personally supplicate to Allah ﷻ and intercede on one's behalf on the Day of Judgement by saying:

يَارَبِّ حُلَّهُ، فَيلْبِسُ تَاجَ الكَرَامَةِ، ثُمَّ يَقُولُ: يَارَبِّ زِدْهُ، فَيَلْبِسُ حُلَّةَ الكَرَامَةِ، ثُمَّ يَقُولُ: يَارَبِّ اِرْضَ عَنْهُ، فَيَرْضَى عَنْهُ.

"[The Qur'ān will say:] 'O Lord, decorate him,' so he will be adorned with the crown of nobility. Then it will say, 'O Lord, increase him [in good].' As a result, he will be clothed with a suit of nobility. Then it will say: 'O Lord, be pleased with them.' Subsequently, Allah will be pleased with them."

In fact, through Allah's divine justice and unlimited favours, one will be even further honoured by being allowed to rise in rank for every verse one recites:

فَيُقَالُ لَهُ: إِقْرَأْ وَارْقَ وَتُزَادُ بِكُلِّ آيَةٍ حَسَنَةً.

"It will be said to him: 'Recite and ascend in nobility for every verse you recite.'"

Such blessings are not restricted to the reciter and companion of the Qur'ān. In fact, the Prophet ﷺ said that the parents of such a person will also be blessed by being dressed in elegant and exquisite garments that will be incomparable to any forms of attire found in this world. Amazed at their good fortune, the parents will not be able to hide their happiness:

فَيَقُولَانِ: بِمَ كُسِينَا؟

"They will both say: 'For what reason have we been dressed in these garments?'"

The following response will be issued:

فَيُقَالُ: بِأَخْذِ وَلَدِكُمَا الْقُرْآنَ.

"It will be said: 'Due to your child's memorisation of the Qur'ān.'"

Another key form of protection that will manifest in the Day of Judgement consists of the various forms of charity expended in this temporal world. Such acts of generosity need not be strictly material in order for one to benefit from them in the Hereafter. For instance, in one notable report, the Prophet ﷺ said:

مَا مِنْ مُؤْمِنٍ يُعَزِّي أَخَاهُ بِمُصِيبَةٍ إِلَّا كَسَاهُ اللهُ مِنْ حُلَلِ الْكَرَامَةِ يَوْمَ الْقِيَامَةِ.

"There is no believer who consoles his brother at the moment of calamity except that Allah will dress him in noble garments on the Day of Resurrection."

But perhaps the most powerful narration in this regard is the one which indicates how Allah ﷻ will return the favour for any act of generosity or benefit that a Muslim confers upon his brother. In this moving *ḥadīth*, the Prophet ﷺ said:

وَأَيُّمَا مُؤْمِنٍ كَسَا مُؤْمِنًا عَلَى عُرْيٍ كَسَاهُ اللهُ مِنْ خُضْرِ الجَنَّةِ.

"Any believer who clothes a naked believer in this world will be clothed by Allah with the green garments of Jannah."

Thus, the Muslim should be aware that Allah ﷻ will recompense any act of good done in this world with a greater good in the Hereafter. If one aspires to be honoured with the noble garments of Paradise in the Hereafter, then one must consistently perform good deeds in this temporal world, especially by honouring one's needy brothers and sisters.

فَأَمَّا مَن ثَقُلَتْ مَوَازِينُهُ فَهُوَ فِي عِيشَةٍ رَاضِيَةٍ

"So as for those whose scales are heavy with good deeds, they will be in a life of bliss."

AL-QĀRIʿAH, 6–7

4

With Those Whom One Loves

In this temporal world, surrounding oneself with people of a certain temperament or value system will almost always translate into acquiring their beliefs and characteristics. For instance, having a good friend or companion will likely lead to the attainment of virtues and noble values. Conversely, having a morally iniquitous acquaintance will adversely affect one's lifestyle choices; people may even assign negative values to a person due to his problematic associations.

On the Day of Judgement, one will be resurrected among the people one associated with or with those one has admired, even if one did not manage to meet them in person. For this reason, every Muslim should reflect on his or her current friendships and associations and ask whether they would wish to be resurrected with such personalities on the Last Day. This question should determine one's friend making process from beginning to end, just as one should be mindful that the Prophet ﷺ once remarked that no person loves a people or folk except that he will be resurrected with them in the Afterlife. Obviously, considering the fact that, in the next life Paradise and Hell will be brought in close proximity to every being in this planet, the intelligent person wishes to stand with and accompany the people of Paradise, not the people of Hellfire.

In a very powerful report, the Prophet ﷺ said:

يُؤْتَى بِجَهَنَّمَ يَوْمَئِذٍ لَهَا سَبْعُونَ أَلْفِ زِمَامٍ، مَعَ كُلِّ زِمَامٍ سَبْعُونَ أَلْفِ مَلَكٍ يَجُرُّونَهَا.

"On that Day, Hellfire will be brought forth with 70,000 bridles, with each bridle being tugged forward by 70,000 Angels."

After making the necessary calculations, one will reach the conclusion that an astronomical figure of Angels—approximately 4.9 billion of them—will be hauling Hellfire and bringing it forward before the wicked. This will be a horrifying sight for the evildoers and oppressors, since not only will they be staring at the dreadful abyss that awaits them, but they will also be overwhelmed by the line of Angels facing them, which will include the chief Archangel Jibrīl ﷺ. This awesome and powerful setting has been discussed in the following Qur'ānic verse:

يَوْمَ يَقُومُ الرُّوحُ وَالْمَلَائِكَةُ صَفًّا ۖ لَّا يَتَكَلَّمُونَ إِلَّا مَنْ أَذِنَ لَهُ الرَّحْمَٰنُ وَقَالَ صَوَابًا.

"On the Day the spirit and the Angels will stand in ranks. None will talk, except those granted permission by the Most Compassionate and whose words are true."[7]

---

[7] *Al-Nabā'*, 38.

In another verse, Allah ﷻ also states:

وَتَرَىٰ كُلَّ أُمَّةٍ جَاثِيَةً ۚ كُلُّ أُمَّةٍ تُدْعَىٰ إِلَىٰ كِتَابِهَا الْيَوْمَ تُجْزَوْنَ مَا كُنتُمْ تَعْمَلُونَ.

"And you will see every faith-community on its knees. Every community will be summoned to its record. [They all will be told:] 'This Day you will be rewarded for what you used to do.'"[8]

Throughout the period in which *Jahannam* is flaring and prepared to receive the wicked oppressors, Allah ﷻ will also bring forth the permanent abode of bliss and peace for the believers:

وَأُزْلِفَتِ ٱلْجَنَّةُ لِلْمُتَّقِينَ غَيْرَ بَعِيدٍ هَٰذَا مَا تُوعَدُونَ لِكُلِّ أَوَّابٍ حَفِيظٍ مَّنْ خَشِيَ الرَّحْمَٰنَ بِالْغَيْبِ وَجَاءَ بِقَلْبٍ مُّنِيبٍ.

"And Paradise will be brought near to the righteous, not far off. [And it will be said to them:] 'This is what you were promised, for whoever turned and kept up—[those] who were in awe of the Most Compassionate without seeing, and have come with a heart turning.'"[9]

If one carefully reflects on this passage of three verses, they will deduce that the people of *Jannah* are characterised with five noble traits. First and foremost, they are *muttaqīn* (God-fearing), i.e. they have a propensity to performing acts of righteousness and avoiding acts of evil. Secondly, they are *awwābīn*, i.e. they always immediately return to their Lord ﷻ in repentance after

---

[8] *Al-Jāthiyah*, 28.

[9] *Qāf*, 31–33.

committing sins. Thirdly, they are *ḥāfiẓīn*, i.e. they meticulously observe Allah's ordinances, such as the religious obligations. Fourthly, they are "in awe of the Most Compassionate without seeing Him" by being conscious of His omniscience at all times, even when they are in private settings. Thus, they do acts of righteousness even when none can see them except Allah ﷻ. Lastly, such individuals come to Allah with a *qalb munīb*, i.e. with a heart predisposed towards sincerity, purity, and repentance. A person possessing such a heart carefully maintains all the religious obligations, loves performing voluntary acts of good, and avoids the commission of sins.

On the Day of Judgement, every nation will be resurrected and gathered together, including the nation of Prophet Muhammad ﷺ. Different peoples and communities will be divided into various clusters depending on their level of piety and sincerity. Taking this into account, and as someone who belongs to the Muslim Ummah, one's priority should be to join the master of this nation and the best of all humanity: Prophet Muhammad ﷺ. On one occasion, a man directly addressed the Prophet ﷺ by stating:

يَا رَسُولَ اللهِ، مَتَى السَّاعَةُ؟

"O Messenger of Allah, when will the Final Hour occur?"

In response, the Messenger of Allah ﷺ said:

مَاذَا أَعْدَدْتَ لَهَا؟

"What have you prepared for it?"

True love in relation to the Prophet ﷺ must be constantly reflected in one's heart, tongue, and deeds. The Prophet ﷺ must always be the normative standard that one follows. One cannot be close to Allah عَزَّ وَجَلَّ on the Day of Judgement without being close to the Prophet ﷺ.

The man gave a frank and solemn reply: "Nothing at all, except the fact that I love Allah and His Messenger."

After hearing this rejoinder, the Prophet ﷺ beautifully said:

أَنْتَ مَعَ مَنْ أَحْبَبْتَ.

"You will be with those whom you love."

One can only imagine one's immense pleasure upon standing, on the Day of Judgement, in close proximity to the Messenger of Allah ﷺ, his Companions ﷺ, and kinfolk. For this to happen, it is necessary that one exhibits true and sincere love towards him by following his commands and prohibitions. In a beautiful verse of poetry, Imām al-Shāfiʿī ﷺ once said about the servant's relationship with Allah ﷻ:

لَوْ كَانَ حُبُّكَ صَادِقاً لَأَطَعْتَهُ ... إِنَّ المُحِبَّ لِمَنْ يُحِبُّ مُطِيعُ

*"Had your love been sincere, you would have obeyed Him...
For surely the lover is always compliant and dutiful to
his beloved."*

Thus, to ensure that one's love for the Prophet ﷺ is sincere, it is imperative for one to exhibit genuine love towards him spiritually and practically. For instance, one must attempt to emulate the personality and behavioural standards of the Prophet by carefully reflecting on his *Sīrah* (life and conduct) to let its spiritual fragrance waft through one's life and conduct. Whenever one reads a report transmitted from the Prophet ﷺ, or reflects on his lifetime experiences, one should attempt to emulate an aspect of the Prophet's character and behavioural traits. Taking these aforementioned facts into consideration, one can appreciate the following *ḥadīth* in which the Prophet ﷺ addressed his community by asking:

أَلَا أُخْبِرُكُمْ بِأَحَبِّكُمْ إِلَيَّ وَأَقْرَبِكُمْ مِنِّي مَجْلِسًا يَوْمَ الْقِيَامَةِ؟

"Shall I not inform you of the ones who will be most beloved and closest in proximity to me on the Day of Judgement?"

The Companions were awed by such a question, and did not immediately respond. After the Prophet repeated the question a few times, they finally replied by saying: "Yes, indeed, O Messenger of Allah, who are they?" The Messenger of Allah ﷺ replied by stating:

أَحْسَنُكُمْ خُلُقًا.

"Those of you who are best in character."

Furthermore, the Prophet ﷺ provided concrete examples to illustrate how excellent character is actualised in real life. For instance, Anas رضي الله عنه reported that the Prophet ﷺ said: "Whoever raises two daughters properly and takes care of their needs until they reach the age of maturity, I and he will , on the Day of Judgement, be close to one another like these two." He then joined his two fingers.

Upon reading his *Sīrah* and evaluating his relationship with his daughter Fāṭimah رضي الله عنها, one will not fail to notice that the Prophet ﷺ was the best father that this world has ever seen. The person who emulates his spiritual mode of parenting will be bestowed with the honour of standing by his side on the

Day of Judgement. Of course, one who loves the Prophet's style of parenting will naturally also aspire to adopt his moral example in other spheres of life. That way, one can ensure that one will enjoy the companionship of the Prophet on the Day of Judgement. Lastly, the more one reads about the Prophet's life and unparalleled mission, the more one will recite *ṣalawāt* (prayers) on him whenever his blessed name is mentioned. As confirmed in the following *ḥadīth*, this practice will also allow one to earn a blessed station on the Day of Judgement:

أَوْلَى النَّاسِ بِي يَوْمَ القِيَامَةِ أَكْثَرُهُمْ عَلَيَّ صَلاَةً.

"The people who have a better right on me on the Day of Judgement are those who send the most prayers and blessings upon me."

In order to be a recipient of the above-mentioned virtues, it is imperative to note that true love in relation to the Prophet must be constantly reflected in one's heart, tongue, and deeds. The Prophet ﷺ must always be the normative standard that one follows. The Prophet ﷺ is most deserving of this level of deference and love since humanity only recognised Allah ﷻ through his noble teachings. Thus, one cannot be close to Allah ﷻ on the Day of Judgement without being close to the Prophet ﷺ. If one is blessed with the opportunity of standing beside him on Judgement Day, one's heart will be spared from all fears and anxieties.

5

When Allah Addresses the Gathering

Imagine corresponding with a pen pal or an overseas friend for a number of years, only to then enjoy the opportunity of meeting him or her in person for the first time. Such a first encounter will undoubtedly be a thrilling experience. Now, as a thought experiment, calculate the value of five prayers done over the span of five years, without considering the Sunnah prayers or independent acts of *du'ā'* (supplication) done during the day. At a minimum, one would be performing 10,000 iterations of prayer during this relatively short time.

This means that one will be directly maintaining contact with one's Lord for at least 10,000 occasions. If one fails to develop a relationship with Allah ﷻ or remains incapable of addressing the Lord of the worlds through this multitude of conversations, then this would be a significant loss indeed. For one should understand that developing a spiritual bond with Him in this *dunyā* (temporal world) will translate into success in the *ākhirah* (Hereafter). The Prophet ﷺ reiterated this latter point in the following ḥadīth:

وَلَا يَتَوَلَّى اللهُ عَزَّ وَجَلَّ عَبْدًا فِي الدُّنْيَا، فَيُوَلِّيهِ غَيْرَهُ يَوْمَ القِيَامَةِ

"Allah will not take someone as a friend in this lower world only to then entrust his affairs to someone else on the Day of Judgement."

This report highlights how splendid the affair of the believer will be on the Day of Judgement, as Allah ﷻ will ensure he or she is fittingly judged. The great ascetic Abū Ḥāzim رحمه الله was asked how the process of returning to Allah ﷻ in the Hereafter will be like for a person. So he said:

أَمَّا المُحْسِنُ كَالغَائِبِ يَقْدُمُ عَلَى أَهْلِهِ، وَأَمَّا المُسِيءُ كَالآبِقِ يُقْدَمُ بِهِ عَلَى مَوْلَاه.

"As for the obedient one, it will be like an absent person returning to his or her family. But as for the wrongdoer, it will be like a runaway captive who is returned to his master."

This ultimately means that the Day of Judgement does not constitute a meeting with one's deeds. Instead, it represents the moment *one meets one's Lord with one's deeds.* As Abū Ḥāzim noted, such a meeting with Allah must not be an introductory encounter but a pleasant reunion with one's loved one, which is devoid of any fear or distress. This is indicated in the following verse:

إِنَّا نَخَافُ مِنْ رَبِّنَا يَوْمًا عَبُوسًا قَمْطَرِيرًا فَوَقَاهُمُ اللَّهُ شَرَّ ذَٰلِكَ الْيَوْمِ وَلَقَّاهُمْ نَضْرَةً وَسُرُورًا.

"[They will say to themselves:] 'We fear from our Lord a horribly distressful Day.' So Allah will deliver them from the horror of that Day, and grant them radiance and joy."[10]

In a famous holy saying (*ḥadīth qudsī*), the Prophet ﷺ related that Allah ﷻ said:

وَعِزَّتِي لَا أَجْمَعُ عَلَى عَبْدِي خَوْفَيْنِ وَأَمْنَيْنِ: إِذَا خَافَنِي فِي الدُّنْيَا أَمِنْتُهُ يَوْمَ الْقِيَامَةِ وَإِذَا أَمِنَنِي فِي الدُّنْيَا أَخَفْتُهُ يَوْمَ الْقِيَامَةِ.

"By My might, I will never combine for My servant two fears or two securities. Should he fear Me in this temporal world, I will provide him security on the Day of Judgement. And if he feels secure from Me in this temporal world, then I shall instil fear in him on the Day of Judgement."

10 *Al-Insān*, 10–11.

Thus, according to this narration, the ones who are neglectful of Allah's message and ignore His call will be barred from seeing Him on the Day of Judgement. Regarding this matter, Allah ﷻ states in the Qur'ān:

كَلَّآ إِنَّهُمْ عَن رَّبِّهِمْ يَوْمَئِذٍ لَّمَحْجُوبُونَ.

"Undoubtedly, they will be sealed off from their Lord on that Day."[11]

Such a serious void and disconnection will cause the wrongdoers to feel greater apprehension; for while they may not be able to see Allah ﷻ, they will be aware of His presence and even sense His anger. In addition to being barred from seeing Him, they will be deprived of security and comfort. The believers will be granted the privilege of seeing Him during the Assembly, though this initial vision will be of a lesser degree than the beatific vision that they will enjoy in Paradise. In any case, Allah ﷻ will come and introduce Himself in a splendid manner to His righteous and God-fearing servants. The Prophet ﷺ described the Lord's appearance by stating:

يَتَجَلَّى لَنَا رَبُّنَا عَزَّ وَجَلَّ يَوْمَ القِيَامَةِ ضَاحِكًا.

"Our Lord will manifest Himself before us on the Day of Judgement while He is laughing."

[11] *Al-Muṭaffifīn*, 15.

When the Companion Abū Razīn ﵁ heard the Prophet ﷺ describe Allah's attribute of laughter, he became overjoyed and exclaimed:

لَنْ نُعْدَمَ مِنْ رَبٍّ يَضْحَكُ خَيْرًا.

"We will never be deprived of good by a Lord Who laughs."

Such a sight will undoubtedly be a gift that shall comfort the believers and put their hearts at ease. This then naturally leads to the question of determining who these special classes of believers are. If one peruses the *Ḥadīth* literature, one will notice that many narrations highlight the notions of humility and forbearance. For instance, in one beautiful narration, the Prophet ﷺ states:

وَمَنْ كَظَمَ غَيْظَهُ وَلَوْ شَاءَ أَنْ يُمْضِيهِ أَمْضَاهُ، مَلأَ اللهُ صَدْرَهُ رِضًا يَوْمَ القِيَامَةِ.

"Whoever checks his anger despite being able to react upon it, Allah will fill his heart with contentment on the Day of Judgement."

Interestingly, there is a series of narrations which mention how Allah ﷻ openly announces to humanity the qualities that will bestow upon them serenity in the most difficult day. In one report—whose chain has a minor degree of weakness—the Prophet ﷺ said that Allah ﷻ Himself will announce on the Day of Judgement:

سَيَعْلَمُ أَهْلُ الجَمْعِ مَنْ أَهْلُ الكَرَمِ.

"The people of the Gathering will know who the people of magnanimity are."

The people present asked, "And who are the people of *magnanimity*, O Messenger of Allah?" In response to them, the Prophet ﷺ said:

أَهْلُ الذِّكْرِ فِي المَجَالِسِ.

"They are the people who are distinguished by their dhikr (remembrance) of Allah in their gatherings."

As noted in this *ḥadīth*, there is a firm nexus between being a person of *dhikr* in this world and being allotted contentment on the Day of Judgement. This theme has in fact been further reiterated in other reports as well. For instance, ʿImrān ibn Ḥusayn ﷺ related that the Messenger of Allah ﷺ said:

إِنَّ أَفْضَلَ عِبَادِ اللهِ يَوْمَ القِيَامَةِ الحَمَّادُونَ.

"Indeed the best servants of Allah on the Day of Judgement are the ḥammadūn (those who praise Allah often)."

On another occasion, the Prophet ﷺ was in the presence of his Companions and then suddenly pronounced:

سَبَقَ المُفَرِّدُونَ سَبَقَ المُفَرِّدُونَ.

"The forerunners have excelled and moved ahead. The forerunners have excelled and moved ahead."

In response, the Companions said: "O Messenger of Allah! Who are those people?" The Prophet ﷺ explained his initial proclamation by stating:

الْمُسْتَهْتَرُونَ فِي ذِكْرِ اللهِ.

"They are the ones who are completely immersed in the dhikr of Allah."

The Prophet ﷺ further explained the righteousness of this elite group of people by stating:

يَضَعُ الذِّكْرُ عَنْهُمْ أَثْقَالَهُمْ فَيَأْتُونَ يَوْمَ الْقِيَامَةِ خِفَافًا.

"Their dhikr has freed them of the burden of their sins, such that they will come on the Day of Judgement light."

At this point, one may ask: why are the people of *dhikr* bestowed such a lofty rank on the Day of Judgement? The answer lies in the fact that they are the ones who frequently visit the most beloved of places to Allah ﷻ, namely the mosques. After all, it is in the mosques that Allah's name is frequently mentioned and glorified. For this reason, it is no surprise to find that on one occasion the Prophet ﷺ related that Allah ﷻ Himself once asked:

أَيْنَ جِيرَانِي؟ أَيْنَ جِيرَانِي؟

"Where are My neighbours? Where are My neighbours?"

Upon hearing this query, the Angels responded by saying:

رَبَّنَا وَمَنْ يَنْبَغِي أَنْ يُجَاوِرَكَ؟

"Our Lord! Who ought to be Your neighbour?"

Allah clarified who the recipients of this noble rank are by asking:

أَيْنَ عُمَّارُ المَسَاجِدِ.

"Where are those who frequent the mosques?"

In this context, one may also mention the virtues of the scholars, since they also will have a unique status on the Day of Judgement. In a *ḥadīth* mentioning the exceptional groups and classes that will be honoured by Allah ﷻ on the Last Day, the Messenger of Allah ﷺ said:

ثُمَّ يُمَيِّزُ العُلَمَاءَ.

"Allah will then set aside the scholars [from the rest of humanity]."

The preferential status conferred upon the scholars should not come as a surprise, for Allah has labelled them as *ahl al-dhikr* (the people of remembrance) in the Qur'ān. Opposed to this group are the hypocrites who fail to mention Allah's name and will face the utmost humiliation on the Day of Judgement. As for the sincere scholars, they are the ones who fear standing before Allah and acquire knowledge in order to draw near to their Lord ﷻ. This point has been underscored in the following verse of the Qur'ān:

إِنَّمَا يَخْشَى اللهَ مِنْ عِبَادِهِ العُلَمَاءُ.

"Of all Allah's servants, only the savants ('ūlamā') are in awe of Him."[12]

---

[12] *Fāṭir*, 28.

Because of their sincerity and love for the Truth, the scholars will not be fearful on the Last Day. In fact, Allah ﷻ will directly address them and comfort them with the following words:

يَا مَعْشَرَ العُلَمَاءِ: إِنِّي لَمْ أَضَعْ عِلْمِي بَيْنَكُمْ إِلَّا لِعِلْمِي بِكُمْ وَلَمْ أَضَعْ عِلْمِي فِيكُمْ لِأُعَذِّبَكُمْ؛ اِذْهَبُوا فَقَدْ غَفَرْتُ لَكُمْ.

"O company of scholars! I did not intend to waste My knowledge among you by having you punished. Proceed forward, for I have forgiven you."

One can detect a consistent theme in these aforementioned narrations. In this temporal world, while these people of knowledge have led circles of divine remembrance, unbeknownst to them they were protected and honoured through being shaded by the angels and praised by Allah ﷻ in His divine assembly. While none of these metaphysical manifestations of praise could be heard or seen, they are nevertheless felt. But in the Hereafter, these words of praise will be directly issued in the greatest of assemblies and gatherings, where all the angels and members of humanity will be present. These eminent stars of knowledge will be able to hear and enjoy these words of praise from their Creator ﷻ.

The Prophet ﷺ taught his Ummah a specific formula of *dhikr* which can be recited for obtaining the pleasure and praise of the Lord in the Hereafter. In a beautiful narration, he said:

مَا مِنْ عَبْدٍ مُسْلِمٍ يَقُولُ حِينَ يُصْبِحُ وَحِينَ يُمْسِي ثَلَاثَ مَرَّاتٍ: رَضِيتُ بِاللهِ رَبًّا وَبِالإِسْلَامِ دِينًا وَبِمُحَمَّدٍ صَلَّى اللهُ عَلَيْهِ وَسَلَّمَ نَبِيًّا، إِلَّا كَانَ حَقًّا عَلَى اللهِ أَنْ يُرْضِيَهُ يَوْمَ القِيَامَةِ.

"There is no Muslim servant who says three times upon the advent of the morning and evening , 'I am pleased with Allah as my Lord, with Islam as my religion, and with Muhammad as my Prophet' except that Allah takes it upon Himself to please him on the Day of Judgement."

A person who consistently recites this supplication will be readily prepared to answer the three questions that will be posed in the grave. This very conclusion has in fact been implicitly supported by the following Qur'ānic verse:

أَلَا بِذِكْرِ ٱللَّهِ تَطْمَئِنُّ ٱلْقُلُوبُ.

"Surely in the remembrance of Allah do hearts find comfort."[13]

As for the ones who do not, then they will be subject to a depressing and suffocating state instead in their resting place:

وَمَنْ أَعْرَضَ عَن ذِكْرِي فَإِنَّ لَهُۥ مَعِيشَةً ضَنكًا.

"But whoever turns away from My Reminder will certainly have a miserable life."[14]

---

13 *Al-Ra'd*, 28.

14 *Ṭāhā*, 124.

6

Two Faces and One Tongue

The eminent Companion ʿUmar ibn al-Khaṭṭāb ﵁ is reported to have once said:

عَلَيْكُمْ بِذِكْرِ اللهِ فَإِنَّهُ شِفَاءٌ، وَإِيَّاكُمْ وَذِكْرُ النَّاسِ فَإِنَّهُ دَاءٌ.

"Hold fast to remembering Allah for it is a a healing. And beware of referring to people for it is a disease."

In essence, this wise saying reminds one that the tongue is a double-edged sword: by using it for *dhikr*, one is able to elevate onself. But if it is used in frivolous matters, then it can debase the purity of one's soul. In fact, if one speaks excessively about the affairs of others, one will eventually meet a tremendous downfall. ʿUmar ibn al-Khaṭṭāb ﵁ himself warned of the moral dangers found in this habit by stating:

مَنْ كَثُرَ كَلَامُهُ كَثُرَ سَقَطُهُ.

"The one whose speech is excessive will frequently commit errors and slip-ups."

Intuitively, when errors are frequent, the possibility of committing sins increases, which ultimately puts one in danger of falling in Hellfire. The tongue is a very powerful instrument and can be used for hurtful and damaging ends. Through a few choice words, the reputation of a person can be tarnished or destroyed. Through making slanderous and libellous remarks, a whole community can be held hostage. The potential for damage is further exacerbated by the proliferation of the internet and social media platforms. One should note that the greater the moral chaos and disorder one causes with one's tongue (or pen), the more one will damage one's state and rank in the Hereafter. At the same time, however, the opposite is also true. For instance, one may utter a simple phrase of kindness or exhibit gratitude to a fellow brother or sister, and—unbeknownst to one—through that action one will earn the pleasure of Allah ﷻ. In sum, through the tongue one may earn the pleasure and praise of one's Creator, or subject oneself to His wrath and then be thrown into the deepest abysses of Hellfire.

The majority of Prophetic sayings that have been transmitted concerning the defects of the tongue are disconcerting and terrifying. But it is necessary to know of the punishments prepared for those who transgress verbally, so one may learn to restrain one's tongue from uttering any ill or frivolous words. Upon evaluating these reports, one will immediately notice that there is an intricate connection between the tongue and the face. In this regard, one may consider one of the disturbing spectacles that the Prophet ﷺ witnessed during the miraculous night journey of *al-Isrāʾ waʾl-Miʿrāj*:

مَرَرْتُ بِقَوْمٍ لَهُمْ أَظْفَارٌ مِنْ نُحَاسٍ يَخْمِشُونَ وُجُوهَهُمْ وَصُدُورَهُمْ فَقُلْتُ: مَنْ هؤُلَاءِ يَا جِبْرِيلُ؟ قَالَ: هَؤُلَاءِ الّذِينَ يَأْكُلُونَ لُحُومَ النَّاسِ، وَيَقَعُونَ فِي أَعْرَاضِهِمْ.

"I passed by a group of people who were using copper nails to scratch their faces and chests. So I said: 'O Jibrīl, who are these people?' He said: 'These are the people who eat the flesh of others and slander their honour.'"

The scholars who commented on this *ḥadīth* have provided a number of reasonable explanations for why the face is the object of punishment. They note that the person whose reputation is defamed avoids showing his or her face in public. Such an oppressed person is so to speak banished from society. As a fitting and parallel form of punishment, Allah ﷻ will make those oppressors who slandered him or her disfigure and tear their own faces in the next world. These themes are further reiterated and stressed in other reports as well. For instance, in one narration, the Prophet ﷺ said:

إِنَّ شَرَّ النَّاسِ ذُو الوَجْهَيْنِ الذي يَأْتِي هَؤُلَاءِ بوَجْهٍ وهَؤُلَاءِ بوَجْهٍ.

"The worst of people is the two-faced person, that is, the one who appears before some people with one face and then goes to a different group with another face."

On the Day of Judgement, the faces of the righteous will be glowing with a shimmering light and they will be content, while the faces of the wrongdoers and oppressors will be gloomy and dark.

In a report bearing a similar message, the Prophet ﷺ said that the worst of people on the Day of Resurrection will be the man who shares the intimate secrets of his wife. In another *ḥadīth*, he stated that the most wicked of people is the one who has a foul mouth such that the people cease to correct him out of fear of being the target of his vile words.

The collective theme found in this group of narrations is that the worst of people are those who use their tongues to hurl abuses at, or betray the trust of, their fellow believers. These vile people will be exposed to the greatest form of punishment on the Day of Judgement and humiliated in front of the whole of humanity. In one chilling report, the noble Companion ʿAmmār ibn Yāsir ؓ related that he heard the Messenger of Allah ﷺ say:

مَنْ كَانَ لَهُ وَجْهَانِ فِي الدُّنْيَا كَانَ لَهُ يَوْمَ الْقِيَامَةِ لِسَانَانِ مِنْ نَارٍ.

"Whoever is two-faced in this world will have two tongues of fire on the Day of Judgement."

In this latter report, one acutely notes how fire is used as a means of punishment against such wrongdoers. This is because the secrets and trusts of others are considered sacred in the sight of Allah ﷻ. When these consigned trusts are violated, it is as if the transgressor is engulfing his or her ears and tongue in a branding fire. This in fact explains why the Prophet ﷺ said that one who eavesdrops on the private conversations of others will have molten lead poured into one's ears on the Day of Judgement. However, the spiritual outcome will not be bleak and grievous for everyone. Conversely, there will be people whose faces and limbs will be honoured on the Day of Resurrection as a result of their virtuous deeds. For instance, in one key report, the Prophet ﷺ said:

مَنْ رَدَّ عَنْ عِرْضِ أَخِيهِ رَدَّ اللَّهُ عَنْ وَجْهِهِ النَّارَ يَوْمَ الْقِيَامَةِ.

"Whoever safeguards the honour of his brother in the latter's absence Allah will protect his face from Hellfire on the Day of Resurrection."

The people who protect the honour and reputation of their brothers and sisters are rarer than precious gems, but they can be found in some gatherings and sittings. They are the individuals who refuse to remain silent and clearly voice their disapproval when one of their Muslim brothers or sisters is slandered or mocked. They are the ones who do not hesitate to condemn such transgressions, even if they ensue from their closest friends and companions. In fact, such morally upright people are even willing to defend the integrity of individuals they do not particularly admire. Upon evaluating these various reports, one notices a striking point of differentiation: as opposed to the slanderer and transgressor who will have their face disfigured, the defender of a Muslim's reputation will have his face shielded from the horrors and trials of Hellfire.

On the Day of Judgement, the faces of the righteous will be glowing with a shimmering light and they will be content, while the faces of the wrongdoers and oppressors will be gloomy and dark. In a series of verses, Allah ﷻ provides vivid descriptions of the beauty of the believers on the Day of Judgement. In one verse, Allah ﷻ states:

وُجُوهٌ يَوْمَئِذٍ نَاعِمَةٌ لِسَعْيِهَا رَاضِيَةٌ.

"On that Day faces will be glowing with bliss, pleased with their striving."[15]

Such people will be content and pleased with the salvation that they attained through their good deeds. This very point is reiterated in another verse:

وُجُوهٌ يَوْمَئِذٍ مُسْفِرَةٌ ضَاحِكَةٌ مُسْتَبْشِرَةٌ.

"On that Day faces will be bright, laughing and rejoicing."[16]

Once again, the deeds of the believer are what will cause them to rejoice and smile at their newfound fortune in the Afterlife. But as another set of verses indicates, the believers will be filled with joy due to another blessing that they will be showered with on the Day of Resurrection:

وُجُوهٌ يَوْمَئِذٍ نَاضِرَةٌ إِلَىٰ رَبِّهَا نَاظِرَةٌ.

"On that Day faces will be bright, looking at their Lord."[17]

---

[15] *Al-Ghāshiyah*, 8–9.

[16] *'Abasa*, 38–39.

[17] *Al-Qiyāmah*, 22–23.

In other words, the faces of the believers will be glowing with happiness due to the blessing of directly seeing their Lord ﷻ, Who will be pleased with them and they with Him. At the same time, however, it is important to note that the faces of the believers will actually be illuminated in this world as well. It is reported that al-Ḥasan al-Baṣrī ﵀ was once asked about the worshippers who performed *tahajjud* (the late-night prayer) and how they had illuminating faces despite their overall lack of sleep. Al-Ḥasan responded with the following rejoinder:

لِأَنَّهُمْ خَلَوْا بِالرَّحْمَنِ فَأَلْبَسَهُمْ مِنْ نُورِهِ.

"This is due to the fact that they secluded themselves with al-Raḥmān (the All-Merciful) in worship, so He dressed them with His light."

While this is the case in this temporal world, one can only imagine how intense and amplified the light of the worshippers will be when Allah ﷻ gazes and smiles at them on the Day of Judgement.

7

Long Necks and Grey Hair

The first grey hair that is found on one's head can be a sobering and stressful experience. For the Muslim, a grey hair is a warning sign and a reminder that this life is transient and fleeting. There is in fact a Qur'ānic verse which indirectly points to this conclusion. In the passage in question, Allah ﷻ states:

أَوَلَمْ نُعَمِّرْكُم مَا يَتَذَكَّرُ فِيهِ مَنْ تَذَكَّرَ وَجَاءَكُمُ النَّذِير.

"Did We not give you lives long enough so that whoever wanted to be mindful could have done so? And the warner came to you." [18]

According to many scholars and Qur'ānic exegetes, the *nadhīr* (warner) mentioned in this verse is actually a reference to grey hairs, since they constitute a sign that one is nearing the end

[18] *Fāṭir*, 37.

of one's lifetime and will soon meet Allah ﷻ. This in fact explains why the Prophet once said:

أَعْذَرَ اللَّهُ إِلَى امْرِئٍ أَخَّرَ أَجَلَهُ حَتَّى بَلَّغَهُ سِتِّينَ سَنَةً.

"Allah will forgive a person whose lifetime is extended until they reach the age of 60."

This *ḥadīth* clearly demonstrates that once one reaches sixty years of age, one will have no excuse whatsoever for one's lapses and transgressions, as enough proofs have been fully established against one. Besides old age, another key factor that contributes to the development of grey hairs is stress. This variable has also been indirectly indicated in the following verse, whereby Allah ﷻ warns of the extreme fear and stress found on the Day of Judgement:

فَكَيْفَ تَتَّقُونَ إِن كَفَرْتُمْ يَوْمًا يَجْعَلُ ٱلْوِلْدَٰنَ شِيبًا.

"If you persist in disbelief, then how will you guard yourselves against a Day which will turn children's hair grey?"[19]

The Prophet ﷺ did not have many grey hairs during his life, but there was one particular period of time when a substantial portion of his hair started to thin and whiten. When Abū Bakr al-Ṣiddīq رضي الله عنه asked him about this, he said:

شَيَّبَتْنِي هُودٌ وَأَخَوَاتُهَا.

"(Sūrah) Hud and its sister Sūrahs have turned my hair grey."

---

[19] *Al-Muzzammil*, 17.

Such a transformation in one's hair should never be perceived in a negative manner. This is because anything that has aged or been expended for the sake of Allah ﷻ should be perceived in a positive light, as it is an honour to sacrifice something for Allah alone. This includes sustaining a wound for the sake of Allah ﷻ, experiencing pain in one's joints due to performing acts of worship, or developing a mark on one's forehead due to excessive prostration. The key analytical conclusion of this discussion is that the physical and mental strains that the righteous believers have to sustain in this world will be transformed into marks of light in the Hereafter.

But if one fails to attain any moral development with the advancement of age, one will expose oneself to the wrath of Allah ﷻ. This is why the Prophet ﷺ said that one of the people whom Allah ﷻ will not look at on the Day of Judgement is the *al-shaykh al-zānī*, i.e. the old man who commits adultery; the reason why his crime is considered doubly inappropriate is because he disregarded Allah's prohibition and fell into illegal sexual intercourse despite his advanced age.

Conversely, there are morally upright individuals who expend their long lives in the obedience and worship of Allah ﷻ. Such people are paragons of moral virtue and should be honoured by the Muslim community. In a noteworthy tradition, the Prophet ﷺ said:

لَيْسَ مِنَّا مَنْ لَمْ يَرْحَمْ صَغِيرَنا وَلَمْ يَعرِفْ شَرَفَ كَبِيرِنا.

"He is not of us whoever does not show mercy to our young ones and does not appreciate the honour of our elders."

As this *ḥadīth* indicates, it is imperative for Muslims to show mercy to their youth rather than showing them harsh words and actions. Additionally, the seniors of the community should be respected and honoured to the utmost degree; any acts denoting mockery or disrespect towards them should never be tolerated. Through such initiatives, a community based on Prophetic values can be generated.

An old person will be honoured on the Day of Judgement through a series of elaborate markers and signs. In one key *ḥadīth*, the Prophet ﷺ said:

مَنْ شَابَ شَيْبَةً فِي الْإِسْلَامِ كَانَتْ لَهُ نُورًا يَوْمَ الْقِيَامَةِ.

"Whoever grows grey hair in Islam, it will be an illuminating light for him on the Day of Judgement."

In light of this report, one understands why the Prophet ﷺ prohibited his nation from plucking grey hairs, for doing so means that one will be depriving oneself of this great blessing on the Day of Judgement. Alternatively, he permitted senior members of his community to dye their hair with different colours, to the exclusion of black. Moreover, there is nothing in the Islamic legal tradition which prohibits one from trimming grey hairs. But plucking them entirely from their roots is detested from a Shariah standpoint, since it is ideal to have them radiate and glitter like gold on the Day of Judgement.

The grey hair, stress, and sleeplessness that one experiences due to one's grief and concern for the plight of the Ummah will all be taken into account on the Day of Judgement and handsomely rewarded by Allah عزّ وجلّ.

Continuing on this theme, Imām al-Ḥasan al-Baṣrī ﷺ said:

أَفْضَلُ النَّاسِ ثَوَابًا يَوْمَ الْقِيَامَةِ الْمُؤْمِنُ الْمُعَمَّرُ.

"The best of people in terms of reward on the Day of Judgement are the believers who have long lives."

Of course, if the status of the old believer is examined in a broader light, his or her virtue does not simply lie in his or her grey hairs. Instead, the grey hair is merely a manifestation or signpost of his or her acts of righteousness and sacrifices for the sake of Allah ﷻ. Such signs and markers can be found in other virtuous classes of believers as well. For instance, when outlining the merits of the martyr (*shahīd*) , the Prophet ﷺ said:

مَا مِنْ مَجْرُوحٍ يُجْرَحُ فِي سَبِيلِ اللهِ، وَاللهُ أَعْلَمُ بِمَنْ يُجْرَحُ فِي سَبِيلِهِ، إِلَّا جَاءَ يَوْمَ الْقِيَامَةِ وَالْجُرْحُ كَهَيْئَتِهِ يَوْمَ جُرِحَ، اللَّوْنُ لَوْنُ دَمٍ، وَالرِّيحُ رِيحُ مِسْكٍ.

"No one is wounded in the cause of Allah—and Allah knows who is sincerely wounded for His cause—except that he will appear on the Day of Judgement with his wounds exactly as it was on the day he was injured. But while its colour will be that of blood, its smell will be that of musk."

Thus, the *shahīd* will enjoy an unparalleled rank on the Last Day, where his body will be exuding bright light and the most pleasant scent imaginable. When reading this report, one can only wonder how beautiful Ḥamzah ibn ʿAbd al-Muṭṭalib ؓ will be, as his chest and other wounded areas will be discharging light. The same can be said about the great Companion Khālid ibn al-Walīd ؓ who led countless battles and military expeditions, sustaining in the process wounds in every limb of his body.

Similar virtues can be attributed to other categories of believers as well. For instance, the great Companion and *mu'adhdhin* (caller to prayer) Bilāl ﷺ will appear on the Day of Judgement with a long and elegant neck, as will the rest of the callers to prayer who came after him throughout the history of Islam. This is because the Prophet ﷺ said:

الْمُؤَذِّنُونَ أَطْوَلُ النَّاسِ أَعْنَاقاً يَوْمَ الْقِيَامَةِ.

"The mu'adhdhins will have the longest necks on the Day of Judgement."

In his commentary of this *ḥadīth*, the great medieval scholar al-Nawawī ﷺ mentioned that the Arabs used the expression "long neck" as a description for individuals of high standing and nobility. Thus, the people who call the Muslims to prayer in this world will be leaders in the Hereafter. It is true that some scholars have stated that the role of the *mu'adhdhin* is strictly confined to the mosque, since it is the primary place for prayer and intuitively the ideal place where it should be performed. However, if one carefully evaluates the words of the *adhān*, one will find that it is a wide-ranging formula of *dhikr* which helps raise one's position in the Hereafter. The Companion Abū Saʿīd al-Khudrī ﷺ was a shepherd, which meant that sometimes he found himself alone in the wilderness with his cattle. The Prophet ﷺ taught him the following form of advice:

إِنِّي أَراكَ تُحِبُّ الغَنَمَ والبادِيَةَ، فإذا كُنْتَ في غَنَمِكَ وبادِيَتِكَ، فأَذَّنْتَ بالصَّلاةِ، فارْفَعْ صَوْتَكَ بالنِّداءِ، فإنَّه لا يَسْمَعُ مَدَى صَوْتِ المُؤَذِّنِ جِنٌّ وَلَا إِنْسٌ وَلَا شَيْءٌ إلَّا شَهِدَ لَهُ يَومَ القِيامَةِ.

"I notice that you enjoy staying among your sheep or dwelling in the wilderness. Should you happen to be engaged in such areas and proceed to call the adhān, then ensure that you raise your voice during the process. For the echo of the mu'adhdhin's voice is not heard by a jinn, human, or any other being except that it will testify for them on the Day of Judgement."

But a Muslim may not fall under any of the aforementioned categories—the warrior, the elder, or the *mu'adhdhin*—and naturally wonder whether he or she may derive any spiritual benefits promised in the *ḥadīths* cited above. The answer to this can be found in a beautiful narration in which the Prophet ﷺ mentioned that one of the key questions that one must answer on the Day of Judgement is regarding one's body and how one had expended it in this temporal world. From this statement, one can deduce that any mental or physical sacrifices that one has made for the sake of Allah ﷻ will be recompensed in the Hereafter. For instance, a pregnant woman who experiences pain during the main stages of labour will be rewarded for all the struggles she had to endure and the stretch marks her body developed during this difficult process. Moreover, the grey hairs, stress, and sleeplessness that one experiences due to one's grief and concern for the plight of the Ummah will all be taken into account on the Day of Judgement and handsomely rewarded. Thus, any physical or mental sacrifice expended in this world should not be deemed to be a blemish, as it will illuminate one and raise one's rank in the Hereafter.

8

Under Which Banner?

As times become more deceiving and delusive, it becomes relatively more difficult to identify who the fraudsters are. The Prophet described the interval preceding the Day of Judgement as being *sanawāt khaddā'āt* (deceptive years), and further said:

يُصدَّقُ فيها الكاذِبُ، ويُكذَّبُ فيها الصادِقُ.

"In those years the truthful one is belied, while the liar is believed."

In essence, all conventional standards of credibility will be abandoned, and the overwhelming majority of people will become unprincipled. The liars will be able to materially flourish since they will be unbridled by any moral principles. In such a corrupt setting, the sincere and truthful members of society will face severe difficulties, since they will refuse to compromise their moral principles for the sake of progressing in society.

Each individual person has a particular moral orientation or bearing, but his or her personal nature is hidden from others. One can only imagine what it would be like if the angels provided their own reviews of the people they surround and observe. That way, one would be able to know the level of credibility of a person before befriending him or her or engaging in transactions with him or her. Such a certification process would be immensely useful, especially if such information could be provided in front of a person's business or household. In the spiritual realm, such modes of accreditation and labels do in fact exist. In a notable *ḥadīth*, the Prophet ﷺ mentioned that no one leaves his home except that he will be followed by two banners, one banner held by an Angel and the other banner raised by a devil. If the person plans to undertake an action that Allah ﷻ loves, then he will traverse his path under the banner hoisted by the angel. However, if he decides to go and commit a forbidden action, then he will be accompanied by the devil's emblem until he returns home. While these banners and symbols are concealed from the human eye in this world, they will be fully visible in the Hereafter, such that every human being will be able to see them. At the same time, however, it is true that the identities of some figures will be clearly illustrated. For instance, with regard to the *Dajjāl* (Antichrist), the Prophet ﷺ said:

وَإِنَّ بَيْنَ عَيْنَيْهِ مَكْتُوبٌ كَافِرٌ.

"Between his two eyes the word disbeliever (kāfir) is written."

That way, every true believer will be able to identify the *Dajjāl* and thus avoid his call to disbelief and falsehood. Afterwards, he will be vanquished by the true Messiah, and the earth will enter into a period of stability and faith. But after humankind once again descends into disbelief and injustice, Allah ﷻ will cause the world's destruction and bring forth the Day of Judgement. On the Day of Judgement, every standing person will have a unique identity that is determined by his or her deeds. The Prophet ﷺ alluded to this reality when he said:

إِنَّ الصِّدقَ يَهْدِي إِلَى البِرِّ وَإِنَّ البِرَّ يَهْدِي إِلَى الجَنَّةِ وَإِنَّ الرَّجُلَ لَيَصْدُقُ وَيَتَحَرَّى الصِّدْقَ حَتَّى يُكْتَبَ عِنْدَ اللَّهِ صِدِّيقًا وَإِنَّ الكَذِبَ يَهْدِي إِلَى الفُجُورِ وَإِنَّ الفُجُورَ يَهْدِي إِلَى النَّارِ وَإِنَّ الرَّجُلَ لَيَكْذِبُ وَيَتَحَرَّى الكَذِبَ حَتَّى يُكْتَبَ عِنْدَ اللَّهِ كَذَّابًا.

"Truthfulness leads to righteousness and righteousness leads to Paradise. A man will keep saying the truth and does his utmost to be truthful until he is registered with Allah as a truthful person. Lying leads to wickedness, and wickedness leads to the Hellfire. A man will keep lying and does his utmost to lie until he is registered with Allah as a liar."

On the Day of Judgement, the distinction between the two categories of people will be most evident, with each group bearing the recompense for their deeds. For instance, it is well known that in this temporal world, being truthful sometimes causes one to face material disadvantage, while lying may lead to profitable gains. Interestingly, the Qur'ān alludes to this fact when it provides the following portrayal of the Day of Judgement:

قَالَ ٱللَّهُ هَٰذَا يَوْمُ يَنفَعُ ٱلصَّٰدِقِينَ صِدْقُهُمْ.

"Allah will declare, 'This is the Day when the ṣādiqūn (truthful) will benefit from their ṣidq (truthfulness).'"[20]

[20] *Al-Mā'idah*, 119.

The point of benefit becomes clear once one takes into account the fact that the truthful will have banners that will point to their virtue. As for the people of deceit and evil, they will have their status exposed on the Day of Judgement in front of every member of the human race. In a chilling report, the Prophet ﷺ said:

يُرْفَعُ لِكُلِّ غَادِرٍ لِوَاءٌ، فَيُقَالُ: هَذِهِ غَدْرَةُ فُلانِ بْنِ فُلانٍ.

"A banner will be raised over every treacherous person, and it will be announced: here is the betrayal of so-and-so, the son of so-and-so."

As a result, their transgressions and deceit will be exposed before everyone, as opposed to the power and influence they exercised in the world. Their names and reputations will be fully tainted, as they await their proceedings before the Lord of the worlds ﷻ. In the case of the believers, they will have banners hoisted over them that relate words of praise. This blessed group will be led by the greatest person to have lived on this planet, namely Prophet Muhammad ﷺ, and his banner will be the greatest. The Prophet ﷺ clearly outlined his eminent status and the Banner of Praise that will be bestowed upon him on the Day of Judgement:

أَنَا سَيِّدُ وَلَدِ آدَمَ يَوْمَ القِيَامَةِ وَلَا فَخْرَ ، وَبِيَدِي لِوَاءُ الحَمْدِ وَلَا فَخْرَ ، وَمَا مِنْ نَبِيٍّ يَوْمَئِذٍ آدَمَ فَمَنْ سِوَاهُ إِلَّا تَحْتَ لِوَائِي.

"I am the master of the children of Adam on the Day of Judgement, and I am not boasting. And the banner of praise will be placed on my hand, and I am not boasting. And there will be no Prophet on that Day—whether Adam and those after him—except that they will be standing under my banner as well."

Taking this report into consideration, the scholars and commentators deduced that, on the Day of Judgement, the Prophet ﷺ will be provided the prominent and high-ranking *liwāʾ al-ḥamd* (Banner of Praise), which will attract the attention of people around it. Every person who sees it will want to be standing under its protection. It is important to note, however, that members of other praiseworthy classes will also be granted banners of their own, despite being less prominent in their size and image. Those belonging to the ranks of the *ṣādiqūn* (people of truthfulness), *ṣābirūn* (people of patience), and *shākirūn* (people of gratitude) will be blessed with their own banners. In order to be one of the receiver of a banner of praise, one must ascend to a virtuous station accepted in the religion. For instance, a merchant or tradesperson may be committed to uttering the truth in all circumstances, even if it causes him socioeconomic disadvantages when concluding deals with his customers. Because of his willingness to accept material loss in order to uphold the truth, the Prophet ﷺ stated that the sincere traders will be resurrected among the martyrs (*shuhadāʾ*) on the Last Day. Just as the latter group was sincere and faithful to their Creator when facing the enemy in the battlefield, the former class of individuals feared their Lord, were cognisant of His presence, and made sure that the material rights of their customers were not violated under any circumstances.

There are numerous stories from the pious predecessors which illustrate the type of behaviour and moral integrity needed to secure a banner of praise in the Hereafter. For instance, Ṣāliḥ, the son of Imām Aḥmad ibn Ḥanbal ﷺ, mentioned that his father forgave every individual who slandered or tortured him

The believers will have banners hoisted over them that relate words of praise. This blessed group will be led by the greatest person to have lived on this planet, namely Prophet Muhammad ﷺ, and his banner will be the greatest.

during the *miḥnah* (inquisition). This was the case despite the fact that numerous actors—rulers, viziers, guards, and even religious figures—made sure that he was persecuted and imprisoned for several years. Despite the great injustices that he faced, the Imām did not hesitate to forgive his oppressors. It is narrated that some of the guards who tortured and even whipped the Imām until he lost consciousness visited him and begged for his forgiveness. The Imām unhesitatingly pardoned all of them. Likewise, those who slandered the Imām sought his pardon, and he duly obliged. In sum, the Imām never mistreated his opponents and was a paragon of forgiveness.

What makes this account even more beautiful is that Ṣāliḥ asked his father what his position was regarding his persecutors and oppressors who had already passed away and failed to ask for his forgiveness. Remarkably, the Imām indiscriminately forgave all of them, stating:

لَقَدْ جَعَلْتُ المَيِّتَ فِي حِلٍّ مِنْ ضَرْبِهِ إِيَّايَ.

"I have forgiven even the dead for all the different forms of harm and punishment they meted against me."

Afterwards, Imām Aḥmad ﵀ reminded his son of the following verse:

فَمَنْ عَفَا وَأَصْلَحَ فَأَجْرُهُۥ عَلَى ٱللَّهِ.

"But whoever pardons and seeks reconciliation, then their reward is with Allah."[21]

---

[21] *Al-Shūrā*, 40.

In other words, Allah has guaranteed that He will address the plight of the oppressed victims and receivers of injustice by handsomely rewarding them. Through his own chain of narration, the Imām provided further insights into the verse by mentioning the following report from al-Ḥasan al-Baṣrī ﵀:

إِذَا جَثَتِ الْأُمَمُ بَيْنَ يَدَيْ رَبِّ الْعَالَمِينَ يَوْمَ الْقِيَامَةِ ، نُودُوا: لِيَقُمْ مَنْ كَانَ أَجْرُهُ عَلَى اللَّهِ، فَلَا يَقُومُ إِلَّا مَنْ عَفَا فِي الدُّنْيَا

"When the various nations are brought forth before the Lord of the worlds on the Day of Judgement, they will be addressed with the following call: 'Let the one whose reward with Allah is guaranteed stand up.' At that point, no one will stand except those who pardoned others in the temporal world."

In light of this powerful report, Imām Aḥmad forgave every oppressor who harmed him, even if he failed to come to him and seek his forgiveness. He even went as far as saying:

وَمَا عَلَى رَجُلٍ أَلَّا يُعَذِّبَ اللَّهُ تَعَالَى بِسَبَبِهِ أَحَدًا

"A man should not wish that Allah Most High punishes anyone because of him."

Admittedly, one must have a generous and compassionate heart if one wishes to replicate the approach of Imām Aḥmad. But it cannot be denied that any person who emulates such a model will be a direct recipient of Allah's grace, such that he or she will be awarded with the largest and most beautiful of banners. If one wishes to be a member of this noble class, one must ensure that one's interactions with one's Lord ﷻ and other individuals are in accordance with Islamic normative standards.

9

Pulpits of Light

Should one enter a mosque and find a person presiding over the pulpit, it would be reasonable to assume that that person enjoys a privileged and honourable position in that place of worship. There are individuals who settle interpersonal affairs in a fair and impartial manner, thereby keeping their desires for power and material gain in check. There are others who are disinterested in obtaining authority over others. But when others entrust them with such positions, they accomplish their responsibilities with the required level of fidelity (*amānah*).

Yet, there are some people who are eager to form relations and ties with others, but in a solely altruistic manner; they have no hidden desire to attain monetary or social rewards from other people. Regarding these themes, Allah ﷻ establishes a decisive otherworldly principle:

تِلْكَ الدَّارُ الْآخِرَةُ نَجْعَلُهَا لِلَّذِينَ لَا يُرِيدُونَ عُلُوًّا فِي الْأَرْضِ وَلَا فَسَادًا ۚ وَالْعَاقِبَةُ لِلْمُتَّقِينَ.

"That Home in the Hereafter We reserve for those who seek neither tyranny nor corruption on the Earth. The ultimate outcome belongs to the muttaqīn (righteous)."[22]

Furthermore, the aforementioned points explain why ʿIsā ibn Maryam ﷺ once said:

طُوبَى لِلْمُتَوَاضِعِينَ فِي الدُّنْيَا هُمْ أَصْحَابُ الْمَنَابِرِ يَوْمَ الْقِيَامَةِ.

"Glad tidings to the humble and meek ones in the temporal world. For they will be the possessors of the pulpits (manābir) on the Day of Judgement."

There will be multiple levels of eminence and grandeur on the Day of Judgement, with every particular level being assigned its own specific status. While many individuals may have heard of the pulpits of light, there are in fact noteworthy stations and ranks besides them. For instance, the Prophet ﷺ highlighted three specific categories of people who will be protected from the horrors of the Day of Judgement by having their sessions of accountability (*ḥisāb*) waived altogether. In fact, the Prophet said that while the rest of humanity is

---

22 *Al-Qaṣaṣ*, 83.

being judged and appraised by Allah ﷻ, members of these three groups will be resting upon a dune made of precious musk (*kathīb min misk*). They will find themselves secluded in this fragrant and pleasant environment while Allah holds the rest of humanity to account for their actions. Once the proceedings are complete, Allah ﷻ will allow these three groups to directly enter Paradise without any hearing or accountability for their deeds. After mentioning these various privileges, the Prophet ﷺ proceeded to enumerate these three categories one after the other. The first represents the reciters of the Qur'ān, who read it with full sincerity and solely for the sake of Allah ﷻ. Moreover, they lead people in prayer with the recitation of Allah's Book, while they are pleased with him. In essence, these reciters are epitomes of the *ahl al-Qur'ān* (the folk of the Qur'ān). The second encompasses the caller (*dā'ī*) who humbly entreats the people to observe their daily prayers, while making such pleas only for the sake of Allah ﷻ. The third group is represented by the God-fearing servants who fulfil the various duties and rights entrusted to them by Allah ﷻ and other people.

Upon reflection, it becomes apparent why these three groups attain such a privileged position in the Hereafter. Both the reciters and the callers have the ability to perform these acts for worldly gains and privileges, but they choose to do so for Allah ﷻ alone. Those who belonged to the third category may be engaged in interpersonal relations whereby they are the dominant party, such that they could exploit the other side and exact concessions from them, if they wished to do so. However, they fear Allah and ensure that their interpersonal affairs are set in order. Conversely, the most despised of people are the tyrants, who are further subdivided into various groups and classes. From the moment the Resurrection begins, Allah ﷻ will make His detestation of them abundantly clear. In a noteworthy report, the Prophet ﷺ said:

يُحْشَرُ الْمُتَكَبِّرُونَ الْجَبَّارُونَ يَوْمَ الْقِيَامَةِ فِي صُورَةِ الذَّرِّ.

"The arrogant individuals and the tyrants will be resurrected on the Day of Judgement in the form of atoms."

Such oppressive figures will be minuscule in size, even smaller than ants. Through this form of humiliation Allah ﷻ will illustrate to them their true worth and rank before Him. In fact, the Prophet ﷺ noted that their status will be so diminished that the rest of people—who will be normal in size—will step over them and show them no consideration whatsoever. In stark contrast to these figures, there will be towering stations of light that will dazzle the eyes of the onlookers. The paragons of justice and righteousness will be awarded this eminent rank. In a beautiful report, the Prophet ﷺ said:

إِنَّ الْمُقْسِطِينَ عِنْدَ اللَّهِ عَلَى مَنَابِرَ مِنْ نُورٍ عَنْ يَمِينِ الرَّحْمَنِ عَزَّ وَجَلَّ وَكِلْتَا يَدَيْهِ يَمِينٌ، الَّذِينَ يَعْدِلُونَ فِي حُكْمِهِمْ وَأَهْلِيهِمْ وَمَا وَلُوا.

"The people who exact justice will be with Allah, elevated on pulpits made of light. They will be on the right Hand of al-Raḥmān (the All-Merciful), and both of His Hands are right. These are the ones who are just in their judgements and in their engagements with their families, and in whatever they were entrusted with."

Noble stations and pulpits will be given to individuals who faithfully fulfilled the tasks and responsibilities enjoined upon them without falling in dubious practices. They loved Allah ﷻ and His Prophet ﷺ and so Allah will raise them to the highest of stations with His grace.

These are the people who uphold justice in their private and public affairs and ensure that their judgements are fair and equitable. While this *ḥadīth*'s import is general, there is no doubt that it applies more to individuals entrusted with powerful positions. For instance, many presiding judges are granted unchecked powers and prerogatives in the courtroom. If they use their power lawfully and responsibly, by ensuring that just rulings are issued, they will be able to mount a marvellous pulpit on the Day of Judgement, while all the onlookers look at them with admiration. While the tyrants and oppressors of this world are being punished, the people of righteousness and justice will be granted these elevated stations.

There is another group of righteous people who are allotted their own platforms and pulpits of light. But as opposed to the former group, their virtue lies in the fact that they upheld virtuous and loving ties with their religious brethren for the sake of Allah ﷻ. In other words, they supported their brothers and sisters in faith by reminding them of their religious responsibilities before their Creator. One can appreciate the importance of this category by considering its direct antithesis, namely the individuals who support one another in misguidance and evil. Members belonging to the latter form of association will be engaged in fierce disputes with one another on the Day of Judgement, with every person blaming the other for his or her ultimate loss. They will even go as far as asking Allah ﷻ to permit them to strike and trample on their evil companions for leading them to the wrong path. Allah ﷻ describes this level of discord and antagonism by stating:

ٱلْأَخِلَّآءُ يَوْمَئِذٍۭ بَعْضُهُمْ لِبَعْضٍ عَدُوٌّ إِلَّا ٱلْمُتَّقِينَ.

"Close friends will be enemies to one another on that Day, except the righteous."[23]

On that day, tensions will be high, with these disconcerted individuals wishing they did not befriend one another or follow the path of evil. In quiet voices, they will say to themselves in regret:

يَا وَيْلَتَىٰ لَيْتَنِي لَمْ أَتَّخِذْ فُلَانًا خَلِيلًا.

"Woe to me! I wish I had never taken so-and-so as a close friend."[24]

While the people of misguidance engage in these altercations and condemnation of each other, Allah ﷻ will direct His attention to the people of righteousness—who will preside on pulpits of light—and address them by saying:

المُتَحَابُّونَ فِي جَلَالِي لَهُمْ مَنابِرُ مِنْ نُورٍ يَغبِطُهُمُ النَّبِيُّونَ وَالشُّهَدَاءُ.

"The people who loved each another for My glory will have pulpits of light, and they will even be acclaimed by the prophets and the martyrs."

---

[23] *Al-Zukhruf*, 67.

[24] *Al-Furqān*, 28.

In one version of this report, the Companions sought further clarification and said: "O Messenger of Allah, inform us of these people and their identity." The Prophet ﷺ provided the following description of them:

نَاسٌ مِن أَفنَاءِ النَّاسِ، ونَوَازِعِ القَبَائِلِ، لَمْ تَصِلْ بَيْنَهُمْ أَرْحَامٌ مُتَقَارِبَةٌ، تَحَابُّوا فِي اللَّهِ وَتَصَافَوا، يَضَعُ اللَّهُ لَهُمْ يَوْمَ القِيَامَةِ مَنَابِرَ مِنْ نُورٍ، فَيَجْلِسُونَ عَلَيْهَا، فَيَجْعَلُ وُجُوهَهُمْ نُورًا وَثِيَابَهُمْ نُورًا، يَفْزَعُ النَّاسُ يَوْمَ القِيَامَةِ وَلاَ يَفْزَعُونَ، وَهُمْ أَوْلِيَاءُ اللَّهِ لاَ خَوْفٌ عَلَيْهِمْ وَلاَ هُمْ يَحْزَنُونَ.

"They consist of a group of people belonging to different tribes and nationalities that have no family ties, but they love one another for the sake of Allah and stand united for His sake. On the Day of Judgement Allah will erect for them pulpits made of light, upon which they will sit. While the other people are fearful and trembling, they will be fearless. For they are the friends of Allah, who shall have no fear and will never grieve."

Thus, such noble stations and pulpits will be given to individuals who had renounced this world and its transient pleasures; they faithfully fulfilled the tasks and responsibilities enjoined upon them without falling in dubious practices such as corruption or nepotism. They loved Allah ﷻ and His Prophet ﷺ, while also ensuring His light illumined their intentions and deeds. As a result, Allah will raise them to the highest of stations with His grace, such that even the Messengers and martyrs will look at them with admiration.

10

Under the Shade of Allah ﷻ

Broadly speaking, humanity may be divided into three groups: (1) those who are predominantly evil, (2) those who are predominantly upright, and (3) those who are paragons of virtue by exercising the standards of *iḥsān* (religious excellence) in their daily lives. Ideally, individuals belonging to the second group should be striving to become members of the third group, i.e. people of *iḥsān*. One of the key indicators which can be used to differentiate between the two stations is how one hasten to respond to the ordinances of Allah and the quality of one's deeds. Thus, the two key variables which distinguish the people of *iḥsān* from the ordinary believers consist of the urgency and resoluteness found in their actions. In other words, the key distinction between the *muttaqūn* (the righteous) and the *muḥsinūn* (paragons of religious excellence) is that while the former walk towards Allah, the latter hasten towards their Creator.

The state of these three groups and their respective characteristics have been outlined in the following Qur'ānic verses:

وَكُنْتُمْ أَزْوَاجًا ثَلاثَةً فَأَصْحَابُ الْمَيْمَنَةِ مَا أَصْحَابُ الْمَيْمَنَةِ وَأَصْحَابُ الْمَشْأَمَةِ مَا أَصْحَابُ الْمَشْأَمَةِ وَالسَّابِقُونَ السَّابِقُونَ أُولَئِكَ الْمُقَرَّبُونَ.

"You will be three groups: the people of the right, how (blessed) will they be; the people of the left, how (miserable) will they be; and the foremost (in faith) will be the foremost (in Paradise). They are the ones nearest to Allah."[25]

On one occasion, I recall asking one of my teachers why the martyrs (*shuhadā'*) are not mentioned in the famous *ḥadīth* which enumerates the seven groups of people that will be protected under the shade of Allah's Throne. In response, my teacher pointed out that the *shuhadā'* will enjoy a high and uncontested rank because they will be situated in glittering chandeliers that will be hanging from the sides of the Throne of Allah ﷻ, they will ultimately not be in need of any shade on the Last Day. As for the believers who are below them in rank and standing, they will be provided shade which is commensurate with their deeds. For instance, as noted in a previous chapter, a person's voluntary charity (*ṣadaqah*) will provide him or her shade and protection on that stressful day. However, there will be an elite class of believers who will be provided shade under the Throne of Allah ﷻ. They will be comprised of several groups, and collectively they will belong to a celebrated and praised group known as the forerunners (*sābiqūn*) who will supersede the *muttaqūn* in virtue.

[25] *Al-Wāqi'ah*, 7–11.

One of the most beautiful facts about the *ḥadīth* outlining the seven groups that will be shaded by Allah is that it can potentially encompass every Muslim, regardless of his or her socioeconomic status, age, or gender. The only thing needed in order to attain this special privilege is having genuine sincerity and love towards the religion of Allah ﷻ and exerting efforts to gain His pleasure. It is not necessary for one to be a special or high-ranking figure, such as a friend of Allah (*walī*) or an ascetic (*zāhid*). The full text of the *ḥadīth* in question states:

سَبْعَةٌ يُظِلُّهُمُ اللَّهُ تَعَالَى فِي ظِلِّهِ يَوْمَ لَا ظِلَّ إِلَّا ظِلُّهُ إِمَامٌ عَدْلٌ، وَشَابٌّ نَشَأَ فِي عِبَادَةِ اللَّهِ، وَرَجُلٌ قَلْبُهُ مُعَلَّقٌ فِي الْمَسَاجِدِ، وَرَجُلَانِ تَحَابَّا فِي اللَّهِ اجْتَمَعَا عَلَيْهِ وَتَفَرَّقَا عَلَيْهِ، وَرَجُلٌ دَعَتْهُ امْرَأَةٌ ذَاتُ مَنْصِبٍ وَجَمَالٍ فَقَالَ: إِنِّي أَخَافُ اللَّهَ، وَرَجُلٌ تَصَدَّقَ بِصَدَقَةٍ فَأَخْفَاهَا حَتَّى لَا تَعْلَمَ شِمَالُهُ مَا تُنْفِقُ يَمِينُهُ وَرَجُلٌ ذَكَرَ اللَّهَ خَالِيًا فَفَاضَتْ عَيْنَاهُ.

"Seven categories of people will be shaded by Allah on a day when there is no shade except His: a just ruler, a young man who is raised in the worship of Allah, a man whose heart is attached to the mosques, two men who love each other for the sake of Allah, whereby they meet and depart from one another for His sake alone, a man who is called to commit illegal sexual intercourse by a woman who has wealth and beauty, but he says: 'I fear Allah', a man who gives alms and conceals it such that his left hand does not know what his right hand has given, and a man who remembers Allah when he is alone and weeps [out of fear of Allah]."

The qualities and virtues highlighted in this report include: just governance, piety during one's youth, exhibiting love for the mosques, loving a fellow believer for the sake of Allah ﷻ, protecting oneself from engaging in evil acts, giving charity in

The key distinction between the muttaqūn (the righteous) and the muḥsinūn (paragons of religious excellence) is that while the former walk towards Allah, the latter hasten towards their Creator.

secret, and remembering Allah ﷻ in private to the extent that one is overwhelmed with tears. It is important to note that other versions of the *ḥadīth* mention additional categories as well, with their scope going beyond these seven. Most interestingly, the famous scholar Ibn Ḥajar al-ʿAsqalānī ﵀ gathered all these various versions in his book *Maʿrifah al-Khiṣāl al-Mūṣilah ilā al-Ẓilāl*. By looking at the different wordings of these versions, a number of tentative conclusions can be drawn. First, many of these causes are somehow tied to extending generosity and charitable acts and words to others. This requires much reflection, since it may explain why Allah gives these categories of people His protection in the otherworld. First and foremost, it is understood that when one provides charity to others, one is in fact granting a form of protective shade to the selected recipients. Likewise, as noted in another version of the same *ḥadīth*, the one who indefinitely defers the payment back of what he loaned to someone else, or forgives it altogether, will be protected under the shade of Allah's Throne. When one gives an unlimited extension to one's debtor or even goes as far as paying off a defaulter's loan, in essence one has provided security to such vulnerable and exploitable individuals. Therefore, to reciprocate his act, Allah ﷻ will reward one's leniency with protection in the otherworld.

Imām Ibn Qayyim al-Jawziyyah ﵀ derives an additional insight from these reports. He notes that each one of these seven groups reflects a powerful manifestation of *mukhālafat al-hawā* (going against one's whimsical desires). In a certain way, each one of these categories rejects their sensual impulses through giving preponderance to the will of Allah ﷻ.

To further elaborate, the ruler gives up worldly gains and benefits and instead exerts his efforts to exact justice at any cost; the young man shuns vain desires and sources of amusement in order to restrict himself to worship of the divine; the person attached to the mosques avoids this-worldly and pleasure-inducing centres of entertainment; the young man tempted to commit fornication suppresses his sexual desires to gain the pleasure of his Lord ﷻ; the person who gives charity resists the temptations of wealth and materialism; and the person who devotes himself to private worship closes all the avenues leading to transgression in seclusion. In essence, each one of these categories embodies the opposition of innate desires in order to gain the pleasure of Allah ﷻ.

Moreover, further themes can be derived upon careful study of the seven categories mentioned above. For instance, it is evident that the actions of every individual from amongst these groups constitute obedience to Allah ﷻ. But as the scholars and commentators note, Allah's obedience can be subdivided into two categories: private and public. The former includes acts of worship done in a closed and private setting, while the latter constitutes noble acts done at the interpersonal level for the sake of Allah ﷻ. Interestingly, the first four groups of people mentioned in this report performed noble actions publicly. The final three, on the other hand, performed virtuous deeds in private. From this arrangement and presentation found in the *ḥadīth*, one can infer a golden ethical principle: one must reform one's conduct in public in order to improve one's religious undertakings in private.

Commentators of *Ḥadīth* also note that just as the gates of *Jannah* are numerous, the people of virtue covered in this *ḥadīth* also belong to several categories. In fact, they point out that Prophet Yūsuf ﷺ is perhaps the only person who will be included in all the seven categories, due to the number of remarkable transformations and stages found in his miraculous life. It is also interesting to note that the first group—the people of authority who rule with justice—is extremely rare and beyond the reach of most people, since the number of rulers in the world is very limited. On the other hand, the last category—those who remember Allah ﷻ and cry out of fear of His punishment—is potentially attainable by all people, regardless of their socioeconomic status or political standing. After all, one does not need to enjoy political privileges to reflect on one's Creator and appreciate His all-inclusive power over the world. Undoubtedly, one who belongs to the first and last categories is stamped with a beautiful spiritual temperament. One of the heroes of Islamic history who achieved this very feat was none other than 'Umar ibn al-Khaṭṭāb ؓ, the second Caliph of Islam. Besides being a morally scrupulous and religiously conscious ruler, he was known for his generous charity efforts—he carried bags of staple goods on his own shoulder—and his habit of praying at night. In fact, as a result of frequently shedding tears at night-time, it is said that he developed marks under his eyes.

Commentators also note that, although the various versions of this *ḥadīth* mention the seven categories in different sequences, one key regularity which persists in all these versions is the initial mention of the just ruler. This remarkable consistency is not without its wisdom, since it is well-known that when the head of political authority is morally upright in his conduct and rule, civil society will flourish and become a bastion of religious goodness and spiritual consciousness. This explains why the noble Imām and ascetic Sufyān al-Thawrī ؒ uttered his famous statement:

صِنْفَانِ إِذَا صَلَحَا صَلَحَتِ الأُمَّةُ وَإِذَا فَسَدَا فَسَدَتِ الأُمَّةُ: الحُكَّامُ وَالعُلَمَاءُ.

"If two classes of people are morally upright, the Ummah will be morally upright as well. But if they are corrupt, then the entire Ummah will be corrupted as well. These two groups consist of the political authorities and the scholars."

It is interesting to note how every group, in the abovementioned Prophetic saying, is intricately connected to the one that is mentioned after it, sometimes even in causal terms. For instance, a noble and religious ruler facilitates the worship of Allah ﷻ by financing the construction of mosques and encouraging his subjects to pray there frequently. Through the noble initiatives of the ruler, the youth will be motivated to attend these mosques and develop a moral compass oriented towards the worship of Allah ﷻ. But such a highly spiritual mode of upbringing is impossible unless the mosque is built first, a process which strictly falls within the prerogative of the ruler. The pious ruler's role in the activation of religious consciousness cannot be underestimated. For history reveals

The eye which sheds tears for the sake of Allah will be made unlawful for the Fire to graze it. Upon seeing His slave privately express khashyah (fear) towards his Creator, Allah will provide him comfort and tranquillity in this life and the Hereafter.

that when political authorities are unjust and oppose the observance of religion, then the mosques become manipulated or even destroyed by tyrannical forces.

If one reflects even more carefully, further connections can be drawn between the various categories mentioned in the *ḥadīth* above. When the mosques are maintained by the rulers and a new generation of religious youth is fostered, the hearts of people will be intricately connected with the houses of Allah ﷻ. Over time, the worshippers will begin to meet their fellow attendees and develop deep-rooted ties; they will eventually love one another for the sake of Allah, with the mosque firmly anchoring their spiritual bonds. Furthermore, this high degree of spiritual consciousness will provide the worshippers with a religious stamina to resist any evil calls or sinful endeavours. Instead of positively responding to such opportunities, they will resist and proclaim: "I fear Allah." Ultimately, these attendees and worshippers will develop such a strong degree of faith and love for Allah ﷻ that they will perform private acts of good as well. Instead of succumbing to their desires and committing sins in their private quarters, they will instead secretly give charity for the sake of Allah alone. With the acts of piety now spilling over to the private sphere, one's goodness can now culminate in the form of the last category: remembering Allah ﷻ in private and weeping in astonishment of His power and command over one.

The final two categories are not only deeply intimate and private affairs, but they are actions which can be undertaken by all people, irrespective of their state or status. In fact, it is well-established that the *Salaf* (pious predecessors) often alternated between these two actions over the span of a twenty-four-hour cycle. Regarding some of them, it was said:

يُنْفِقُ فِي النَّهَارِ وَيَبْكِي فِي اللَّيْلِ.

"He would give wealth in charity during the day and cry during the night."

In other words, the sixth and seventh categories are intricately tied with one another, since the optimal period to remember Allah ﷻ is immediately after giving some wealth in charity. The Prophet ﷺ mentioned in a *ḥadīth* that the latter softens one's heart thereby opening it to spiritual reflection. Additionally, the opposite causal relationship can be invoked as well. Giving charity *after* remembering Allah ﷻ at night-time is also a praiseworthy act, since through such religious reflection one's attachment to the *dunyā* (temporal world) is diminished. This means that any subsequent acts of charity will be sincere and purified from base intentions and thoughts.

As explicitly mentioned in a *ḥadīth*, Allah ﷻ is more merciful towards us than our own mothers are. When our mothers witness us cry or fall in a deeply emotional state, they become concerned and immediately rush to our aid. One can only imagine the aid and facilitation that Allah ﷻ provides to His crying slave. The Prophet ﷺ highlighted the significance of this matter by stating that the eye which sheds tears for the sake of Allah will be made unlawful for the Fire to graze it. Upon seeing His slave privately express *khashyah* (fear) towards his Creator, Allah will provide him comfort and tranquillity in this life and the Hereafter. The great Companion 'Abdullāh ibn 'Umar ﷺ underscored these aforementioned themes by making the following statement:

لَأَنْ أَدْمَعَ دَمْعَةً مِنْ خَشْيَةِ اللهِ أَحَبُّ إِلَيَّ مِنْ أَنْ أَتَصَدَّقَ بِأَلْفِ دِينَارٍ، فَإِنْ أَنْفَقْتُ أَلْفَ دِينَارٍ لَا أَدْرِي أَضَمِنْتُ مِنَ النَّارِ.

"Crying due to the fear of Allah is more beloved to me than giving 1000 dinars in charity, since if I were to spend the latter amount, I would not know whether they would secure me from the Hellfire."

Through this statement, Ibn 'Umar emphasised the value of shedding tears out of fear of Allah. Regardless of whether it is done after the commission of a good deed or a sin, such a manifestation of sincere *khashyah* will ensure one is shaded from the scorching heat of the Day of Judgement. Moreover, the tears shed due to such fear will protect one from the chastisement of Hellfire.

11

When He Asks About One's Prayer

The first thing that will rush to one's aid in the grave will be one's *ṣalāh* (prayer). When one awakens in one's grave one's commitment to the *ṣalāh* will be immediately tested. Moreover, during the period of reckoning on the Day of Judgement, the first thing that one will be asked about is one's *ṣalāh*. All these facts make it abundantly clear that one must ensure that *ṣalāh* is performed in the best possible manner throughout one's life. The Prophet ﷺ also underscored the priceless value of the *ṣalāh* when he stated:

إِذَا كَانَ أَحَدُكُمْ فِي الصَّلَاةِ فَإِنَّهُ يُنَاجِي رَبَّهُ.

"When one of you is engaged in prayer, he is engaged in an intimate conversation with his Lord."

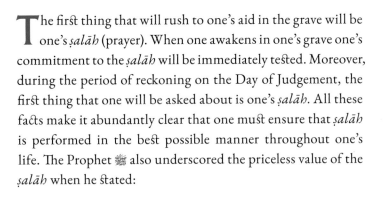

One should also carefully study the structure of the *ṣalāh* as well. After immediately emphasising Allah's mercy in *Sūrah al-Fātiḥah* by reading His names al-Raḥmān (the All-Merciful) and al-Raḥīm (the Giver of Mercy), one then reads the following verse, which reminds one of accountability in the other world:

مَٰلِكِ يَوْمِ ٱلدِّينِ.

"Master of the Day of Judgement."[26]

The relationship between these two verses is not coincidental, since through them one is reminded that obtaining the mercy of Allah ﷻ is pivotal, especially on the Day of Judgement. In fact, throughout the pillars and motions of the *ṣalāh*, not only does one feel closer to one's Lord, but one is also acutely reminded of the Day of Judgement and the necessity of preparing for it by reading its title in *Sūrah al-Fātiḥah* and seeking refuge from its horrors and trials before concluding one's act of worship.

There is no doubt that the best *ṣalāh* occurs when one's heart is fully engaged with the Creator ﷻ to the extent that the soul yearns to meet Him on the Day of Judgement. For this reason, Ibn Qayyim al-Jawziyyah ؒ stated that the person who masters his standing before his Lord in this world will also master it in the other world. The best way for one to be included among the *sābiqūn* (forerunners) is to pray punctually and avoid any unnecessary delays in performing it, since this is one of the deeds which Allah ﷻ intensely loves. In fact, one who performs the prayers regularly on time will oftentimes carry out other worldly and religious responsibilities in a diligent manner. In the *dunyā* (temporal world), when the time for

[26] *Al-Fātiḥah*, 4.

prayer enters, the believers turn to their lord and abandon other responsibilities and the gatherings they are present in. On the Day of Judgement, one will also depart from one's point of gathering and proceed to meet one's Lord. But instead of going to pray, one will approach one's Lord in order to be questioned and held to account for one's deeds.

The Prophet ﷺ has vividly described how the process of accountability will unfold in the Hereafter. He stated that, upon dividing humankind into various categories, Allah ﷻ will then begin the accountability process, whereby His individual servants will be called, one after the other. In this report, the Prophet ﷺ describes how a person will be brought before his Lord and addressed by Him directly:

فَيَلْقَى العَبْدَ فَيَقُولُ: أَيْ فُلْ أَلَمْ أُكْرِمْكَ وَأُسَوِّدْكَ وأُزَوِّجْكَ وَأُسَخِّرْ لَكَ الخَيْلَ وَالإِبِلَ.

"He will bring His slave forward and say: 'O so-and-so! Did I not honour you, make you a leader, provide you with a spouse, and put at your disposal various means of transportation?'"

One by one, Allah ﷻ will enumerate the blessings He granted His slave. Afterwards, Allah will ask His slave whether he acknowledges all these blessings. The latter will reply in the positive. Subsequently, Allah ﷻ will ask:

أَفَظَنَنْتَ أَنَّكَ مُلَاقِيَّ؟

"Did you not ever come to the realisation that you will be meeting Me?"

The person will respond, "No." Allah ﷻ will then condemn this individual by stating:

فَإِنِّي أَنْسَاكَ كَمَا نَسِيْتَنِي.

"So I shall forget you today, as you have forgotten Me."

If one carefully reflects on this narration, one will realise that Allah ﷻ first enumerated the blessings He bestowed on this servant and then proceeded to condemn him for his contempt of Him. There is a strong connection between these two states, as ungratefulness leads to forgetfulness of Allah. Conversely, gratitude (*shukr*) of Allah leads to greater remembrance of Him through performing more acts of worship. This connection is further highlighted in the famous *ḥadīth*:

إِنَّ أَوَّلَ مَا يُحَاسَبُ بِهِ العَبْدُ يَوْمَ القِيَامَةِ مِنْ عَمَلِهِ صَلَاتُهُ.

"The first deed about which the slave will be taken to task is the ṣalāh."

The main reason why the *ṣalāh* is highlighted and stressed so much in the Islamic tradition is because it is the yardstick by which one's remembrance of Allah ﷻ is measured. Without performing it, one's remembrance of, and gratitude towards, Allah will always be deficient. In fact, in the following verse of the Qur'ān, one may even be tempted to deduce that the *ṣalāh* is the sole means of remembering Allah ﷻ in this life:

وَأَقِمِ الصَّلَاةَ لِذِكْرِي.

"And establish prayer for My remembrance."[27]

The one who consistently prays with an attentive heart can never be amongst those who forget Allah ﷻ. This causal relationship is further underscored in another verse, whereby Allah issues the following set of imperatives:

بَلِ اللَّهَ فَاعْبُدْ وَكُنْ مِنَ الشَّاكِرِينَ

"Rather, worship Allah and be one of the grateful."[28]

Furthermore, when the Prophet ﷺ was once asked why he constantly observed the night prayers even though all his sins were forgiven, he hypothetically asked:

أَفَلَا أَكُونُ عَبْدًا شَكُورًا؟

"Shall I not be a grateful servant?"

---

[27] *Ṭāhā*, 14.

[28] *Al-Zumar*, 66.

The best way for one to be included among the sābiqūn (forerunners) is to pray punctually and avoid any unnecessary delays in performing it, since this is one of the deeds which Allah عز وجل intensely loves. The first deed about which we will be taken to task is the ṣalāh.

In another powerful report, the Prophet ﷺ gave glad tidings to the one who consistently observes his prayers:

مَنْ حَافَظَ عَلَيْهَا كَانَتْ لَهُ نُورًا وَبُرْهَانًا يَوْمَ الْقِيَامَةِ.

"Whoever attentively upholds their performance, it will be a shimmering light and a decisive evidence for him on the Day of Judgement."

Conversely, the Prophet issued the following warning for the one who is neglectful of his prayers:

وَمَنْ لَمْ يُحَافِظْ عَلَيْهَا لَمْ يَكُنْ لَهُ نُورٌ وَلَا بُرْهَانٌ وَلَا نَجَاةٌ، وَكَانَ يَوْمَ الْقِيَامَةِ مَعَ قَارُونَ وَفِرْعَوْنَ وَهَامَانَ وَأُبَيِّ بْنِ خَلَفٍ.

"And whoever fails to uphold them, he will be devoid of any shimmering light, decisive evidence, and salvation. On the Day of Judgement, he will be raised with Qārūn, Firʿawn, Hāmān, and Ubayy ibn Khalaf."

In other words, the person who fails to observe his prayers will be resurrected amongst the tyrants and oppressors. This fact may be shocking to many people, for there are many non-religious individuals who attempt to justify their non-observance of prayers by claiming that they pray in their heart and treat people with kindness and generosity. Why then will they be raised with the people of evil? First and foremost, the *ṣalāh* is what differentiates the believer from the disbeliever. The connection between the non-observant person—who misses his prayers—and the aforementioned tyrants lies in the fact that all of them are heedless of Allah ﷻ and unmindful of His favours upon them. By forgetting Allah, these oppressors became haughty and egoistic. They failed to appreciate the blessings conferred upon them by their Creator ﷻ and the message of truth that He delivered to them through His Prophets. The key upshot is that without prayer, one will die in a state of spiritual poverty. The story of the man who was called and judged before Allah in the aforementioned *ḥadīth* also underscores this point, since he failed to reflect on the various blessings that Allah granted him through turning to Him in worship. As he forgot Allah in this world, Allah will forget him on the Day of Judgement.

At this juncture, it is important to note that people can never actually recompense Allah ﷻ for everything He has given them through the performance of prayer, since His blessings are unlimited. In fact, the Prophet ﷺ once related that a man who performs the prayer for more than 500 years cannot repay Allah for the blessing of his eyes and vision. On the Day of Resurrection, it will become evident that any amount of prayer presented to Allah ﷻ will prove deficient and insufficient to pay Him for the smallest of blessings given in this world. Moreover, in a sound narration, the Prophet ﷺ said:

لَوْ أَنَّ رَجُلًا يُجَرُّ عَلَى وَجْهِهِ مِنْ يَوْمِ وُلِدَ إِلَى يَوْمِ يَمُوتُ هَرَمًا فِي مَرْضَاةِ اللهِ عَزَّ وَجَلَّ
لَحَقَّرَهُ يَوْمَ الْقِيَامَةِ.

"Were a man to be dragged on his face from the day he is born until the day he dies in order to attain the pleasure of Allah, He would still deem this to be insignificant on the Day of Judgement."

Instead of seeking rewards from Allah ﷻ, the believer's true concern should be to receive deliverance from punishment, since the acts of prayer performed by humans are always beset by imperfections and errors. However, Allah ﷻ has assured His servants that He will judge them mercifully, and even forgive their sins by cancelling them with their good deeds, such as the prayer. Such an act of kindness exceeds and supersedes any form of blessing that Allah could give the believers in this world.

At this stage, it is worthwhile to further explore the *ḥadīth* cited earlier in this chapter, in which the Prophet ﷺ is reported to have said: "The first thing that the slave will be held to account is the *ṣalāh*." In the same report, the Prophet ﷺ further said:

فَإِنْ صَلَحَتْ فَقَدْ أَفْلَحَ وَأَنْجَحَ.

"If it was performed properly and as required, then he has succeeded and attained his salvation."

But then the Prophet ﷺ warns:

وَإِنْ فَسَدَتْ فَقَدْ خَابَ وَخَسِرَ.

"But if it was not performed as ordered, then he has failed and lost."

At first sight, this report seems to suggest that one who falls short in one's prayers will be held to account and punished. Such an inference would undoubtedly be terrifying, since the worship of every Muslim is deficient and lacking in some respects.

But Allah ﷻ will not leave His servant disappointed on that Day. He will address the angels and say:

هَلْ لِعَبْدِي مِنْ تَطَوُّعٍ؟

"Does My servant have any voluntary prayers in his record?"

This latter part of the *ḥadīth* reflects the mercy of Allah ﷻ. While the servant is having his deeds weighed and judged in the most stupendous test for humanity, Allah will ensure that his supererogatory prayers are also counted and used to mend any imperfections found in his obligatory worship. The Prophet ﷺ further noted that other supererogatory acts of worship will also be considered to mend any deficiencies in their respective obligatory categories. This relevant portion of the *ḥadīth* states:

ثُمَّ يَكُونُ سَائِرُ عَمَلِهِ عَلَى ذَلِكَ.

"The rest of his actions will be taken to account in the same manner."

By way of example, if one failed to consistently fast every month of Ramadan during one's life, Allah ﷻ will determine whether one has performed any voluntary fasts that could help correct that deficiency. Likewise, should one's payment of *zakāt* payments be outstanding and in arrears, it will be evaluated whether one has given any alms (*ṣadaqah*) during one's lifetime that matches or comes close to the amount of *zakāt* one owes. The same procedure will be undertaken for the rest of his deeds.

One will recall that the greatest category of believers is that which includes those who will be protected under the throne of Allah. Such believers will be bestowed the eminent title of *al-muqarrabūn* (the ones who are brought nigh to Allah). In a very beautiful holy saying (*ḥadīth qudsī*), the Prophet ﷺ related the following words from Allah ﷻ:

وَمَا تَقَرَّبَ إِلَيَّ عَبْدِي بِشَيْءٍ أَحَبَّ إِلَيَّ مِمَّا افْتَرَضْتُ عَلَيْهِ، وَمَا يَزَالُ عَبْدِي يَتَقَرَّبُ إِلَيَّ بِالنَّوَافِلِ حَتَّى أُحِبَّهُ.

"My servant does not draw near to Me with anything more beloved to Me than what I have made obligatory on him. And my servant keeps drawing close to Me through voluntary deeds until I end up loving him."

This *ḥadīth* underscores the importance of attaining closeness (*qurb*) to Allah ﷻ. When one undertakes the actions that bring one in spiritual proximity to Allah, one will be included among the beloved of Allah and thus benefit from His shade on the Day of Judgement. Undoubtedly, the first decisive step to achieving this *qurb* is to perform the compulsory acts of worship prescribed in the religion. Secondly, one should also strive to perform the voluntary acts of prayer as well. To illustrate these two categories in the form of a concrete example, one may consider the five daily prayers. No one who claims to love Allah and His Messenger will disregard the *adhān*, which directly addresses every listener with the phrases *ḥayya 'alā al-ṣalāh* (come to prayer) and *ḥayya 'alā al-falāḥ* (come to success). Moreover, one who punctually observes the five daily prayers will gradually develop the habit of performing voluntary prayers as well. This will inevitably lead to a heightened state of spirituality and a religious consciousness and, as a result, every prayer will be performed with fewer errors and deficiencies. Not only will one's quantity of worship increase then, but its overall quality will also be amplified. On the Last Day, Each one of these obligatory and voluntary prayers—such as *tahajjud* (the late-night prayer) and *tarāwīḥ* (the special Ramadan night prayer)—will appear as clusters of light, testifying on one's behalf, and ensuring that one attains salvation in the eternal abode of bliss.

فَأَمَّا مَن ثَقُلَتْ مَوَٰزِينُهُۥ فَهُوَ فِى عِيشَةٍ رَّاضِيَةٍ

"So as for those whose scales are heavy with good deeds, they will be in a life of bliss."

AL-QĀRIʿAH, 6–7

12

Mountains and Mirages

The true and sincere believer evaluates everything in this world while being cognisant of Allah's greatness and mercy. Subsequently, he will never deem a good deed to be insignificant, since he is well aware of the greatness of its recipient: the Lord of the worlds ﷻ. On this matter, the Prophet ﷺ has stated:

لَا تَحْقِرَنَّ مِنَ الْمَعْرُوفِ شَيْئًا.

"Do not belittle the slightest of good deeds."

With the same logic in mind, the Prophet ﷺ warned against *muḥaqqarāt al-dhunūb* (sins deemed to be insignificant), since the wise believer must always bear in mind the magnificence of the One Who he is sinning against.

The believer knows that regardless of the good he undertakes, Allah ﷻ is deserving of what is greater and better both quantitatively and qualitatively. Likewise, whenever he commits a sin, he recalls the textual proofs that stress Allah's mercy, and thus ultimately turn to Him in repentance. Sometimes, though, it may be difficult for one to be motivated by one's good actions: in one's mind a small *duʿā'* (supplication) or an insignificant amount of charity is inconsequential in the grander scale of things. When such thoughts cross one's mind, it is important to recall that the role of humans, when it comes to actions and deeds, is to sincerely sow seeds of good in their environment. It is their Creator ﷻ Who then causes these kernels to sprout and mature into flourishing structures.

Before one stands before Allah ﷻ on the Day of Judgement, one must undertake the necessary preparations by performing as many good deeds as possible, while ensuring that one's intention is to please Him alone. On the Day of Judgement, these deeds will not simply be weighed, but they will also be assessed directly by Allah. Allah—Whose knowledge is complete—will not only assess deeds on account of their value in the world, but also the intentions and motivations that triggered them in the first place. On the Day of Judgement, the sincerity and intent behind one's actions will be the decisive factor in raising the value of one's deeds. Without these noble aims and objectives, one's deeds will be hollow and devoid of any moral worth.

In the texts of the Qur'ān and Sunnah, one often finds the invocation of mountains and mustard seeds as metaphors for the value of one's deeds. For instance, Allah ﷻ has declared that even a deed which is as small as a mustard seed will in fact be recompensed by Him on the Day of Judgement:

فَمَنْ يَعْمَلْ مِثْقَالَ ذَرَّةٍ خَيْرًا يَرَهُ وَمَنْ يَعْمَلْ مِثْقَالَ ذَرَّةٍ شَرًّا يَرَهُ.

"So whoever does an atom's weight of good will see it. And whoever does an atom's weight of evil will see it."[29]

In another verse, He ﷻ states:

وَإِنْ كَانَ مِثْقَالَ حَبَّةٍ مِنْ خَرْدَلٍ أَتَيْنَا بِهَا.

"And if a deed is the weight of a mustard seed, we will bring it forth."[30]

While any good deed done today—even if it is as minuscule as a seed—will be accepted and registered in one's account, Allah ﷻ has declared that no offering or good deed on the Day of Judgement will avail one as a ransom, even if is a mountain of gold. The people of wickedness lack foresightedness and only live for the present moment; they fail to show any concern for the next world that awaits them. For this reason, the evildoers—who lacked the urgency to perform acts of good in this temporal world—will become panic-stricken and desperate on the Day of Judgement, and even go as far as offering ten times the world in gold to secure their salvation.

29 *Al-Zalzalah*, 7–8.

30 *Al-Anbiyā'*, 47.

On the Day of Judgement, the sincerity and intent behind one's actions will be the decisive factor in raising the value of one's deeds. Without these noble aims and objectives, one's deeds will be hollow and devoid of any moral worth.

Allah ﷻ will remind them that He never sought such a thing from His servants; instead, they were simply required to consistently perform acts of good while they were in this world. But because the evildoers let this world pass by them and now observe the punishment that awaits them, they end up extending such exorbitant offers. The greedy and godless mentality of the short-sighted evildoers is encapsulated in the following narration:

لَوْ أَنَّ لِابْنِ آدَمَ وَادِيًا مِنْ ذَهَبٍ أَحَبَّ أَنْ يَكُونَ لَهُ وَادِيَانِ، وَلَنْ يَمْلأَ فَاهُ إِلَّا التُّرَابُ.

"Were the son of Adam to be given a valley of gold, he would love to have two of them. But nothing will fill his mouth except dust."

This narration indicates that the materialist impulses of the this-worldly person will not cease until he enters the grave. The greatest tragedy in such a mentality is that it can never consider rewards and punishments, nor preparing for the Hereafter. The Prophetic Companions completely eschewed such short-sighted and materialist tendencies, and instead fully invested their actions and efforts in preparing for the Hereafter, thereby attaining Allah's pleasure. This explains why the Prophet ﷺ said:

لَا تَسُبُّوا أَحَدًا مِنْ أَصْحَابِي ، فَإِنَّ أَحَدَكُمْ لَوْ أَنْفَقَ مِثْلَ أُحُدٍ ذَهَبًا مَا أَدْرَكَ مُدَّ أَحَدِهِمْ ، وَلَا نَصِيفَهُ

"Do not vituperate any of my Companions, for if one of you were to spend the weight of Uḥud in gold, he would not match [the merit and worth of] a handful or even half a handful of what they had spent."

It was the noble and righteous intentions of the Companions which magnified their actions to the extent that they towered like mountains in the sight of their Creator ﷻ. While the virtues described in this report are unique to the Companions, nevertheless the same logic is applicable to the rest of Muslims, in the sense that a sincere deed is magnified in the sight of Allah ﷻ. This explains why the Prophet ﷺ said that even if one hears the Trumpet announcing the Day of Resurrection, one should still sow the seed of a plant that is in one's hand, thereby starting a good deed with a well-intentioned heart. In another report, the Prophet ﷺ said:

إنَّ اللهَ ليُربِّي لأحدِكم التَّمرةَ واللُّقمةَ كما يُربِّي أحدُكم فَلُوَّه أو فصيلَه حتَّى تكونَ مثلَ أُحُدٍ.

"Indeed, Allah shall cultivate for one of you the date or morsel that he gives in charity in the same way that one of you nurtures a foal or young camel until it reaches the size of Uḥud."

In another report, the Prophet ﷺ said:

مَا تَصَدَّقَ أَحَدٌ بِصَدَقَةٍ مِنْ طَيِّبٍ ، وَلَا يَقْبَلُ اللَّهُ إِلَّا الطَّيِّبَ ، إِلَّا أَخَذَهَا الرَّحْمَنُ بِيَمِينِهِ ، وَإِنْ كَانَتْ تَمْرَةً ، فَتَرْبُو فِي كَفِّ الرَّحْمَنِ حَتَّى تَكُونَ أَعْظَمَ مِنَ الْجَبَلِ ، كَمَا يُرَبِّي أَحَدُكُمْ فَلُوَّهُ أَوْ فَصِيلَهُ.

"None of you gives ṣadaqah from that which is pure and wholesome—and Allah does not accept anything except what is pure and wholesome—except that al-Raḥmān (the All-Merciful) will accept it with His Right Hand. Even if the offering is as small as a date, al-Raḥmān will nurture it in His Hand until it becomes greater than a mountain, just as one of you raises his foal or young camel."

For this reason, the *Salaf* (pious predecessors) made sure that their offerings were given with a sincere and pure heart. The Mother of the Believers 'Ā'ishah ﵂ put perfume on her money before distributing it to the poor and needy. She was conscious that this would be received by *al-Raḥmān* ﷻ, Who would then cultivate it for her. The concept of having good deeds multiplied is further highlighted in the following verse:

مَنْ ذَا الَّذِي يُقْرِضُ اللَّهَ قَرْضًا حَسَنًا فَيُضَاعِفَهُ لَهُ وَلَهُ أَجْرٌ كَرِيمٌ.

"Who is it that will lend to Allah a good loan which Allah will multiply for them, and they will have an honourable reward?"[31]

The aforementioned narrations demonstrate that sincerity is the essential building block of deeds, and, through it, the smallest of actions can grow into the size of mountains on the Day of Judgement. At the same time, however, the opposite is also true: virtuous actions can be downgraded or thwarted through impure intentions and transgressions. In a chilling *ḥadīth*, the Companion Thawbān narrated that the Prophet ﷺ said:

لَأَعْلَمَنَّ أَقْوَامًا مِنْ أُمَّتِي يَأْتُونَ يَوْمَ الْقِيَامَةِ بِحَسَنَاتٍ أَمْثَالِ جِبَالِ تِهَامَةَ بِيضًا فَيَجْعَلُهَا اللَّهُ عَزَّ وَجَلَّ هَبَاءً مَنْثُورًا.

"I certainly know of groups of people from my Ummah who will come on the Day of Judgement with sparkling virtuous deeds the size of the mountains of Tihāmah. Yet, Allah will turn those deeds into scattered dust."

---

[31] *Al-Ḥadīd*, 11.

Thawbān ؓ said:

يَا رَسُولَ اللَّهِ صِفْهُمْ لَنَا جَلِّهِمْ لَنَا أَنْ لَا نَكُونَ مِنْهُمْ وَنَحْنُ لَا نَعْلَمُ.

"O Messenger of Allah, describe and clarify them to us, lest we
become of them without realizing it."

The Prophet ﷺ replied by stating:

أَمَا إِنَّهُمْ إِخْوَانُكُمْ وَمِنْ جِلْدَتِكُمْ وَيَأْخُذُونَ مِنْ اللَّيْلِ كَمَا تَأْخُذُونَ وَلَكِنَّهُمْ أَقْوَامٌ إِذَا
خَلَوْا بِمَحَارِمِ اللَّهِ انْتَهَكُوهَا.

"They are your brothers and members of your people, and
spend the night in worship as you do. However, when they
find themselves alone with the sanctities of Allah, they
transgress them."

The message encapsulated in this *ḥadīth* is echoed in the
following verse:

وَقَدِمْنَا إِلَى مَا عَمِلُوا مِنْ عَمَلٍ فَجَعَلْنَاهُ هَبَاءً مَّنْثُورًا.

"Then We will turn to whatever deeds they did, reducing them
to scattered dust." [32]

These sacred texts indicate how one's mountains of good deeds
can be turned into nothingness: exhibiting piety in front of
people but demonstrating blatant disregard for Allah ﷻ by
sinning in one's private quarters can lead to one's devastation
and agony in the Hereafter. This analytical conclusion may
be *prima facie* problematic for some observers, since there

---

[32] *Al-Furqān*, 23.

The believer does not belittle any small deed, nor does he underestimate any sin. Even an atom of good can become a towering mountain on the Last Day if it is done with sincerity. Likewise, multitudes of good deeds can be destroyed through a single sin done in abject disregard of Allah.

are other *ḥadīths* which suggest that Allah ﷻ will forgive the private sins of His Muslim servants. The scholars have resolved this apparent conflict by asserting that the *ḥadīth* of Thawbān refers to the hypocrites who only act in public spaces, while the other reports pointing to Allah's forgiveness apply to Muslims who sincerely strive not to sin in private. By his very nature, the hypocrite gives no consideration to the fact that Allah is observing his actions, and instead is strictly concerned with his conduct in the presence of other people. On the other hand, the believer pays little or no attention to what people think of him; his hopes and fears are solely attached to his Creator ﷻ.

Another decisive factor which distinguishes the Companions and makes their deeds like the size of Uḥud is the fact that they deemed any sin—regardless of its degree of severity—to be destructive and dangerous to their faith. The prominent Companion Anas ibn Mālik ﵁ sternly reminded the Successors (*Tābiʿūn*)—who were people of piety as well—of this fact and urged them to exercise greater diligence in their inner and outer conducts:

إِنَّكُمْ لَتَعْمَلُونَ أَعْمَالًا هِيَ أَدَقُّ فِي أَعْيُنِكُمْ مِنَ الشَّعَرِ، إِنْ كُنَّا لَنَعُدُّهَا عَلَى عَهْدِ النَّبِيِّ صَلَّى اللَّهُ عَلَيْهِ وَسَلَّمَ مِنَ المُوبِقَاتِ.

"You often perform actions which you deem to be insignificant and minor. But during the time of the Prophet ﷺ, we used to consider them to be major destructive sins."

ʿAbdullāh ibn Masʿūd ﵁ said:

إنَّ المُؤْمِنَ يَرَى ذُنُوبَهُ كَأنَّهُ قاعِدٌ تَحْتَ جَبَلٍ يَخافُ أنْ يَقَعَ عَلَيْهِ، وَإنَّ الفَاجِرَ يَرَى ذُنُوبَهُ كَذُبابٍ مَرَّ عَلَى أنْفِهِ فَقَالَ بِهِ هَكَذَا.

"The believer sees his sins and considers himself as if he is sitting at the foot of a mountain, fearing that it will fall on him at any moment while the wicked person perceives his sin to be like flies hovering around his nose, which he simply waves away."

Thus, the believer does not belittle any small deed, nor does he underestimate any sin. This is because even an atom of good can prospectively become a towering mountain on the Last Day, provided it is done with sincerity. Likewise, multitudes of good deeds can be destroyed through a single sin done in abject disregard of Allah. Yet, there is another ethical dimension of the Companions which requires some consideration. For if they believed that every sin was an enormity and potential source of damnation, should this not have psychologically burdened them and caused them to become emotionally insecure? We know for a fact that this was not the case, since they were people of ambition and vitality. The reason why this was the case is that they grasped that, no matter how sinful one may be, Allah's door of mercy and forgiveness are always open.

In a widely-cited *ḥadīth qudsī*, the Prophet ﷺ related the following from Allah ﷻ:

يَا ابْنَ آدمَ ! إِنَّكَ مَا دَعَوْتَنِي وَرَجَوْتَنِي غَفَرْتُ لَكَ عَلَى مَا كَانَ فِيكَ وَلاَ أُبَالِي يَا ابْنَ آدمَ! لَوْ بَلَغَتْ ذُنُوبُكَ عَنَانَ السَّمَاءِ ثُمَّ اسْتَغْفَرْتَنِي غَفَرْتُ لكَ وَلاَ أُبَالِي؛ يَا ابْنَ آدمَ! لَوْ أَتَيْتَنِي بِقُرَابِ الأَرْضِ خَطَايا ثُمَّ لَقِيْتَنِي لاَتُشْرِكُ بِي شَيْئًا لأَتَيْتُكَ بِقرَابِهَا مَغْفِرَةً.

"O son of Adam! As long as you call upon Me and have hope in Me, I will not mind forgiving you any lapses done on your part. O son of Adam! Even were your sins to reach the height of the clouds and then you seek My forgiveness, I will forgive you without minding. O son of Adam! Were you to come to Me with sins reaching the depths of the Earth and then encounter Me while not ascribing to Me any partners, I would come to you with the same amount of forgiveness."

This narration beautifully illustrates the vast and limitless mercy of Allah ﷻ. The Muslim who commits numerous sins can be fully forgiven and have his vices replaced with rewards. In this regard, Imām Ibn Qayyim al-Jawziyyah ؒ has said:

إِنَّ العَبْدَ لَيَأْتِي يَوْمَ القِيَامَةِ بِسَيِّئَاتٍ أَمْثَالَ الجِبَالِ، فَيَجِدُ لِسَانَهُ قَدْ هَدَمَهُ مِنْ كَثْرَةِ ذِكْرِ اللهِ تَعَالَى".

"The servant will come on the Day of Judgement with sins the size of mountains, but then finds that his tongue has completely demolished them due to his oft remembrance (dhikr) of Allah."

We ask Allah ﷻ to shower us with His mercy and generosity by upgrading our insignificant virtuous deeds into mountains and causing our mountains of sins to disintegrate into minute atoms.

13

One's Limbs Will Testify

What would your reaction be if every object or thing in your possession—including your limbs—spoke and relayed all the actions that you performed throughout your life? As a thought experiment, one could imagine one's own mobile phones and electronic devices speaking and relating what one types and searches on one's respective keyboard every day. One's hands and feet would be sharing details of one's daily activities and destinations. Undoubtedly, if such was the case, many of us would likely feel insecure and exercise extreme caution in the performance of their day-to-day actions. But no one would disagree that the most frightening and terrifying form of testimony in this regard will come from the heart, since it is a sensitive organ whose state changes drastically depending on one's spiritual states and environments. Occasionally one's intentions—despite apparently seeming noble and righteous—are contaminated by insincere desires. To demonstrate this fact, one may consider a moving interaction between the prominent authorities and authors in the science of *Ḥadīth*, Imām Abū

Dāwūd and Imām Aḥmad ibn Ḥanbal ﷺ. After compiling his *magnum opus*, the *Sunan*, Imām Abū Dāwūd told Imām Aḥmad: "I wrote this work for the sake of Allah." The latter responded by stating: "That is a serious claim. Instead say: "This is something that my heart was disposed towards doing, so I obliged." One must be careful before claiming that they did something for the sake of Allah ﷻ, since intentions are fluid and subject to change with the passage of time. As a general rule, one must pay heed to the prohibition found in the following verse:

فَلا تُزَكُّوا أَنفُسَكُمْ هُوَ أَعْلَمُ بِمَنِ اتَّقَى.

"So do not elevate yourselves. He knows best who is righteous."[33]

Thus, one should avoid praising oneself or informing others of any good acts that one has undertaken, lest one acts contrary to this verse's import. When speaking or assessing a fellow believer, one must always have a good opinion of him or her. But in such circumstances, declarations of praise should be qualified and carefully issued. In this regard, the Prophet ﷺ said:

إِذَا كَانَ أَحَدُكُمْ مَادِحًا صَاحِبَهُ لا مَحَالَةَ، فَلْيَقُلْ: أَحْسِبُ فُلَانًا، وَاللَّهُ حَسِيبُهُ، وَلَا أُزَكِّي عَلَى اللهِ أَحَدًا.

"If one of you must praise his fellow companion, then let him say: 'I consider so-and-so to be such-and-such, but Allah alone is his true assessor. And I do not definitively claim anyone is pious, for Allah alone knows the state of everyone.'"

---

[33] *Al-Najm*, 32.

On the Day of Judgement, Allah ﷻ will animate every silent object in this world and allow it to speak for or against every person that possessed or used it. As pointed out in the first chapter, the deeds of every person will assume a human character while he is in the grave and speak on his behalf. But once a person is resurrected and brought forth to his Creator, many other things will attain the ability to converse and testify. In an earlier chapter, a *ḥadīth* was cited in which Allah ﷻ reminds a person of the blessings He gave him in this world, and ultimately reprimands him for failing to give thanks to the Creator. In that same narration, it is mentioned that Allah ﷻ will bring forth another servant before Him. The Prophet ﷺ explains this exchange by stating:

فَيَقُولُ لَهُ مِثْلَ ذَلِكَ.

"Allah will say to him the same thing (which he told the earlier servant)."

In other words, Allah ﷻ will enumerate the various blessings and favours He bestowed upon this servant. But in this conversation, the servant will claim that he did remember and prepare for his meeting with Allah ﷻ on the Day of Judgement. In fact, he will assert that he followed all the divine rules and regulations of the religion of Islam:

فَيَقُولُ: يَا رَبِّ آمَنْتُ بِكَ وَبِكِتَابِكَ وَبِرُسُلِكَ وَصَلَّيْتُ وَصُمْتُ وَتَصَدَّقْتُ.

"O Lord, I believed in You, in Your Book, and in Your Messengers. I also prayed, fasted, and gave alms."

The limbs will be given the ability to speak and relate what their possessor did with them during his lifetime. Even a person's skin will speak and testify in this regard. This should cause one to pause and reflect on the prospective trials that lie ahead on the Day of Judgement.

This person will continue to praise his actions and conduct until Allah ﷻ will interrupt him and state:

هَاهُنَا الآنَ، نَبْعَثُ شَاهِدَنَا عَلَيْكَ.

"Stop at this point. We will now send Our witnesses to testify against you."

The man will be puzzled to hear such an announcement. In fact, the *ḥadīth* notes that the inner state of the man will be burning with questions:

وَيَتَفَكَّرُ فِي نَفْسِهِ مَنْ ذَا الذِي يَشْهَدُ عَلَيَّ.

"He will think to himself: 'Who is this that will testify against me?'"

Of course, he will assume that no one had the ability to witness his private statements and actions. In fact, as another version of the report mentions, the man will go as far as attempt to challenge Allah's proclamation by stating:

لَا أُجِيزُ عَلَى نَفْسِي إِلَّا شَاهِدًا مِنِّي.

"I will not permit anyone to testify against me except a witness from me."

Allah ﷻ will respond to his challenge by stating:

كَفَى بِنَفْسِكَ الْيَوْمَ عَلَيْكَ شَهِيدًا وَبِالْكِرَامِ الْكَاتِبِينَ شُهُودًا.

"Your own self and the honourable angelic scribes are sufficient witnesses against you."

This marks the dramatic point of the *ḥadīth* as the man will be suddenly silenced and rendered mute. Then, one by one, his limbs will testify against him:

فَيُخْتَمُ عَلَى فِيهِ، وَيُقَالُ لِفَخِذِهِ وَلَحْمِهِ وَعِظَامِهِ: انْطِقِي، فَتَنْطِقُ فَخِذُهُ وَلَحْمُهُ وَعِظَامُهُ بِعَمَلِهِ.

"His mouth will be sealed, and it will then be said to his thighs, flesh, and bones: 'Speak!' Then his thighs, flesh, and bones will begin to relate his deeds."

This terrifying episode has also been confirmed and related in the Qur'ān as well:

الْيَوْمَ نَخْتِمُ عَلَى أَفْوَاهِهِمْ وَتُكَلِّمُنَا أَيْدِيهِمْ وَتَشْهَدُ أَرْجُلُهُم بِمَا كَانُوا يَكْسِبُونَ.

"On this Day We will seal their mouths, their hands will speak to Us, and their feet will testify to what they used to commit."[34]

Every limb and part of the body will assume a human character of their own and relate what their possessor did with them during his lifetime. Even a person's skin will speak and testify in this regard. Amazed and baffled at this sight, the person will address his own skin and say:

وَقَالُوا لِجُلُودِهِمْ لِمَ شَهِدتُّمْ عَلَيْنَا.

"They will ask their skin, 'Why have you testified against us?'"[35]

---

[34] *Yā-Sīn*, 65.

[35] *Fuṣṣilat*, 21.

The person will be confused and angered, since by testifying against him, the skin will cause itself and the rest of the person's body to enter Hellfire. But the skin will explain that the matter is beyond its own control:

قَالُوا أَنْطَقَنَا اللَّهُ الَّذِي أَنْطَقَ كُلَّ شَيْءٍ.

"It will say, 'We have been made to speak by Allah, Who causes all things to speak.'"[36]

Thankfully, the person who is being described in this *ḥadīth* is not a believer. The Prophet ﷺ provided us a clear picture of this individual's identity:

وَذَلِكَ الْمُنَافِقُ وَذَلِكَ الَّذِي يَسْخَطُ اللَّهُ عَلَيْهِ.

"That is the hypocrite, and that is the one who Allah is angry with."

This narration clearly establishes that the limbs will be given the ability to speak. This should cause one to pause and reflect on the prospective trials that lie ahead on the Day of Judgement. The deeds, limbs, and inanimate objects that used to harm others in this world will be animated and personified in the other world. But the *ḥadīth* also indirectly reminds us to avoid the characteristics and traits of the hypocrites. One of the defining features of this immoral class was that they were fanatical materialists and lovers of wealth. Consequently, they disliked the notion of spending any wealth in the path of Allah ﷻ. After the death of the Prophet ﷺ, they attempted

---

36 *Fuṣṣilat*, 21.

to repeal the obligation of *zakāt* so that they could amass and hoard wealth without any restrictions. To avoid the development of such unhealthy hedonistic tendencies, Allah and His Prophet have declared that not paying the necessary due *zakāt* is a major sin. In one *ḥadīth*, the Prophet ﷺ warned that the one who fails to pay his or her *zakāt* will experience the following form of punishment in the Hereafter:

مَنْ آتَاهُ اللَّهُ مَالاً فَلَمْ يُؤَدِّ زَكَاتَهُ ، مُثِّلَ لَهُ مَالُهُ شُجَاعًا أَقْرَعَ ، لَهُ زَبِيبَتَانِ يُطَوَّقُهُ يَوْمَ الْقِيَامَةِ ، يَأْخُذُ بِلِهْزِمَتَيْهِ - يَعْنِي بِشِدْقَيْهِ - يَقُولُ: أَنَا مَالُكَ أَنَا كَنْزُكَ

"The one whom Allah has given wealth Allah but fails to pay the obligated zakāt shall have his wealth appear in the form of a bald and giant snake that has two poisonous glands in its mouth. It will circle around him on the Day of Judgement and bite his face, saying: 'I am your wealth. I am your hoarded treasure."

The Prophet ﷺ completed his statement by reciting the following verse:

وَلَا يَحْسَبَنَّ الَّذِينَ يَبْخَلُونَ بِمَا آتَاهُمُ اللَّهُ مِنْ فَضْلِهِ هُوَ خَيْرًا لَهُمْ بَلْ هُوَ شَرٌّ لَهُمْ سَيُطَوَّقُونَ مَا بَخِلُوا بِهِ يَوْمَ الْقِيَامَةِ.

"And do not let those who withhold Allah's bounties think it is good for them—in fact, it is bad for them! They will be leashed on the Day of Judgement with whatever they used to withhold."[37]

---

[37] *Āl 'Imrān*, 180.

After a righteous person passes away, all the locations where he or she made prostration (sajdah) will cry and yearn for them. These places will re-appear on the Day of Judgement and bear witness to this person's piety.

Furthermore, on the Day of Judgement, all the various places that one had visited and all the possessions one had owned will be granted the ability to speak. As Allah ﷻ indicates in the Qur'ān, all one's hidden actions or undertakings in this world will be revealed in the Hereafter:

يَوْمَ تُبْلَى ٱلسَّرَآئِرُ.

"On the Day all secrets will be disclosed."[38]

In the case of the sincere and repentant believer, Allah ﷻ will wipe away his or her sins and give him or her the glad tiding of Paradise. The blessed locations and places that one had visited during one's life will come to one's aid and testify. If one did fear Allah ﷻ during one's life in this world, had attempted to adopt a righteous life and was cognisant of Allah's presence, then He will shower one with His mercy. He will even forgive one for the various transgressions pointed out by one's limbs and the objects one had used and the places one had visited. But this is on the condition that such sins were not done in a state of hypocrisy or with complete disregard of Allah.

The people of evil will be cursed and remembered for their transgressions, and no place in the universe will mention them with good. For as Allah ﷻ states:

فَمَا بَكَتْ عَلَيْهِمُ ٱلسَّمَآءُ وَٱلْأَرْضُ.

"Neither Heaven nor Earth wept over them."[39]

---

[38] *Al-Ṭāriq*, 9.

[39] *Al-Dukhān*, 29.

The case of the believer will be the complete opposite. As Ibn 'Abbās mentioned, after a righteous person passes away, all the locations where he or she made prostration (*sajdah*) will cry and yearn for them. These places will re-appear on the Day of Judgement and bear witness to this person's piety. In addition, a person's *Ḥajj* and *'Umrah* will also appear and testify on his or her behalf. Specifically, there is a report in which the Prophet ﷺ said that the Black Stone (*al-Ḥajar al-Aswad*) will be resurrected on the Day of Judgement and will praise the ones who approached it and touched it with sincerity:

وَاللهِ لَيَبْعَثَنَّ اللهُ الحَجَرَ يَوْمَ القِيَامَةِ وَلَهُ عَيْنَانِ يُبْصِرُ بِهِمَا وَلِسَانٌ يَنْطِقُ بِهِ
يَشْهَدُ بِهِ عَلَى مَنْ اِسْتَلَمَهُ بِحَقٍّ.

"By Allah, Allah will raise it on the Day of Judgement possessing two eyes with which it sees and a tongue with which it will be able to speak. It will then testify in favour of whoever touched it with its due right."

In another report, the Prophet ﷺ described how another landmark of the sacred area of Makkah will appear on the Day of Judgement and speak in favour of the pilgrims who touched it:

يَأْتِي الرُّكْنُ يَوْمَ القِيَامَةِ أَعْظَمُ مِنْ أَبِي قُبَيْسٍ لَهُ لِسَانٌ وَشَفَتَانِ يَتَكَلَّمُ عَمَّنِ اسْتَلَمَهُ بِالنِّيَّةِ.

"The (Yemeni) Corner will appear on the Day of Judgement with its dimensions greater than those of Abū Qubays mountain. It will have a tongue and two lips, speaking on behalf of those who touched it with a sincere intention."

Furthermore, animals will also speak on the Day of Judgement and relate to their Lord ﷻ the various interactions they had with humans. In this world, we know that some animals—such as birds and camels—spoke with the Prophet ﷺ and complained about how they were mistreated by their owners. However, on the Day of Judgement, the animals who testify against the humans who harmed them will speak in a language that is understood by everyone present. By way of example, the Prophet said that a sparrow killed spitefully in this world will come before its Lord ﷻ on the Day of Judgement and say:

يَا رَبِّ إِنَّ فُلَانًا قَتَلَنِي عَبَثًا ، وَلَمْ يَقْتُلْنِي لِمَنْفَعَةٍ

"O Lord, So-and-so killed me for sport and did not do so to derive any benefit."

In stark contrast, the Prophet ﷺ mentioned that the person who studies sacred knowledge will be honoured by every entity in the universe:

وَإِنَّ العَالِمَ لَيَسْتَغْفِرُ لَهُ مَنْ فِي السَّمَاوَاتِ وَمَنْ فِي الأَرْضِ حَتَّى الحِيتَانُ فِي جَوْفِ المَاءِ.

"Everything in the Heavens and the Earth, including the fish in the depths of the water, seeks forgiveness for the scholar."

As a result of his or her knowledge, the scholar is cognisant of his or her responsibility as a vicegerent and exercises a spiritual form of stewardship whenever he or she interacts with other human beings, beasts or forests. If Allah ﷻ will cause the animals, plants, physical objects, locations, and limbs to testify on the Last Day, one can only imagine the momentous significance that will be found in the testimony of one's fellow humans for or against one.

14

Justice for the Oppressed

One cannot be observant of one's religious obligations and, at the same time, be evil in one's personal conduct towards one's fellow co-religionists. On the Day of Judgement, Allah ﷻ will gather the testimonies of people regarding a given individual and divide them into two classes: (1) the witnesses of those who benefitted from the individual in question, and (2) the witnesses of those who were harmed by him. The testimonies issued from these respective groups will leave a decisive impact on the individual as he stands before his Lord. These witnesses will assess an individual person on the basis of how he or she treated them at a personal and interactional level. There is no scriptural indication which can be understood to imply that Allah ﷻ will ask these witnesses to appraise a person's religious conduct in terms of his or her prayer and fasting. Allah is already aware of each individual's level of religious observance and, instead, will ask the witnesses to confirm whether the person was a source of moral assistance or harm in this world.

When discussing Allah's evaluation of His human servants, it is necessary to consider two key variables: His justice and His mercy. Divine justice refers to Allah's review of a person's deeds through the testimonies of his or her limbs as well as other objects and subjects which interacted with him or her in the life of this world. On the other hand, Allah's mercy refers to His inclination to pardon and forgive one for these faults. In terms of application, if one has harmed or wronged another person, Allah ﷻ will exclusively impose His divine justice on one—the possibility of divine mercy in such a scenario is restricted or negated altogether. When one disobeys or transgresses against Allah, He has the prerogative to forgive one for one's faults and erase one's sins. However, if the wronged party is a human, then Allah ﷻ cannot readily forgive one, since the basic principles of justice dictate that the injured party cannot be denied his right, as he has to be avenged or compensated. This explains why the noble Imām Sufyān al-Thawrī ؒ once said: "To meet Allah with seventy sins relating to Allah's rights is much easier than meeting Him with a single sin involving the rights of His servants."

In a narration, the Prophet ﷺ stated that Allah's adjudication between the people on the Day of Judgement will relate to exacting justice for those who were murdered. Of course, almost everyone knows of the *ḥadīth* in which the Prophet said that the first thing which Allah will ask His slave about on the Day of the Judgement is the *ṣalāh* (prayer). However, scholars have reconciled these apparently contradictory reports by noting that while the former *ḥadīth* relates to interpersonal affairs, the latter refers to the relations between Allah and His servants. Regarding the issue of the person who is unjustly killed and comes on the Day of Judgement seeking justice, the Prophet ﷺ said in a remarkable and striking narration:

يَجِيءُ المَقْتُولُ بِالقَاتِلِ يَوْمَ القِيَامَةِ نَاصِيَتُهُ وَرَأْسُهُ بِيَدِهِ وَأَوْدَاجُهُ تَشْخَبُ دَمًا يَقُولُ يَا رَبِّ هَذَا قَتَلَنِي حَتَّى يُدنيَهُ مِنَ العَرْشِ.

"The murdered person will come on the Day of Judgement with his murderer—holding his forelock and head in his hand with his jugular vein dripping with blood—saying: 'O Lord, this man killed me,' until he takes him close to the Throne."

This scene is undoubtedly chilling and shocking: the people who were murdered in this world will virtually drag their murderers to the Supreme Judge ﷻ in order to exact retributive justice. Because of the punishments that await the oppressors and wrongdoers in the Hereafter, the Prophet ﷺ imparted the following golden words of advice to the members of his nation:

كُنْ عَبْدَ اللهِ المَظْلُومَ، وَلَا تَكُنْ عَبْدَ اللهِ الظَّالِمَ.

"Be the servant of Allah who is wronged, and do not be the servant of Allah who wrongs others."

In a similar report, the Prophet ﷺ said:

تَكُونُ فِتَنٌ فَكُنْ فِيهَا عَبْدَ اللهِ المَقْتُولَ وَلَا تَكُنْ القَاتِلَ.

"There shall be seditions, therefore be the servant of Allah who is killed [in these seditions]*, and do not be the killer."*

The reason why the Prophet ﷺ issued these imperatives to his Ummah is explained in another *ḥadīth* which states that the supplication (*du'ā'*) of the oppressed (*maẓlūm*)—even if he be a disbeliever—will be heard directly by the Lord ﷻ, with no veil or barrier in the Heavens coming in its way. Regarding protecting the rights of the disbeliever from all forms of oppression, the Prophet ﷺ said:

أَلَا مَنْ ظَلَمَ مُعَاهِدًا أَوِ انْتَقَصَهُ أَوْ كَلَّفَهُ فَوْقَ طَاقَتِهِ أَوْ أَخَذَ مِنْهُ شَيْئًا بِغَيْرِ طِيبِ نَفْسٍ فَأَنَا حَجِيجُهُ يَوْمَ الْقِيَامَةِ.

"Whoever wrongs a protected non-Muslim, or violates his rights, or burdens him with more than he can bear, or takes anything from him in a disagreeable manner, I shall be his opponent on the Day of Judgement."

The protected non-Muslims are the People of the Book or other religious minority communities whose protection is guaranteed by the Sacred Law. In this report, the Prophet ﷺ warns that, on the Day of Judgement, He will Himself institute proceedings against anyone who harms a disbeliever, even if the transgressor is a Muslim. This is because the religion of Islam stresses the restoration of justice, regardless of the status or faith of people. In the case of those who consume or partake in *ribā* (usury), the punishment will be even more severe. Allah ﷻ has issued the following warning to those who engage in this unjust financial practice:

فَإِنْ لَمْ تَفْعَلُوا فَأْذَنُوا بِحَرْبٍ مِنَ اللَّهِ وَرَسُولِهِ.

"If you do not (refrain from partaking in ribā), then beware of a war with Allah and His Messenger!"[40]

---

40 *Al-Baqarah*, 279.

In his commentary on this verse, the great Companion Ibn
'Abbās ؓ stated:

يُقَالُ يَوْمَ القِيَامَةِ لِآكِلِ الرِّبَا خُذْ سِلَاحَكَ لِلْحَرْبِ.

*"The consumer of ribā will be issued the following
directive on the Day of Judgement: 'Take your weapon
and prepare for war.'"*

At first sight, this harsh and condemnatory stance against *ribā*
may seem severe. But it is important to note that it is a mistake
to assume that *ribā* is simply a crime against the Creator ﷻ.
In actual fact, it is a multifaceted offence, since it also
plunges the economically lower classes into impoverishment
and unjustly exploits sincere and hard-working borrowers.
One could even consider it to be a latent or obscure form of
monetary theft and plundering that occurs on a daily basis in
the modern economy.

However, the most common means through which people sin
and oppress others is the tongue. This in fact explains why
the Prophet ﷺ once rhetorically asked in a tone that conveyed
his disapproval:

وَهَلْ يُكَبُّ النَّاسُ عَلَى وُجُوهِهِمْ إِلَّا حَصَائِدُ أَلْسِنَتِهِمْ.

*"Is there anything else that causes people to be thrown face first
into the Hellfire except the harvests of their tongues?"*

People who freely malign others with their destructive tongues
will find on the Day of Judgement that their good deeds are

The most common means through which people sin and oppress others is the tongue. People who freely malign others with their destructive tongues will find on the Day of Judgement that their good deeds are reduced or eliminated altogether.

reduced or eliminated altogether. In a well-known *ḥadīth*, it is related that the Prophet ﷺ once asked his Companions:

أَتَدْرُونَ مَنِ المُفْلِسُ؟

"Do you know who the bankrupt one is?"

The Companions provided an intuitive answer: "The bankrupt person is the one who lacks any money or possessions." The Prophet ﷺ gently indicated that their instinctive reply missed the mark by saying:

إِنَّ الْمُفْلِسَ مِنْ أُمَّتِي مَنْ يَأْتِي يَوْمَ الْقِيَامَةِ بِصَلاَةٍ وَزَكَاةٍ وَصِيَامٍ ، وَيَأْتِي قَدْ شَتَمَ عِرْضَ هَذَا ، وَقَذَفَ هَذَا ، وَأَكَلَ مَالَ هَذَا ، وَضَرَبَ هَذَا.

"In actual fact, the bankrupt person is the one who comes on the Day of Judgement with a lifetime of good deeds, such as prayer, fasting, and zakāt. But he comes while he has insulted one individual, cursed another, consumed the wealth of a different person, killed another person, and beat an additional figure."

All the victims of this oppressor will stand before Allah ﷻ and ask for justice. Allah will positively respond to their request, and the following retributive measures will be undertaken:

فَيَقْعُدُ فَيَقْتَصُّ هَذَا مِنْ حَسَنَاتِهِ ، وَهَذَا مِنْ حَسَنَاتِهِ ، فَإِنْ فَنِيَتْ حَسَنَاتُهُ ، قَبْلَ أَنْ يَقْضِيَ مَا عَلَيْهِ مِنَ الْخَطَايَا ، أُخِذَ مِنْ خَطَايَاهُمْ ، فَطُرِحَتْ عَلَيْهِ ، ثُمَّ طُرِحَ فِي النَّارِ.

"The first victim will be given some of his good deeds, and the second will also take a share of them, and so on and so forth. If his good deeds are depleted before the retributive process is completed, then the sins of his victims will be removed from them and added to him instead, and then he will be thrown in Hellfire."

The prominent Successor to the Companions Saʿīd ibn Jubayr ﷦ related that, on the Day of Judgement, the servant will be summoned before his Lord ﷻ and the register of his deeds will be presented to him. But, to his astonishment, he will find that despite apparently living a life of piety, all his good acts are missing from this register, which prompts him to address his Lord by saying:

يَا رَبِّ هَذَا كِتَابُ غَيْرِي.

"O Lord, this is someone else's register."

This person will be certain that a mistake occurred, as the register in his hands fails to give an adequate account of his behaviour and code of conduct in the temporal world. But Allah ﷻ will correct his misconception by pointing out that, in actual fact, his register is devoid of good deeds because he destroyed his good works by frequently indulging in backbiting (*ghībah*). He will be accordingly issued the following response: "Indeed your Lord does not overlook anything or forget. Your good deeds have disappeared as a result of your *ghībah*." Such narrations serve as a striking reminder that one should refrain from speaking ill of others or spreading gossip about them, as that will thwart one's good deeds in the Hereafter.

However, it should be noted that these aforementioned facts can yield positive benefits for those at the receiving end of injustice or *ghībah*. On the Day of Judgement, they will be granted numerous good deeds due to the physical and moral harms they suffered in this temporal world. Abū Umāmah narrated that the Prophet ﷺ said:

إِنَّ الْعَبْدَ لَيُعْطَى كِتَابَهُ يَوْمَ الْقِيَامَةِ مَنْشُورًا ، فَيُرِيهِ فِيهِ حَسَنَاتٍ لَمْ يَعْمَلْهَا.

"On the Day of Judgement, the servant will be given a scroll [enumerating his deeds], and he will see in it good deeds that he did not do during his life."

This Muslim slave will be in a state of incredulity, since he will be surprised to see his register of deeds brimming with good deeds that he never undertook in the temporal world. Naturally, he will turn to Allah ﷻ and ask:

يَا رَبِّ مِنْ أَيْنَ لِي هَذَا.

"O Lord, from whence did I get all this?"

Allah ﷻ will explain his surplus of good deeds with the following answer:

هَذَا مَا اغْتَابَكَ النَّاسُ وَأَنْتَ لَا تَشْعُرُ.

"This is a result of the people backbiting against you while you were unaware."

This surprising discovery will cause those who were backbitten against to be pleased that they were backbitten by others, since such backbiting dramatically improves their register of deeds.

In fact, it is reported that Imām ʿAbd al-Raḥmān ibn Mahdī ﷺ said:

لَوْلَا أَنِّي أَكْرَهُ أَنْ يُعْصَى اللهُ لَتَمَنَّيْتُ أَنْ لَا يَبْقَى فِي هَذَا الْمِصْرِ أَحَدٌ إِلَّا وَقَعَ وَاغْتَابَنِي وَأَيُّ شَيْءٍ أَهْنَأُ مِنْ حَسَنَةٍ يَجِدُهَا الرَّجُلُ فِي صَحِيفَتِهِ يَوْمَ الْقِيَامَةِ لَمْ يَعْمَلْهَا وَلَمْ يَعْلَمْ بِهَا.

"Where it not for the fact that I hate that Allah be disobeyed, I would have wished that every person living in this city had backbitten me. For what could possibly be sweeter than a man finding a cluster of good deeds in his book that he never performed?"

If these are the deeds given to the passive target of backbiting, then one can only imagine the number of rewards accrued by the active backer and protector of the needy Muslim population.

"So as for those whose scales are heavy with good deeds, they will be in a life of bliss."

AL-QĀRIʿAH, 6–7

Saved for
Saving Others

While he was in prison and being tortured, Imām Aḥmad ibn Ḥanbal 🙵 addressed Aḥmad ibn Abī Du'ād—the prominent Abbasid judge and chief instigator of the Inquisition [against those who refused to accept the heretical view of the createdness of the Qur'ān] (*miḥnah*)—with the succinct yet powerful sentence:

بَيْنَنَا وَبَيْنَكُمُ الْجَنَائِزُ.

*"What distinguishes the likes of us and you are the
funeral processions."*

Imām Aḥmad uttered these golden words when he was still in prison. On the other hand, the one addressed with these words—Ibn Abī Du'ād—was honoured and occupied some of the highest positions in the Abbasid court. Yet, with the passage of time, Imām Aḥmad's statement proved to be fateful and decisive. When Ibn Abī Du'ād passed away, only a few people attended his funeral, as the Muslim community loathed him for his evil and oppression against the institution of scholarship and Islamic orthodoxy as a whole. On the other hand, Imām Aḥmad's funeral was likely one of the greatest in Islamic history, with some historians estimating that it was attended by more than one million people. In the end, truth prevailed over falsehood.

A famous *ḥadīth* relates that the funeral processions of two individuals passed by the Prophet ﷺ and his Companions. When the first one passed by them, the Companions praised the person for his good qualities and enumerated his virtues. In response, the Prophet ﷺ said:

وَجَبَتْ وَجَبَتْ وَجَبَتْ.

"It has become mandatory, it has become mandatory, it has become mandatory."

But when the second one passed by them, the Companions related the vices and harms that the deceased person caused to others during his life. The Prophet ﷺ ultimately issued the same response:

وَجَبَتْ وَجَبَتْ وَجَبَتْ.

"It has become mandatory, it has become mandatory, it has become mandatory."

The Companions were confused by this set of responses, and subsequently asked the Prophet for clarification. The Prophet ﷺ explained his previous declarations with the following statement:

مَن أَثْنَيْتُمْ عليه خَيْرًا وَجَبَتْ له الجَنَّةُ، وَمَن أَثْنَيْتُمْ عليه شَرًّا وَجَبَتْ له النَّارُ.

"Paradise has become mandatory for the person you described in positive terms, while Hellfire has become mandatory for the person you described in negative terms."

He then completed his explanation by delicately noting the final distinction:

المَلَائِكَةُ شُهَدَاءُ اللهِ فِي السَّمَاءِ وَأَنْتُمْ شُهَدَاءُ اللهِ فِي الأَرْضِ.

"The angels are Allah's witnesses in Heaven, while you are the witnesses of Allah on earth."

Of course, no one can presume with absolute certainty that one will enter Hellfire or Paradise, unless one has been identified by Allah ﷻ and His Messenger ﷺ in explicit scriptural texts. For instance, the Qur'ān definitively states that Abū Lahab will be in Hellfire. Likewise, the authentic Prophetic Sunnah mentions that a number of senior Companions—such as Abū Bakr, 'Umar, 'Uthmān, and 'Alī ﷺ—are guaranteed Paradise. However, the final destination of other Muslims cannot be stated for certain, since Allah ﷻ alone knows that. Yet, at the same time, the positive or negative testimonies of people regarding any person will bear an effect on his standing on the Day of Judgement. For instance, an individual has family members and close loved ones who they interact with during his lifetime. These people would certainly amass different kinds of information regarding this individual, which ultimately means they will have to testify regarding him on the Day of Judgement. Thus, on the Day of Judgement, an individual's limbs will not be the only things to testify against him; in fact, his own loved ones will reveal valuable insights regarding his inner character.

The individual who leads a pious life and treats his circle of loved ones decently will be recompensed handsomely by his Creator ﷻ. Allah Himself has guaranteed this in the Qur'ān:

هَلْ جَزَآءُ ٱلْإِحْسَٰنِ إِلَّا ٱلْإِحْسَٰنُ.

"Is there any reward for goodness except goodness?"[41]

In other words, Allah ﷻ will handsomely recompense any doer of good and even bestow him a greater benefit in the Hereafter. In this regard, one may consider the famous story of an evil wrongdoer who was saved because of giving water to a thirsty dog. To fully appreciate the dynamics of this story, its chronology of events must be carefully considered. This individual—who led a life of sinfulness—was wandering and searching for water because of excess thirst. Allah recognised this man's state of need and subsequently directed him to a source of water. Despite being guided to water, this sinner did not immediately rush to quench his thirst. As a token of gratitude to Allah, he first prioritised the welfare of a dog—which was also very thirsty—by filling up his leather shoe with

---

[41] *Al-Raḥmān*, 60.

The individual who leads a pious life and treats his circle of loved ones decently will be recompensed handsomely by his Creator. Allah ﷻ will reward any doer of good and even bestow him a greater benefit in the Hereafter.

water and giving it to the animal. If one carefully reflects on this report, one will be able to appreciate the vastness of Allah's mercy and blessings. One must consider the fact that Allah ﷻ guided this person to a water source in this world, despite his corrupt moral state. But because he helped a thirsty dog and gave it water, Allah will recompense him in the Hereafter with even greater bounties, that is rivers in Paradise. This is because no matter how much gratitude (*shukr*) one shows towards one's Creator in this world, Allah's level of generosity will always be preponderant, since one of His divine names is *al-Shakūr* (the Most Appreciative). Thus, His bounteousness can never be matched.

There are multiple narrations which further reflect on the generosity of the Creator ﷻ. For instance, in one key *ḥadīth*, the Prophet ﷺ mentions that a person belonging to one of the previous nations will stand before Allah ﷻ on the Day of Judgement to be judged. No virtuous deed will be found in his register, except that he demonstrated leniency with partners and customers in his business affairs, and he forgave his debtors who struggled to pay their outstanding debts to him. In light of these few but magnificent acts of virtue, Allah will tell this person:

نَحْنُ أَحَقُّ بِذَلِكَ مِنْهُ تَجَاوَزُوا عَنْهُ.

"We have a better right [to forgiving others and being lenient with them]: overlook his sins."

In an inspirational and moving narration, the Prophet ﷺ said:

مَنْ نَفَّسَ عَنْ مُؤْمِنٍ كُرْبَةً مِنْ كُرَبِ الدُّنْيَا، نَفَّسَ اللَّهُ عَنْهُ كُرْبَةً مِنْ كُرَبِ يَوْمِ الْقِيَامَةِ، وَمَنْ يَسَّرَ عَلَى مُعْسِرٍ، يَسَّرَ اللَّهُ عَلَيْهِ فِي الدُّنْيَا وَالْآخِرَةِ، وَمَنْ سَتَرَ مُسْلِمًا، سَتَرَهُ اللَّهُ فِي الدُّنْيَا وَالْآخِرَةِ.

"Whoever relieves a believer from one of distresses of this world, Allah will alleviate from him one of the distresses of the Day of Judgement. And whoever provides ease to a financially burdened person, Allah will provide him ease in this world and also on the Day of Judgement. And whoever conceals the faults of a Muslim, Allah will conceal his faults in this world and in the Hereafter."

A similarly worded but relatively shorter report reiterates the same thing found in the previous narration:

لَا يَسْتُرُ عَبْدٌ عَبْدًا فِي الدُّنْيَا إِلَّا سَتَرَهُ اللهُ يَوْمَ القِيَامَةِ.

"No servant conceals the faults of another servant in this dunyā (this temporal world) except that Allah will conceal his faults on the Day of Judgement."

Allah ﷻ will give this servant such a special rank on the Day of Judgement because he saved his fellow believer from humiliation in this world by covering his embarrassing faults and defects. In the eyes of many, having one's shortcomings and blemishes exposed in public is more painful than being subject to physical abuse. The Muslim who is cognisant of this fact and protects his brother or sister from such humiliation will find Allah ﷻ to be more considerate and protective towards him in the Hereafter. There are a number of other narrations which further highlight that coming to a fellow Muslim's aid in this world will yield an exponentially greater return in the Hereafter. This principle applies to all virtuous deeds, even if they are deemed to be insignificant and unworthy of recompense by human observers. In a beautiful narration, the Prophet said:

مَنْ أَقَالَ نَادِمًا صَفْقَتَهُ أَقَالَ اللّٰهُ عَثْرَتَهُ يَوْمَ القِيَامَةِ.

"Whoever cancels a transaction after his fellow Muslim regrets it [and changes his mind about it], Allah will cancel his mistakes on the Day of Judgement."

This narration confirms that a small favour conferred on a fellow Muslim will lead to massive benefits on the Day of Judgement. In this report, the act of kindness is minimal, whereby a Muslim seller agrees to cancel a transaction with his Muslim customer after the latter regrets his purchase. Though the former is not legally required to cancel the deal, he is sympathetic to the customer's feelings and thus refunds him. This small act of kindness will allow the Muslim seller to reap massive rewards in the Hereafter.

One of the greatest virtuous deeds in Islam is freeing a person subjected to bondage and servitude. Although slavery no longer exists in its conventional form, there are nevertheless many entrapped and subjugated individuals around the world who require immediate assistance from compassionate forces. The Prophet ﷺ has underscored and highlighted the immense rewards of liberating a slave from his state of captivity:

مَنْ أَعْتَقَ رَقَبَةً أَعْتَقَ اللَّهُ بِكُلِّ عُضْوٍ مِنْهَا عُضْوًا مِنْ أَعْضَائِهِ مِنَ النَّارِ حَتَّى فَرْجَهُ بِفَرْجِهِ.

"Whoever emancipates a believing slave, Allah will free every one of his limbs—including his private parts—from Hellfire, just as he freed every limb of this slave."

In fact, when bestowing rewards to benefactors, Allah ﷻ will not simply take into account the physical forms of assistance given to the disadvantaged. Instead, He will also consider the mental and emotional dimensions of these acts as well. For instance, a person who helps pay off a debtor's outstanding debts may also provide them moral support so the latter may improve his state of mental health. On the Day of Judgement, Allah ﷻ will not only recompense the person for the financial assistance he provided, but He will also consider the intangible forms of support provided as well. One may also consider the continuous forms of aid that benefit communities even after the benefactor has passed away. For instance, during his life, a person may have established an endowment or institution that lasts and continues to benefit future generations. Or it might be that a deceased person has surviving heirs and loved ones who continue to perform good deeds in his name.

Such individuals undoubtedly fall under the virtuous categories mentioned in the following *ḥadīth*:

إِذَا مَاتَ ابنُ آدم انْقَطَعَ عَنْهُ عَمَلُهُ إِلَّا مِنْ ثَلَاثٍ: صَدَقَةٍ جَارِيَةٍ، أو عِلْمٍ يُنْتَفَعُ بِهِ، أَوْ وَلَدٍ صَالِحٍ يَدْعُو لَهُ".

"When a person passes away, all their good deeds come to an end except for three: continuous charity (ṣadaqah jāriyah), beneficial knowledge, or a righteous child that continues to pray for him."

In order to have people make *du'ā'* for one after one's death, it is necessary to leave a positive impact in their hearts by inspiring them to do good or teaching them beneficial knowledge. The golden rule that is applicable in this context is that if one wishes to be remembered and treated with religious excellence (*iḥsān*) after one passes away, then one must exercise the same behavioural standard with others during one's life. On the Day of Judgement, one who endows his community various forms of *ṣadaqah jāriyah*—such as wells, libraries, and seminaries—will find hundreds of people who were born after one's death testifying on one's behalf and praising one for the virtues and benefits that they received as a result of one's generosity. Such a sight will be undoubtedly remarkable, since one will not even know or identify any of these individuals who will speak positively of one. Just like how the target of backbiting unknowingly accrues rewards for every word uttered against him, the benefactor or initiator of any form of *ṣadaqah jāriyah* will receive *du'ā'* and intercession of countless generations to come.

16

Those Who Intercede

Islam encourages its followers to assume high-ranking positions so that they may be providers of help, rather than be receivers of help. One of the most important *ḥadīths* on this theme states:

اليَدُ العُلْيَا خَيْرٌ مِنَ اليَدِ السُفْلَى.

"The upper hand [the hand that gives] is better than the lower hand [the hand that receives]."

Such an approach is not simply highlighted in the area of wealth and financial ventures. The same mentality must be adopted when preparing for the Hereafter (*ākhirah*), whereby one's aspires to attain one of the highest places in Paradise, such that one may intercede and come to the aid of one's relatives. It would be incorrect and dangerous for one to be neglectful of one's religious duties and simply assume that Allah ﷻ will be merciful and grant one the last place in Paradise, or that one's relatives and loved ones would intercede on one's behalf.

In sum, one must aim to secure a pre-eminent position in the Hereafter, so that one may be empowered with the ability to save one's brothers and sisters in need through the power of intercession. Of course, it is true that all members of the Muslim Ummah are in need of the Prophet's intercession in the Hereafter, but one must strive to perform acts of goodness, avoid vices, and treat people with goodness in order to exact as many favourable testimonies as possible in favour of one's uprightness. That way, one will be able to comfortably attain happiness in the Hereafter through the unanimous support of one's peers and loved ones. Otherwise, one will put oneself in an intensely risky situation whereby one's salvation or damnation rests on a single account.

On the Last Day, the privilege of intercession (*shafā'ah*) will be of greater value than the duty of testimony (*shahādah*). Though some scholars label the former as being a category of the latter, they nevertheless consider it to be of a higher and better status. This is because while every individual can be appointed as a witness on the Day of Judgement, only an elite class of individuals will be given the opportunity to intercede on behalf of others. Without any doubt, the best intercessor is the last Messenger sent to all of humankind: Prophet Muhammad ﷺ. Since his status towers above every human and angel, he will actively seek to intercede on behalf of his nation during every step and interval of the Day of Judgement. All the humans resurrected on that Day will appreciate his eminence, since after requesting the earlier Prophets to intercede on their behalf, they will be left empty-handed. These early Messengers will instead advise people to seek Prophet Muhammad ﷺ and request his intervention. In that epic moment, the Prophet ﷺ will announce to his nation that he was destined to save them from the horrors of that Day through his intermediation:

أَنَا لَهَا.

"I am for it."

In the same narration, the Prophet ﷺ relates the dramatic details of this intercession process:

فَأَسْجُدُ تَحْتَ العَرْشِ.

"Then I will prostrate beneath the Throne."

While engaged in this intensive form of worship, Allah ﷻ will directly reveal to the Prophet previously unknown supplicatory words of praise and glorification, which he will then immediately recite. Allah ﷻ will then positively respond to his noble prayers and say:

يَا مُحَمَّدُ ارْفَعْ رَأْسَكَ وَقُلْ يُسْمَعْ لَكَ وَسَلْ تُعْطَ وَاشفَعْ تُشَفَّعْ وَسَلْ تُعْطَ.

"O Muhammad, raise your head. Say what you wish, and you shall be heard. Intercede, and your intercession shall be accepted. Ask, and you shall be given."

Despite being granted an unparalleled form of intercession that will not be rejected by the Lord of the worlds, the Prophet will continue his intensive form of worship by raising his head momentarily but then prostrating once more.

The Prophet Muhammad ﷺ whose status towers above every human and angel, will actively seek to intercede on behalf of his nation during every step and interval of the Day of Judgement. All the resurrected humans will appreciate his ﷺ eminence on that Day.

He will then call out to his Lord and say:

أُمَّتِي يَا رَبِّ أُمَّتِي.

"My Ummah, O Lord, my Ummah."

Allah ﷻ will respond to his supplication by stating:

يَا مُحَمَّدُ! أَدْخِلِ الْجَنَّةَ مِنْ أُمَّتِكَ مَنْ لَا حِسَابَ عَلَيْهِ مِنَ الْبَابِ الْأَيْمَنِ مِنْ أَبْوَابِ الْجَنَّةِ.

"O Muhammad, admit those from your Ummah who will not be brought to account. Have them enter from the right-hand gate of Paradise."

These individuals who enter Paradise through the blessed intervention of the Prophet ﷺ will be from the best of humankind. In a very important *ḥadīth*, the Prophet ﷺ taught his Ummah a beautiful supplication (*du'ā'*) which would help its reciter attain his intercession on the Day of Judgement. As the Prophet ﷺ noted, this *du'ā'* should be recited immediately after one hears the call to prayer (*adhān*):

"اللَّهُمَّ رَبَّ هَذِهِ الدَّعْوَةِ التَّامَّةِ وَالصَّلاَةِ الْقَائِمَةِ آتِ مُحَمَّدًا الْوَسِيلَةَ وَالْفَضِيلَةَ وَابْعَثْهُ مَقَامًا مَحْمُودًا الَّذِي وَعَدْتَهُ".

"O Allah, Lord of this ultimate call and this prayer which will soon be offered, grant Muhammad the privilege of intercession, bestow him a position of grace, and raise him on the praised station which You promised him."

One may also add to this supplication the following closing sentence:

إِنَّكَ لَا تُخْلِفُ الْمِيعَاد.

"Surely You do not fall on Your promises."

This supplication should always be recited at its appropriate times during the day, for the Prophet ﷺ issued the following promise for the one who does so:

حَلَّتْ لَهُ شَفَاعَتِي يَوْمَ الْقِيَامَة.

"My intercession will be granted to him on the Day of Judgement."

The scholars have explained the immense virtues found in this supplication by noting that when one sends prayers (*ṣalawāt*) upon the Prophet ﷺ, one will receive blessings and words of praise from (1) Allah ﷻ, (2) the angels, and (3) the Prophet ﷺ himself. In essence, this implies that when one recites this prayer and asks Allah ﷻ to bestow the Prophet ﷺ the praised station, the Prophet ﷺ uses his privileged position to raise the rank of one.

Anas ibn Mālik رضي الله عنه narrates that on one occasion he asked the Prophet ﷺ where he should meet him on the Day of Judgement in order to obtain his special intercession. The Prophet ﷺ mentioned three locations where he could be located on that Day, in the following order: (1) the *Ṣirāṭ* (Bridge-over-Hell), (2) the *Mīzān* (Scales), and (3) the *Ḥawḍ* (Pool). After highlighting these three central landmarks, the Prophet said:

فَإِنِّي لَا أُخْطِئُ هَذِهِ الثَّلَاثَ الْمَوَاطِنَ.

"Indeed, I will not be missed in these three locations."

This report explicitly indicates that the Prophet ﷺ will be interceding for his people throughout the full range of the Day of Judgement, even as the proceedings progress from one location and site to another. In fact, on that momentous moment, the Prophet will ensure that his intercession is even extended and applied to the lowest members of his Ummah in terms of moral standing and virtue. Ibn 'Umar ﵄ made an astonishing admission when narrating the following report:

"كُنَّا نُمْسِكُ عَنِ الِاسْتِغْفَارِ لِأَهْلِ الْكَبَائِرِ حَتَّى سَمِعْنَا رَسُولَ اللَّهِ صَلَّى اللَّهُ عَلَيْهِ وَسَلَّمَ يَقُولُ: إِنِّي ادَّخَرْتُ دَعْوَتِي شَفَاعَةً لِأَهْلِ الْكَبَائِرِ مِنْ أُمَّتِي.

"We used to refrain from making seeking forgiveness (istighfār) for the perpetrators of major sins (ahl al-kabā'ir) until we heard the Prophet (blessings and peace be upon him) say: 'I have saved my intercession so that it may be used for the ahl al-kabā'ir of my Ummah on the Day of Judgement.'"

Ibn 'Umar revealed that once they heard this statement from the Prophet, their position on their sinful co-religionists changed dramatically:

"قَالَ فَأَمْسَكْنَا عَنْ كَثِيرٍ مِمَّا كَانَ فِي أَنْفُسِنَا ، ثُمَّ نَطَقْنَا بَعْدُ وَرَجَوْنَا".

"As a result, we restrained much of what was inside us and started to have hope for them."

In this report, one derives a number of valuable insights into the lives of the Companions. Initially, they used to believe that those who fell into major sins—such as drinking alcohol, adultery, and theft—were not worthy of their *du'ā'* and prayers. But then they were amazed to find that the Prophet had saved his intercession for this very class of people. Of course, one should never wish to be relegated to such a low level of righteousness and moral standing in the Hereafter, since one will have to wait a considerably long time on the Day of Judgement before one receives the Prophet's intercession. Nevertheless, the fact remains that the Prophet ﷺ will never abandon any member of his Ummah on the Day of Judgement. In fact, there are narrations which mention that the Prophet ﷺ will continue to turn to his Lord ﷻ in prayer and say:

يَا رَبِّ أَدْخِلِ الْجَنَّةَ مَنْ كَانَ فِي قَلْبِهِ خَرْدَلَةٌ.

"O Lord, enter into Paradise anyone who has even a mustard seed's weight of faith in his heart."

Allah ﷻ will positively respond to his request and allow the admission of individuals who meet this criterion. But then the Prophet will once again supplicate to his Lord, this time even further lowering the standard of faith needed for entering Paradise:

أَدْخِلِ الْجَنَّةَ مَنْ كَانَ فِي قَلْبِهِ أَدْنَى شَيْءٍ.

"Enter into Paradise anyone who has even the baseline degree of faith in his heart."

Allah ﷻ will accept this latter supplication as well, thereby increasing the number of people admitted into the gardens of Paradise. In addition, it should be noted that besides the

Prophet ﷺ, the people of righteousness will also have the opportunity to intercede on behalf of their loved ones on the Day of Judgement. Even the angels entrusted with recording the deeds of people will be allowed to speak in favour of them. Every prophet and messenger will come forward and ask Allah to shower His blessings and mercy upon their respective nations. Likewise, the martyrs (*shuhadā'*) will be granted the benefit of interceding for up to seventy family members and loved ones on the Day of Judgement. They will be bestowed this special privilege because they departed from this world relatively early, thereby being separated from their families; they gave up all worldly delights and family ties in order to defend Allah's faith from the internal and external threats. And as they willingly made sacrifices in this temporal world, the *shuhadā'* will be able to intercede for their family members and have them join them in Paradise. Lastly, the *awliyā'* (the friends of Allah) and the pious worshippers (*ṣāliḥūn*) will also be able to stand before Allah ﷻ and act as representatives for their families and loved ones. Undoubtedly, the station of intercession will only be conferred on the servants who are immensely loved by Allah ﷻ. In other words, an individual must have an advantageous position in Allah's sight for him or her to intervene and speak in favour of other people's standing and eligibility for Paradise. In a sound narration, the Prophet ﷺ said:

يَدْخُلُ الجَنَّةَ بِشَفَاعَةِ رَجُلٍ مِنْ أُمَّتِي أَكْثَرُ مِنْ بَنِي تَمِيمٍ

"More people than the population of the Banū Tamīm tribe will enter Paradise through the intercession of a single man of my Ummah."

The Banū Tamīm were one of the biggest clans in the Arabian Peninsula, so quite naturally the Prophet's report immediately stimulated the interest of the Companions. They asked: "Will this be through the intercession of someone other than you, O Messenger of Allah?" The Prophet said:

سِوَايَ.

"It will be someone other than me."

There is a difference of opinion amongst the scholars on the identity of this virtuous and interceding man. Some have opined that the Prophet was referring to 'Uthmān ibn 'Affān ﷺ, while others argued that he was referring to Uways al-Qarnī ﷺ. Though the exact name of the individual in question remains a point of contention, one can still meaningfully conclude that the virtue of some people will be so great that they will be empowered and given the means to intercede for entire communities.

Likewise, children that pass away before the age of puberty will be intercessors for their parents on the Day of Judgement. In fact, as pointed out in a powerful *ḥadīth*, the deceased infants and youngsters will refuse to enter Paradise unless their parents accompany them:

يُقَالُ لِلْوِلْدَانِ يَوْمَ القِيَامَةِ اُدْخُلُوا الجَنَّةَ، قَالَ، فَيَقُولُونَ: يَا رَبِّ حَتَّى يَدْخُلَ آبَاؤُنَا وَأُمَّهَاتُنَا.

"It will be said to the deceased children on the Day of Judgement: 'Enter Paradise.' But they will say: 'O our Lord, we will not enter until our fathers and mothers come with us.'"

The children will be repeatedly informed that the door to Paradise is open for them, and that they should enter it without delay. But they will stay put, insisting that they will not move forward until their parents accompany them as well. At this juncture, Allah ﷻ will ask regarding the children:

مَا لِي أَرَاهُمْ مُحْبَنْطِئِينَ

"Why is it that I see them being hesitant like this?"

The children will repeat their request by stating: "O our Lord, we will not enter until our fathers and mothers come with us." Allah ﷻ will honour their appeal by stating:

ادْخُلُوا الْجَنَّةَ أَنْتُمْ وَآبَاؤُكُمْ.

"Both you and your parents may enter Paradise."

Parents who have a child pass away in this world and accept their loss patiently will have their child's intercession (*shafāʿah*) on the Day of Judgement. There are even a number of explicit *ḥadīths* which indicate that the same ruling applies in the case of the foetus which dies prematurely. In one of these reports, the Prophet ﷺ said:

وَالَّذِي نَفْسِي بِيَدِهِ إِنَّ السَّقْطَ لَيَجُرُّ أُمَّهُ بِسَرَرِهِ إِلَى الْجَنَّةِ إِذَا احْتَسَبَتْهُ.

"By the One in Whose Hand is my soul, the miscarried foetus will continue to pull its mother into Paradise—through its umbilical cord—provided she accept its loss patiently and anticipates Allah's reward for that."

This is a beautiful manifestation of Allah's mercy and how He ensures parents do not experience a tragedy without being handsomely compensated in the Hereafter. There are many parents who make sure that their children receive a proper upbringing so that the latter may supplicate and pray for them after they die. But as for the case of children who die prematurely, the accrued rewards in the Hereafter that parents get from their loss will be much greater; these infants will be physically standing by the gates of Paradise awaiting the arrival of their parents. The mother and father who must face the tragedy of a miscarriage in this world should be content with Allah's decree and apprehend that they have in fact produced for themselves a young intercessor who will lead them to eternal salvation in the next world.

As for acts of worship, two righteous endeavours will present themselves on the Day of Judgement and intercede on one's behalf. These two noble deeds—which are performed in abundance during the month of Ramadan—have been described by the Prophet ﷺ in the following *ḥadīth*:

الصِّيَامُ وَالْقُرْآنُ يَشْفَعَانِ لِلْعَبْدِ، يَقُولُ الصِّيَامُ : أَيْ رَبِّ! إِنِّي مَنَعْتُهُ الطَّعَامَ وَالشَّهَوَاتِ بِالنَّهَارِ، فَشَفِّعْنِي فِيهِ، وَيَقُولُ الْقُرْآنُ: مَنَعْتُهُ النَّوْمَ بِاللَّيلِ، فشَفِّعْنِي فِيهِ؛ فيَشْفَعَانِ.

"The servant's fasting and recitation of the Qur'ān will intercede on his behalf His fasting shall say: 'O Lord, I deprived him of his food and desires throughout the day, so allow me to intercede for him.' The Qur'ān shall say: 'I prevented him from sleeping at night, so allow me to intercede for him.' Then both of them will have their requests to intercede granted."

The mother and father who must face the tragedy of a miscarriage in this world should be content with Allah's decree and apprehend that they have in fact produced for themselves a young intercessor who will lead them to eternal salvation in the next world.

Every type of intercession on the Last Day is a result of Allah's facilitation, since no event or occurrence can take place without His leave. Yet, it is known for certain that no person or thing can compete with Allah's grace and generosity. For this reason, after all the forms of intercession from created beings are articulated, Allah ﷻ will make the following announcement:

بَقِيَتْ شَفَاعَتِي.

"There now remains My intercession (shafā'ah)."

In His infinite mercy, He will remove an unspecified number of individuals who were burned and punished in Hellfire and thereafter submerge them in a river known as *Mā' al-Ḥayāt* (the Water of Life), which is adjacent to Paradise itself. In this divine intercession, Allah ﷻ will allow the bodies of these smouldered individuals to be rejuvenated and regenerated through this blessed water. But the sensible and far-sighted individual should never aspire to be thrown into Hellfire for an unspecified period before being saved. Instead, his priority should be to perform virtuous acts and become a model of goodness, such that he could intercede and save his fellow brothers and sisters on the Last Day. By doing this, one shall be granted an honourable position on the Day of Judgement. For Allah ﷻ says in the Qur'ān:

يَٰٓأَيُّهَا ٱلَّذِينَ ءَامَنُواْ ٱسْتَجِيبُواْ لِلَّهِ وَلِلرَّسُولِ إِذَا دَعَاكُمْ لِمَا يُحْيِيكُمْ.

"O believers! Respond to Allah and His Messenger when he calls you to that which gives you life."[42]

---

[42] *Al-Anfāl*, 24.

17

Saved by Sūrahs

The Qur'ān is unique and miraculous in nature, with every single verse imparting a specific benefit to its reader. However, it is often the case that people have a unique relationship with a particular *Sūrah* or passage of the Qur'ān. This naturally leads to the question of whether or not it is permissible for one to have a preferred or ideal *Sūrah* (chapter). There are many individuals who enjoy frequently reciting a chapter or sequence of verses as a daily routine, because they provide them with a greater sense of comfort and happiness. From an Islamic point of view, there is nothing wrong with such a practice. In fact, there are a number of narrations which demonstrate that the Messenger of Allah ﷺ was emotionally impacted by verses that stressed his moral duties as the last Prophet. For instance, on one occasion *Sūrah al-Nisā'* was recited in his presence and, for the most part, the Prophet quietly listened and enjoyed hearing the recitation of one of his Companions. But everything changed once the reciter began to read the following verse:

فَكَيْفَ إِذَا جِئْنَا مِن كُلِّ أُمَّةٍ بِشَهِيدٍ وَجِئْنَا بِكَ عَلَىٰ هَٰٓؤُلَآءِ شَهِيدًا.

"So how will it be when We bring a witness from every faith community and bring you as a witness against yours?"[43]

Upon hearing this verse, the Prophet ﷺ wept and asked the reciter to stop his recitation, as the emotions that the verse aroused in him were too strong to bear. It is also related that the Prophet ﷺ once spent the whole night repeating just one verse and weeping:

إِن تُعَذِّبْهُمْ فَإِنَّهُمْ عِبَادُكَ وَإِن تَغْفِرْ لَهُمْ فَإِنَّكَ أَنتَ ٱلْعَزِيزُ ٱلْحَكِيمُ.

"If You punish them, they belong to You after all. But if You forgive them, You are surely the Almighty, All-Wise."[44]

On another occasion, the Prophet ﷺ was informed that one of his Companions consistently recited *Sūrah al-Ikhlāṣ* in in all the prayers that he led, to the extent that he earned a reputation for doing so. The Prophet ordered the people to ask the Companion why he was so fond of this particular chapter. The Companion said:

لِأَنَّهَا صِفَةُ الرَّحْمَنِ، وَأَنَا أُحِبُّ أَنْ أَقْرَأَ بِهَا.

"Because it provides a clear description of al-Raḥmān (the All-Merciful), and I love to recite it in prayer."

---

[43] *Al-Nisā'*, 41.

[44] *Al-Mā'idah*, 118.

Upon being provided this explanation, the Prophet ﷺ told the intermediaries to go back and relay the following message to the Companion:

أَخْبِرُوهُ أَنَّ اللهَ يُحِبُّهُ.

"Inform him that Allah loves him."

Interestingly, it is often the case that a particular *Sūrah* revolves around a specific theme or topic, thereby attracting the attention of certain readers. A father currently separated from his son may enjoy reading *Sūrah Yūsuf*, a person wishing to reflect on the bounties of Allah may naturally love *Sūrah al-Raḥmān*, while a person desiring to read the story of one of the most blessed and honourable women in this world would naturally gravitate towards *Sūrah Maryam*. Some of the Companions also had their own favourite chapters and sections of the Qur'ān. For instance, it is related that Ibn Masʿūd ؓ said:

إِذَا وَقَعْتُ فِي آلِ حَم فَقَدْ وَقَعْتُ فِي رَوْضَاتٍ دَمِثَاتٍ أَتَأَنَّقُ فِيهِنَّ.

"When I embark upon reading the interrelated group of Sūrahs beginning with Ḥā-Mīm, I feel as if I am blissfully strolling in delightful meadows."

He is also reported to have stated in a similar narration:

آلُ حمٓ دَيْبَاجُ القُرْآنِ.

"The interrelated group of Sūrahs beginning with Ḥā-Mīm represent the silk covering of the Qur'ān."

The interrelated group of *Sūrah*s referred to in the aforementioned narrations consists of seven *Sūrahs* that all commence with the isolated letters of *Ḥā-Mīm*. They start with *Sūrah Ghāfir*[45] and end with *Sūrah al-Aḥqāf*. Historically, all these chapters were revealed in the Makkan period. Interestingly, none of them address any topics related to the legal rulings and regulations found in the Islamic faith. Instead, their substantive contents focus on the Creator ﷻ and preparing for the Hereafter. Ibn Masʿūd acutely appreciated this thematic focus and ultimately developed a special fondness for this series of chapters. But other individuals may identify different sequences and sections of the Qur'ān that leave a stronger impression on their hearts. Regardless of what section appeals more to one, the ultimate goal should be to develop an intricate bond with the Qur'ān. This is because without reciting and reflecting on the Qur'ān's meanings on a regular basis, one will not be able to purify one's heart from spiritual defects.

---

[45] Also known as *Sūrah Mu'min*.

In fact, reciting the Qur'ān on a regular basis is fundamental to securing one's salvation in the Hereafter. This is because the Book will appear as a personified entity on the Day of Judgement and intercede on behalf of its dedicated reciter and memoriser. For this theme, one can even find narrations which demonstrate that the faithful memoriser of the Qur'ān will enjoy the privilege of intercession on the Day of Judgement. In one key *ḥadīth*, the Prophet ﷺ is reported to have said:

مَنْ قَرَأَ الْقُرْآنَ وَاسْتَظْهَرَهُ فَأَحَلَّ حَلاَلَهُ وَحَرَّمَ حَرَامَهُ أَدْخَلَهُ اللَّهُ بِهِ الجَنَّةَ وَشَفَّعَهُ فِي عَشَرَةٍ مِنْ أَهْلِ بَيْتِهِ كُلُّهُمْ قَدْ وَجَبَتْ لَهُ النَّارُ.

"Whoever recites the Qur'ān, memorises it, and upholds what it rules to be lawful as lawful and abstains from what it deems unlawful, then Allah will admit him into Paradise due to it and grant him intercession (shafāʿah) for ten members of his family, all of whom were originally destined to enter Hellfire."

Several major scholars have deemed this *ḥadīth* to be weak, but they were still expectant that the virtues outlined in its text will be granted to the companion of the Qur'ān. If one wishes to obtain the promised reward found in this narration, then one cannot simply suffice oneself with reading and memorising the Qur'ān. Instead, it is also necessary for one to learn the rulings outlined in its verses and apply them accordingly. The more one strive to memorise and implement the Qur'ānic teachings in one's daily life, the greater the glory that one and one's parents will earn on the Day of Judgement. In a beautiful and exhortative narration, the Prophet ﷺ said:

مَنْ قَرَأَ الْقُرْآنَ وَعَمِلَ بِمَا فِيهِ، أُلْبِسَ وَالِدَاهُ تَاجًا يَوْمَ الْقِيَامَةِ، ضَوْءُهُ أَحْسَنُ مِنْ ضَوْءِ الشَّمْسِ فِي بُيُوتِ الدُّنْيَا، لَوْ كَانَتْ فِيكُمْ.

"Whoever recites the Qur'ān and acts on what is in it, his parents will be crowned on the Day of Resurrection with a crown whose light is brighter than the light of the Sun in your worldly homes."

There are also numerous narrations in which the Prophet describes the specific rewards and benefits that the recitation of a particular chapter will bring in the Hereafter. In one noteworthy narration, he ﷺ encouraged members of his Ummah to read the two longest chapters of the Qur'ān by stating:

اقْرَؤُوا القُرْآنَ فإنَّه يَأْتِي يومَ القِيامَةِ شَفِيعًا لأَصْحابِهِ، اقْرَؤُوا الزَّهْراوَيْنِ البَقَرَةَ، وسُورَةَ آلِ عِمْرانَ، فإنَّهُما تَأْتِيانِ يَومَ القِيامَةِ كَأنَّهُما غَمامَتانِ، أوْ كَأنَّهُما غَيايَتانِ، أوْ كَأنَّهُما فِرْقانِ مِن طَيْرٍ صَوافَّ، تُحاجّانِ عن أصْحابِهِما.

"Recite the Qur'ān, for it will appear on the Day of Resurrection as an intercessor for its companions. Recite the two brightly illuminated chapters: al-Baqarah and Āl 'Imrān, for they will appear on the Day of Resurrection as if they are two clouds, two beneficial bodies of shade, or two flocks of birds that will be arguing on behalf of their companions."

To understand the honour found in this reward, one can reflect on the fact that Prophet Sulaymān عليه السلام used to march with a mass procession of animals and human soldiers, all of which reflect the glory and splendour of his massive kingdom. Similarly, on the Day of Judgement, the regular reciter of *Sūrah al-Baqarah* and *Sūrah Āl 'Imrān* will be accompanied by his own column of birds, clouds, or bodies of shade, which will ultimately raise his status and standing among the rest of the creation. All the onlookers will be dazzled by such a spectacle, and will regret that they did not follow the example of this blessed person by reading these two chapters and acting on their directives. The Prophet ﷺ then said in the same narration:

اقْرَؤوا سُورَةَ الْبَقَرَةِ فَإِنَّ أَخْذَهَا بَرَكَةٌ وَتَرْكَهَا حَسْرَةٌ.

"Recite Sūrah al-Baqarah, for to do so is a blessings, while abandoning it will be a source of bitter regret."

He then mentioned that *Sūrah al-Baqarah* has yet another virtue as well:

وَلَا تَسْتَطِيعُهَا الْبَطَلَةُ.

This short sentence holds a myriad of meanings, and can be translated as: "The people hampered by laziness will not be able to recite it." An alternative translation for it would be: "The practitioners of sorcery will not be able to overcome it."

The Prophet also elucidated the virtues of the short *Sūrahs* that are regularly recited by scholars and laymen alike. On one occasion, the Prophet heard a man complete the recitation of *Sūrah al-Ikhlāṣ*, so he said:

وَجَبَتْ.

"It has become mandatory."

He was then asked: "What has become mandatory?"

The Prophet replied by stating:

وَجَبَتْ لَهُ الجَنَّةُ.

"Paradise has become mandatory for him."

Despite its shortness and simplicity, *Sūrah al-Ikhlāṣ* consists of a powerful sequence of verses that reiterate the fundamental principles of Islamic monotheism. After all, its first verse states:

قُلْ هُوَ ٱللَّهُ أَحَدٌ.

"Say, 'He is Allah—One.'"[46]

In another sound narration, the Prophet ﷺ highlighted the virtues of *Āyah al-Kursī* (the Throne Verse—*Sūrah al-Baqarah*, 255) by stating:

مَنْ قَرَأَ آيَةَ الكُرْسِي دُبُرَ كُلِّ صَلاَةٍ مَا مَنَعَهُ مِنْ دُخُولِ الجَنَّةِ إِلاَّ المَوْتُ.

"Nothing prevents whoever recites Āyah al-Kursī after every prescribed prayer from entering Paradise except death."

In essence, in this report the Prophet ﷺ guarantees his followers who consistently read this verse after each five obligatory prayers that nothing prevents them from entering Paradise except their own demise. There is yet another *Sūrah* which confers immense virtues and rewards upon its reciter. In fact, this *Sūrah* has been assigned a number of names and titles, such as *al-Māni'ah* (the Preventer) and *al-Munjiyah* (the Rescuer). The chapter in question is none other than *Sūrah al-Mulk*, which was praised

46 *Al-Ikhlāṣ*, 1.

and highlighted by the Prophet ﷺ himself in a series of *ḥadīths*. In one key narration, the Prophet ﷺ mentioned that one who recites this chapter every night will be protected from the trials and penalties of the grave. When commenting on this *ḥadīth*, some scholars noted that this chapter helps one attain the level of religiosity and God-consciousness needed to prevent one from engaging in vices and evil deeds, thereby protecting oneself from the punishment of the grave. Moreover, this *Sūrah* is so powerful that it shall be an intercessor for its reciters on the Day of Judgement. In a beautiful narration, the Prophet ﷺ said:

إِنَّ سُورَةً فِي القُرْآنِ - ثَلَاثِينَ آيَةً - شَفَعَتْ لِصَاحِبِهَا حَتَّى غُفِرَ لَهُ.

"There is a Sūrah in the Qur'ān which consists of thirty verses: it intercedes for its [regular] reciter until he is forgiven."

In another version of the *ḥadīth*, the Prophet ﷺ described *Sūrah al-Mulk* with the following words:

خَاصَمَتْ لِصَاحِبِهَا حَتَّى يُغْفَرَ لَهُ.

"It will continue to argue on behalf of its [regular] reciter until he is forgiven."

The Prophet ﷺ then explicitly mentioned that the chapter in question is none other than the following:

تَبَارَكَ الَّذِي بِيَدِهِ المُلْكُ.

"It is the Sūrah which begins with: 'Blessed is the One in Whose Hands rests all authority.'"

Sūrah al-Mulk will assume a unique physical character on the Day of Judgement, persistently arguing on behalf of its regular reciter by requesting Paradise for him and seeking his protection from Hellfire. This should not come as a surprise, for its thirty beautiful verses are replete with the themes of remembering death, fearing Allah ﷻ, and preparing for the Hereafter. In one of its beautiful verses, Allah ﷻ offers the sincere believers the following promise:

إِنَّ ٱلَّذِينَ يَخْشَوْنَ رَبَّهُم بِٱلْغَيْبِ لَهُم مَّغْفِرَةٌ وَأَجْرٌ كَبِيرٌ.

"Indeed, those in awe of their Lord without seeing Him will have forgiveness and a mighty reward."[47]

Thus, while there is no doubt that the Qur'ān is a spiritual and physical healing (*shifā'*), its benefits in the other world will still be exponentially greater. Regardless of whether one is in the grave or standing on the Day of Judgement, the Qur'ān will improve one's condition by elevating one's spiritual rank.

47 *Al-Mulk*, 12.

18

Unanswered *Duʿāʾs*

The eminent Companion Ibn Masʿūd ﵁ once shared an incredible account which demonstrates the perfect knowledge and wisdom of Allah ﷻ:

إِنَّ العَبْدَ لَيَهُمُّ بِالأَمْرِ مِنَ التِجَارَةِ وَالإِمَارَةِ حَتَّى يُيَسَّرَ لَهُ.

"The servant would be on the verge of pursuing trade or political leadership to the point it becomes facilitated for him."

For instance, one may be constantly making *duʿāʾ* (supplication) for a certain worldly benefit or result, and eventually comes close to achieving one's objective. But Ibn Masʿūd notes that once the desired objective is within reach, Allah ﷻ will observe His persistent servant and then issue the following directive to the angels:

اِصْرِفُوهُ عَنْهُ، فَإِنَّهُ إِنْ يَسَّرْتُهُ لَهُ أَدْخَلْتُهُ النَّارَ.

"Direct it away from him, for if I were to make it easy to him, I would then have to put him in Hellfire."

In other words, Allah ﷻ knows that granting this worldly benefit will cause the servant to fall into a path leading to Hellfire. In order to protect the servant's standing and salvation in the Hereafter, Allah takes what he has asked for away from them:

فَيَظَلُّ يَتَطَيَّرُ، يَقُولُ سَبَقَنِي فُلَانٌ دَهَانِي فُلَانٌ، وَمَا هُوَ إِلَّا فَضْلُ اللهِ عَزَّ وَجَلَّ.

"This man will start believing that he is ill-omened, saying, 'So-and-so managed to beat me to it, so-and-so struck me with this misfortune'. Yet, he fails to realise that it was nothing but Allah's favour bestowed upon him."

On the Day of Judgement, the true realities of the seemingly inexplicable events that occurred in this world will become apparent and meaningful. While standing before his Lord ﷻ, the servant will be informed why certain benefits and privileges he desired in this world—such as a dream career, beautiful spouse, or luxury home—were denied him. In one of his works outlining weak and discarded reports, Ibn al-Jawzī ﵀ related a remarkable *ḥadīth qudsī* replete with spiritual wisdom and insights. This narration can be found in some later compilations, such as the *Muʿjam* of Imām al-Ṭabarānī ﵀. Despite deeming the narration to be weak, several scholars—including Ibn Taymiyyah and Ibn Rajab al-Ḥanbalī ﵏—cited it in their respective works and extracted numerous benefits from it. In this report, which was narrated by the Companion Anas ﷺ, the Prophet ﷺ relates that Allah ﷻ said:

إِنَّ مِنْ عِبَادِي الْمُؤْمِنِينَ مَنْ يُرِيدُ بَابًا مِنَ الْعِبَادَةِ فَأَكُفُّهُ عَنْهُ لَا يَدْخُلُهُ عُجْبٌ فَيُفْسِدُهُ ذَلِكَ.

"There are among My believing servants those who seek a particular avenue of worship, but I prevent them from it, lest conceitedness enters their hearts and vitiate it [i.e. the particular worship]."

In His infinite wisdom, Allah ﷻ prevents some of his righteous servants from performing certain acts of worship, so that their hearts are protected from arrogance and self-admiration. Allah continues by stating:

وَإِنَّ مِنْ عِبَادِي الْمُؤْمِنِينَ لَمَنْ لَا يُصْلِحُ إِيمَانَهُ إِلَّا الْغِنَى، وَلَوْ أَفْقَرْتُهُ لَأَفْسَدَهُ ذَلِكَ، وَإِنَّ مِنْ عِبَادِي الْمُؤْمِنِينَ لَمَنْ لَا يُصْلِحُ إِيمَانَهُ إِلَّا الْفَقْرُ، وَلَوْ أَغْنَيْتُهُ لَأَفْسَدَهُ ذَلِكَ، وَإِنَّ مِنْ عِبَادِي الْمُؤْمِنِينَ لَمَنْ لَا يُصْلِحُ إِيمَانَهُ إِلَّا الصِّحَةُ، وَلَوْ أَسْقَمْتُهُ لَأَفْسَدَهُ ذَلِكَ، وَإِنَّ مِنْ عِبَادِي الْمُؤْمِنِينَ لَمَنْ لَا يُصْلِحُ إِيمَانَهُ إِلَّا السَّقَمُ، وَلَوْ أَصْحَحْتُهُ لَأَفْسَدَهُ ذَلِكَ.

"Indeed, there are among My servants those whose faith would not be rectified except through affluence, and were I to deprive them of it, it would corrupt them. And there are among My servants those whose faith would not be rectified except through poverty, and were I to enrich them, it would corrupt them. Furthermore, there are among My servants those whose faith would not be rectified except with good health, and if I were to render them ill, it would corrupt them. Lastly, there are among My servants those whose faith would not be rectified except through poor health, and if I were to give them good health, it would corrupt them."

There are many people who feel that they are ineligible or too lowly to directly address their Lord, yet such worries are baseless; in actual fact, Allah عزّ وجلّ attentively listens to every supplication made to Him.

This remarkable narration closes with the following declaration from Allah ﷻ:

إِنِّي أُدَبِّرُ أَمْرَ عِبَادِي بِعِلْمِي بِقُلُوبِهِمْ، إِنِّي عَلِيمٌ خَبِيرٌ.

"I plan for My servants through My knowledge of what is in their hearts, for I am All-Knowing and All-Aware."

This report provides a number of pivotal lessons for how one should make *du'ā'* to one's Creator. One should not simply call upon Allah ﷻ while being cognisant that He is capable of all things. Instead, one must be acutely aware that Allah alone knows what is most conducive to one's faith and well-being in the Hereafter. In other words, not only do humans sometimes lack the ability to determine what they truly seek and aspire to become in their mortal lives, but they may also fail to realise what is best for them in this world and the Hereafter. These points should be recognised whenever one calls upon one's Lord ﷻ. In an important narration on the proprieties of making *du'ā'*, the Prophet ﷺ said:

لَا يَزَالُ يُسْتَجَابُ لِلْعَبْدِ مَا لَمْ يَدْعُ بِإِثْمٍ أَوْ قَطِيعَةِ رَحِمٍ، مَا لَمْ يَسْتَعْجِلْ.

"The servant's du'ā' will be positively answered as long as he does not pray for something which entails a sin, leads to cutting ties of kinship, or is impatient."

The Companions asked: "O Messenger of Allah? What is meant by impatience?" The Prophet ﷺ then said:

يَقُولُ: قَدْ دَعَوْتُ وَقَدْ دَعَوْتُ، فَلَمْ أَرَ يَسْتَجِيبُ لِي، فَيَسْتَحْسِرُ عِنْدَ ذَلِكَ، وَيَدَعُ الدُّعاءَ.

"It occurs when one says: 'I made du'ā' on numerous occasions, and I did not find Him respond to me.' And as a result, he stops making du'ā' altogether."

Not only does such a person discontinue calling upon his Creator ﷻ, he also develops a negative attitude towards Him. By being dissatisfied with Allah's ability to positively respond, one is in effect assigning to Him the qualities of miserliness (*bukhl*) and weakness (*ḍa'f*), both of which are sacrilegious when ascribed to the Creator.

In another narration, the Prophet ﷺ said:

إِنَّ اللَّهَ حَيِيٌّ كَرِيمٌ يَسْتَحِي إِذَا رَفَعَ الرَّجُلُ إِلَيْهِ يَدَيْهِ أَنْ يَرُدَّهُمَا صِفْرًا خَائِبَتَيْنِ

"Indeed Allah is Compassionate, Diffident, and Generous. He is too diffident for His servant to raise his hands up for Him, and then not place anything good in them."

The beneficence and magnanimity of our Lord ﷻ is so great that He is shy to leave any supplicant, who sincerely calls on Him, empty-handed. There are many people who feel that they are ineligible or too lowly to directly address their Lord, yet such worries are baseless; in actual fact, Allah ﷻ attentively listens to every supplication made to Him. Any disposition and inclination to make *du'ā'* to the Lord of the worlds is a positive development which should be acted upon with confidence.

The great gnostic Ibn 'Aṭā' Allāh al-Iskandarī ﷺ once said:

مَتَى أَطْلَقَ اللهُ لِسَانَكَ بِالطَّلَبِ فَاعْلَمْ أَنَّهُ يُرِيدُ أَنْ يُعْطِيَكَ.

"Whenever Allah let your tongue loose to asking [Allah], then know that He wants to give you."

Similarly, 'Umar ibn al-Khaṭṭāb ﷺ is reported to have said: "Whenever I make *du'ā'*, I only concern myself with the ability to ask, and not with receiving an answer."

This aforementioned report indicates that the true Muslim should never be concerned with obtaining a response from Allah ﷻ. Instead, one should be apprehensive of leaving the practice of *du'ā'* in one's daily routine. The great Companion Abū Hurayrah ﷺ once said:

مَا أَخَافُ أَنْ أُحْرَمَ الإِجَابَةَ، وَلَكِنِّي أَخَافُ أَنْ أُحْرَمَ الدُّعَاءَ.

"I am never fearful of having my supplications left unanswered. But what I do genuinely fear is that I may be deprived of the ability to make supplications."

It is now worthwhile to explore the essential ingredients that produce an effective *du'ā'* for one's worldly affairs as well as for one's Hereafter. First and foremost, it is necessary for the supplicant to use prescribed entreaties and words of praise before making his request. By way of example, one may use words denoting the glorification of Allah (*tasbīḥ*) or oneness of Allah (*tahlīl*) ﷻ, as well as seeking forgiveness (*istighfār*) and sending prayers (*ṣalawāt*) upon the Messenger of Allah ﷺ. Not only are these words intrinsically virtuous insofar as they confer upon one rewards in the Hereafter, they also allow one to assume a stronger religious consciousness before one pleads to one's Lord ﷻ.

Secondly, it is imperative for the supplicant to know that every *duʿā'* consists of two basic elements. The first is the component of praising Allah (*thanā'*), while the second comprises requesting (*ṭalab*). Muslim scholars have noted that the words of *thanā'* expressed in the *duʿā'* will accrue rewards, but the retrieval of these gains and benefits will be deferred until the Hereafter. The benefits produced from the *ṭalab* part will be procured in instalments in this life and the Hereafter. However, it should be noted that in some circumstances getting a response may be postponed in this world, so patience must be exercised by the supplicant. But one must always be grateful and appreciative of the fact, that for every *duʿā'* one makes, one will have virtues and rewards stored for one in the Hereafter.

As for the *ṭalab* part of the supplication, there are a number of narrations which explicitly indicate what type of benefits they will yield. In one report, the Prophet ﷺ said:

مَا مِنْ مُسْلِمٍ يَدْعُو بِدَعْوَةٍ لَيْسَ فِيهَا إِثْمٌ وَلاَ قَطِيعَةُ رَحِمٍ إِلَّا أَعْطَاهُ اللهُ بِهَا إِحْدَى ثَلاَثٍ:
إِمَّا أَنْ يُعَجِّلَ لَهُ دَعْوَتَهُ، وَإِمَّا أَنْ يَدَّخِرَهَا لَهُ فِي الْآخِرَةِ، وَإِمَّا أَنْ يَصْرِفَ عنهُ من السُّوءِ مثلَها.

"There is no Muslim who calls upon Allah for something—as long as it is not a sin or entails cutting one's family ties—except that Allah will grant him for it one of three things: (1) He will immediately fulfil his request; (2) He will drive away from him an evil commensurate with it it; or (3) He will save it for him for the Hereafter."

Upon hearing this beautiful promise made to the Creator ﷻ, the Companions rejoiced and said:

إِذَنْ نُكْثِرُ.

"Then we will make more supplications."

The Prophet responded by stating:

اللهُ أَكْثَرُ.

"Allah has even more than what you ask of Him."

Thus, one can and should make abundant supplications to the Creator ﷻ, since He has limitless provisions at His disposal and gives freely whenever He wishes. One should then be pleased and joyful to know that with every subsequent iteration of *du'ā'*, Allah will reciprocate it with a greater reward.

On the Day of Judgement, every *duʿā'* that one has made in the life of this world will be saved and counted in one's register of good deeds. To illustrate the magnanimity of this point, one may consider a number of thought experiments. Suppose that one has suffered from a grave illness in this world, and to combat its symptoms, one and one's loved ones have made *duʿā'* numerous times for the restoration of one's sound health. Should one fail to have one's health restored in this world, this does not mean that one's continuous *duʿā's* were in vain. Instead, every single supplication made for one's health—whether by them or someone else—will be saved as rewards in the Hereafter. However, now suppose that one was cured and did regain good health after several years of supplicating to Allah ﷻ. With the sole exception of the single *duʿā'* that had proved conducive to one's healing, all the other supplications made during one's illness will be geared towards one's Afterlife and saved as bountiful rewards. Paradoxically, if one knew of the tremendousness of every unanswered *duʿā'* in the Hereafter, one would wish that none of one's supplications are answered in this life. This is because Allah's response in the Afterlife will lead to the accrual of permanent and vast treasures that cannot be rivalled by anything in this world. Just as an act of charity becomes a mountain of gold in the Hereafter, any *duʿā'* whose answer is delayed until the other world will be appreciated to an unimaginable degree.

19

The Reward for One's Patience

The splendour and sublimity of patience is underscored in the following verse:

فَصَبْرٌ جَمِيلٌ.

"So beautiful patience!"[48]

There is nothing more inspirational than seeing a person who is undergoing difficulties leading his life with the ethos of beautiful patience. In fact, for Allah ﷻ, such a sight is even more seemly, since He has perfect knowledge of the physical and psychological struggles that such a person experiences every single day. There are some individuals whose difficulties are apparent to the onlooker, such that others realise the pain they are in and, hence, show them empathy. But there are other individuals whose suffering may be somewhat concealed such that only a discerning observer would be able to perceive it.

---

[48] *Yūsuf*, 18.

And there is yet another category of people who appear to live a materially comfortable and pompous life, yet their spiritual selves are completely empty and devoid of any satisfaction. Their souls are burning with dissatisfaction, yet their physical selves mask their pain.

But the most outstanding category consists of the people of patience (*ṣabr*), for they are the ones who outwardly appear to be undergoing trials and adversities, yet their souls are content and brimming with faith. Despite being materially or physically disadvantaged, their high level of spiritual contentedness is remarkable and miraculous in nature. In fact, the Prophet ﷺ himself remarked that the resilience and stability of the people of patience make a marvellous sight. Undoubtedly, one of the main drivers of their spiritual strength and composure is their realisation that this world is transient. In other words, they are aware that were they to spiritually disassociate themselves from the burdens and temptations of this world, they will be rewarded with Paradise. For this reason, we find Allah ﷻ stating in one key verse:

مَنْ عَمِلَ صَالِحًا مِنْ ذَكَرٍ أَوْ أُنْثَىٰ وَهُوَ مُؤْمِنٌ فَلَنُحْيِيَنَّهُ حَيَاةً طَيِّبَةً ۖ وَلَنَجْزِيَنَّهُمْ أَجْرَهُمْ بِأَحْسَنِ مَا كَانُوا يَعْمَلُونَ.

"Whoever does good, whether male or female, and is a believer, We will surely bless him with a good life, and We will certainly reward them according to the best of their deeds."[49]

[49] *Al-Naḥl*, 97.

Worldly trials serve as a purifier for one's sins and lapses to the extent that one will appear on the Day of Judgement with a clean record of deeds. A patient believer will ultimately rejoice when he receives an unlimited amount of blessings and rewards in the Afterlife.

Commentators of the Qur'ān have noted that the good life (*ḥayāt ṭayyibah*) mentioned in this verse refers to spiritual contentment in this world, while the true reward (*jazā'*) will be granted in the Hereafter. Regarding this very theme, Ibn 'Aṭā' Allah al-Iskandarī ﷺ formulates the following aphorism:

إِنَّمَا جَعَلَ الدَّارَ الآخِرَةِ مَحَلًا لِجَزَاءِ عِبَادِهِ المُؤْمِنِينَ لأَنَّ هَذِهِ الدَّارَ لاتَسَعُ مَا يرِيدُ
أَنْ يُعْطِيَهُمْ , وَلأَنَّه أَجَلَّ أَقْدارَهُمْ عَنْ أَنْ يُجَازِيَهُمْ فِي دَارٍ لا بَقَاءَ لَهَا.

"Allah has made the abode of the Hereafter the location for the reward of His believing servants because this abode is not capacious enough for what He wants to give them and also because He deems their worth to be much greater than to reward them in an abode that has no permanance."

The life of this world is limited in its scope and nature, which means that it cannot appropriately incorporate the types of rewards which Allah ﷻ wishes to give to His servants. For even if Allah gave His servants all the material possessions and pleasures found in this temporal world, they would cease to benefit from them once they die and enter their graves. This explains why in many circumstances Allah ﷻ delays answering supplications in this world, since the benefits granted in the Hereafter are permanent and everlasting.

The Muslim must also perceive worldly trials through the same long-term vision, namely by considering them to be manifestations of Allah's mercy and infinite wisdom. For instance, the wise believer realises that undergoing temporary trials and tribulations in this world is far better than the permanent adversities and hardships of the Afterlife. In other words, the Muslim who is exposed to hardships in this world will be spared any forms of distress in the Hereafter. In an inspiring and thought-provoking *ḥadīth* reported by Anas, the Prophet ﷺ said:

إِذَا أَرَادَ اللّٰهُ بِعَبْدِهِ الخَيْرَ عَجَّلَ لَهُ العُقُوبَةَ.

"If Allah wants good for His servant, He hastens for him punishment in this world."

Secondly, worldly trials serve as a purifier for one's sins and lapses to the extent that one will appear on the Day of Judgement with a clean record of deeds. Thus, worldly tribulations not only efface the tribulations of the Hereafter, but they also blot out one's sins. In a beautiful narration, the Prophet ﷺ said:

مَا يَزَالُ البَلَاءُ بِالمُؤْمِنِ وَالمُؤْمِنَةِ فِي نَفْسِهِ وَوَلَدِهِ وَمَالِهِ حَتَّى يَلْقَى اللّٰهَ وَمَا عَلَيْهِ.

"The male and female believer will be continuously subjected to trials in their own selves, children, and wealth until they meet Allah sinless."

Thirdly, when the servant perseveres and overcomes his worldly trials with the power of faith, Allah ﷻ will grant him an elevated rank in the Hereafter which he would have been unable to attain had he simply experienced a comfortable life. In this regard, the Prophet ﷺ states:

إِنَّ الرَّجُلَ لَيَكُونُ لَهُ عِنْدَ اللَّهِ تَعَالَى الْمَنْزِلَةُ فَمَا يَبْلُغُهَا بِعَمَلٍ ، فَمَا يَزَالُ يَبْتَلِيهِ بِمَا يَكْرَهُ حَتَّى يُبْلِغَهُ إِيَّاهَا.

"A person will have a station in the sight of Allah which he will be unable to attain through his deeds. So Allah will continue to test him with that which he dislikes until He makes him reach that station."

In sum, worldly trials and tribulations eliminate otherworldly afflictions, erase sins and wrongdoings found in one's record, and allow one to attain a station that is unattainable with mere deeds. Because of the immense virtues and blessings found in such trials, on the Day of Judgement, the people who lived trouble-free lives will covet the station granted to the believers who underwent hardships. In fact, in one narration, one reads the following remarkable account which indicates how Allah ﷻ will immensely honour the people who faithfully withstand the trials predestined for them in this world:

يَوَدُّ أَهْلُ العَافِيَةِ يَوْمَ القِيَامَةِ حِينَ يُعْطَى أَهْلُ البَلَاءِ الثَّوَابَ لَوْ أَنَّ جُلُودَهُمْ كَانَتْ قُرِضَتْ فِي الدُّنْيَا بِالمَقَارِيضِ.

"When the people who experienced extreme hardships [in this world] are given their rewards on the Day of Judgement, the individuals who were given well-being in this world would wish that their bodies had been cut [in this world] with scissors."

But at this juncture, one might point out the numerous bouts of depression and mental suffering they went through in this world, and whether any compensation or recompense exists for such experiences. This has been neatly addressed in a beautiful ḥadīth illustrating the unlimited pleasures of Paradise. It discusses how the gloomy and pessimistic outlook of the most unfortunate believer—in terms of health, wealth, and family ties—will instantly change in the Hereafter:

وَيُؤْتَى بِأَشَدِّ الْمُؤْمِنِينَ ضُرًّا وَبَلَاءً، فَيُقَالُ: اغْمِسُوهُ غَمْسَةً فِي الْجَنَّةِ، فَيُغْمَسُ فِيهَا غَمْسَةً، فَيُقَالُ لَهُ: أَيْ فُلَانُ هَلْ أَصَابَكَ ضُرٌّ قَطُّ أَوْ بَلَاءٌ، فَيَقُولُ: مَا أَصَابَنِي قَطُّ ضُرٌّ وَلَا بَلَاءٌ.

"The believer who suffered the most harm and adversity in this world will be brought forth and it will said to him: 'Show him Paradise just for one moment,' and he will accordingly be placed there for one short moment. After that brief experience, he will be asked: 'O so-and-so, have you ever been afflicted with any harm or adversity?' In response, he will say: 'I have never ever experienced any harm or adversity.'"

This report's message is remarkable, since it indicates how one will forget a lifetime of tribulations and misfortunes simply after being immersed in Paradise for a brief moment.

One then can only imagine the degree of pleasure that the dweller of Paradise will experience while he or she is served inside their exquisite palaces. Allah ﷻ guarantees a beautiful reward for those who lead a life of patience:

إِنَّمَا يُوَفَّى الصَّابِرُونَ أَجْرَهُمْ بِغَيْرِ حِسَابٍ.

"Only those who endure patiently will be given their reward without limit."[50]

Unlike the rewards granted for other actions and deeds, the rewards given for patience are unbounded and immeasurable. This is because, as some scholars note, the discomforts experienced as a result of worldly tribulations are prolonged, deep-seated, and multi-dimensional. For this reason, when Allah ﷻ rewards the patient and steadfast believer, He considers the various facets of tribulation that he had to overcome in this temporal world. Such a believer will ultimately rejoice when he receives an unlimited amount of blessings and rewards in the Afterlife. This form of divine reciprocity is a clear manifestation of Allah's mercy, which is sublime and perfect. And on the Day of Judgement, it will be exhibited in its most complete form. In a beautiful and hope-inducing narration, the Prophet ﷺ said:

إِنَّ اللَّهَ خَلَقَ يومَ خَلَقَ السَّمَوَاتِ وَالأَرْضَ مِائَةَ رَحْمَةٍ، كُلُّ رَحْمَةٍ طِبَاقَ ما بيْنَ السَّمَاءِ وَالأَرْضِ، فَجَعَلَ منها في الأرْضِ رَحْمَةً، فَبِهَا تَعْطِفُ الوَالِدَةُ علَى وَلَدِهَا، وَالْوَحْشُ وَالطَّيْرُ بَعْضُهَا علَى بَعْضٍ، فَإِذَا كانَ يَوْمُ القِيَامَةِ أَكْمَلَهَا بِهذِه الرَّحْمَةِ.

---

[50] *Al-Zumar*, 10.

"Indeed, on the very day that Allah created the Heavens and the Earth, He also created one hundred mercies, each of which encompassing what is between the Heavens and earth. He placed one of these mercies on earth, through it a mother shows compassion towards her child, and the animals and birds share empathy for one another. But on the Day of Judgement, Allah will perfect His mercy."

As this report confirms, on this earth, created beings are only experiencing a single unit of divine mercy. But on the Day of Judgement, Allah ﷻ will amplify His mercy to a previously unseen level by incorporating the additional ninety-nine mercies. One then can be assured that, in the other world, one will be judged by a Lord Who is loving and merciful to every created being. When a consoling mother shows love and attention to her distressed child, that reaction simply stems from the one mercy that is present in this world. But on the Day of Judgement, Allah's mercy and compassion to His servants will be represented by the one hundred mercies. This type of divine mercy will not simply relieve the humans who are fearful or distressed on that day, but it will also prove decisive in erasing the spiritual defects and sins of countless individuals.

On this earth, created beings are only experiencing a single unit of divine mercy. But on the Day of Judgement, Allah ﷻ will amplify His mercy to a previously unseen level by incorporating the additional ninety-nine mercies!

20

Deeds Performed Secretly

Every individual has his own fair share of secrets in this temporal world. But it should be the believer's priority to have secrets works that are characterised with purity and virtue, for there is no greater honour than to meet one's Lord ﷻ on the Last Day with a bundle of good deeds that were performed in seclusion, such that He alone was aware of them. As the sacred texts of Islam indicate, Allah's pleasure with such actions will be limitless and beyond description. For instance, in one notable *ḥadīth*, the Prophet ﷺ is reported to have said:

صَدَقَةُ السِّرِ تُطْفِئُ غَضَبَ الرَّبِ.

"The charity given in secret extinguishes the anger of the Lord."

Likewise, the righteous servant who performs good works in secret will be pleased on the Day of Judgement as well. For Allah ﷻ will shower him with praises and enumerate all the private acts of goodness—such as prayer and charity—that His servant performed purely for His sake. Then He will bless this distinguished servant with a unique set of rewards and gifts. At the same time, however, the believer is apprehensive of having the sins he committed in secret exposed by the Lord of the worlds ﷻ. There are many Muslims who are troubled with committing sins in their own private quarters. Though they may be regretful and even repentant of their hidden lapses, such individuals struggle to rectify their affairs and often continue repeating the same sins, with no one having knowledge of them except their Lord.

On the Day of Judgement, Allah ﷻ will reveal His perfect knowledge of these secret sins to the guilty servant and the other members of humanity who are close to him. The ultimate question in this matter is whether Allah will pardon such a servant for his lapses. There is no doubt that Allah will display an inconceivable and unimaginable degree of compassion on the Day of Judgement, to the extent that He will forgive the most serious of sins. However, as a thought experiment, one may ask regarding the fate of the Muslim who happens to be presented with numerous scrolls which enumerate his lifelong sins. Such a person sincerely believed in Allah, but he indulged in a life of sin and debauchery. This may mirror the condition of many Muslims today who register numerous sins in their accounts of deeds. In order to warn these people from treading such a dangerous path, the Prophet ﷺ said:

مَا مِنْكُمْ مِنْ أَحَدٍ إِلَّا سَيُكَلِّمُهُ اللهُ يَوْمَ القِيَامَةِ لَيْسَ بَيْنَهُ وَبَيْنَهُ تَرْجُمَانٌ ، فَيَنْظُرُ أَيْمَنَ مِنْهُ فَلَا يَرَى إِلَّا مَا قَدَّمَ وَيَنْظُرُ أَشْأَمَ مِنْهُ فَلَا يَرَى إِلَّا مَا قَدَّمَ وَيَنْظُرُ بَيْنَ يَدَيْهِ فَلَا يَرَى إِلَّا النَّارَ تِلْقَاءَ وَجْهِهِ.

"There is no one among you except that his Lord will speak to him without any intermediary. He will look to his right and shall not see anything except the deeds he sent forth, and he will look to his left and shall not see anything except the deeds he sent forth, and then he will look in front of him and he shall not see anything except Hellfire facing him."

At this point, the hypocrite will realise that his downfall will occur the moment he receives his register of deeds in his left hand. This devastating sign of doom has been confirmed in the following Qur'ānic verse:

وَأَمَّا مَنْ أُوتِيَ كِتَابَهُ بِشِمَالِهِ فَيَقُولُ يَا لَيْتَنِي لَمْ أُوتَ كِتَابِيَهْ.

"And as for him who is given his book in his left hand, he shall say, 'I wish I had not been given my book.'"[51]

In a desperate attempt to save himself, the hypocrite will place his left hand behind his back. But this will prove to be futile, as a chain will appear and tightly lock his hand, which will be fastened behind his back and make him feel uncomfortable.

[51] *Al-Ḥāqqah*, 25.

Immediately thereafter, he will be handed his record. Any onlooker who is situated behind this hypocrite will witness the latter's shameful end:

وَأَمَّا مَنْ أُوتِيَ كِتَابَهُ وَرَاءَ ظَهْرِهِ فَسَوْفَ يَدْعُو ثُبُورًا.

"And as for him who is given his book from behind his back, he will shall plead without cease for destruction to end him."[52]

Thus, during his examination process, the hypocrite will be abjectly debased and humiliated. By contrast, Allah ﷻ will protect the honour of the genuine believer in the most beautiful of ways. It is reported that a man once came to the noble Companion Ibn ʿUmar and asked him:

كَيْفَ سَمِعْتَ رَسُولَ اللهِ صَلَّى اللهُ عَلَيْهِ وَسَلَّمَ يَقُولُ فِي النَّجْوَى؟

"What did you hear the Prophet ﷺ say about private conversation (najwā)?"

The concept of *najwā* is often cited to refer to a prominent status which denotes the intimate and secret dialogue that the Muslim servant has with his Lord ﷻ. For instance, in a notable *ḥadīth*, the Prophet stated that when the Muslim commences his prayer (*ṣalāh*), he actually initiates an episode of *najwā* with his Lord. But in the question posed to Ibn ʿUmar, the *najwā* that is meant refers to the dialogue that will occur between the Muslim slave and his Creator on the Day of Judgement. Consequently, in order to address

---

52 *Al-Inshiqāq*, 10–11.

the man's question, Ibn 'Umar related the following *ḥadīth* of the Prophet ﷺ:

يُدْنَى الْمُؤْمِنُ يَوْمَ الْقِيَامَةِ مِنْ رَبِّهِ حَتَّى يَضَعَ كَنَفَهُ عَلَيْهِ.

"On the Day of Judgement, the believer will be brought near to his Lord to the extent that He will place His veil over him."

Allah ﷻ will grace the believer with His own veil, which is made of light. In this intimate and spiritual setting, the believing servant will be so close to the Lord that no one will be able to overhear the dialogue that will occur between them. This is an act of mercy from Allah, since it entails that the believing servant's proceedings will occur in a strictly private setting. Allah ﷻ will then reveal the servant's sins and lapses—which he committed in private and concealed from his family and peers—and gently interrogate him by stating:

أَتَعْرِفُ ذَنْبَ كَذَا؟

"Do you recognise and recall such-and-such a sin?"

The believing servant will truthfully respond to his Lord by saying:

رَبِّ أَعْرِفُ.

"O Lord, I do recognise them."

The believer is humbled by these revelations and willingly confesses to committing these faults throughout his life. He will not attempt to falsify any reports or raise his status before the Lord of the worlds ﷻ, nor will he try to evade responsibility by blaming another person or party for these lapses. He will assume sole liability for his sins and transgressions. In recognition of his sincere acknowledgement, Allah ﷻ will say:

فَإِنِّي قَدْ سَتَرْتُهَا عَلَيْكَ فِي الدُّنْيَا، وَأَنَا أَغْفِرُهَا لَكَ الْيَوْمَ.

"Indeed, I had concealed them for you in the temporary life of world and, today, I forgive you for all of them."

The Prophet ﷺ then closed this beautiful narration by stating:

فَيُعْطَى صَحِيفَةَ حَسَنَاتِهِ.

"He will be then given his scroll of his good deeds."

In another narration, the Prophet ﷺ states that, in the Hereafter, the repentant believer will find that every misdeed (*sayy'iah*) he repented from in this world will be replaced with a good deed (*ḥasanah*). This dramatic turn of events will surprise him so much that he will address his Lord ﷻ and say:

يَا رَبِّ لَقَدْ عَمِلْتُ أَشْيَاءَ مَا أَرَاهَا هَاهُنَا.

"O Lord, there are many things (i.e. sins) that I committed which I do not see here."

Allah's mercy on the Day of Judgement will be so great that He will replace the servants' evil deeds with good ones, such that their accounts will be pure and free of any errors. Such a report gives the Muslim glad tidings and hope for the Hereafter. In fact, upon completing this report, the narrator noted that the Prophet ﷺ was seen with a broad and beautiful smile, such that his molars became visible. In fact, as the scholars of *tafsīr*

(Qur'ānic exegesis) mention, the surprising and joyous finding alluded to in the aforementioned *ḥadīth* vividly explains the following Qur'ānic verse:

فَأَمَّا مَنْ أُوتِيَ كِتَابَهُ بِيَمِينِهِ فَيَقُولُ هَاؤُمُ اقْرَءُوا كِتَابِيَهْ إِنِّي ظَنَنتُ أَنِّي مُلَاقٍ حِسَابِيَهْ.

"As for him who is given his book in his right hand, he shall cry, 'Just read, all of you, my record! Verily, I knew I would meet my reckoning.'"[53]

After receiving the record of deeds in his right hand, the believer will rejoice upon all the good deeds registered as a result of his repentance. He will be so ecstatic that he will run around and call his fellow Muslims to come and read his record of virtues. He will share with them the glad tidings and mercy that he received from his Lord ﷻ. In this joyous atmosphere, the believers will pinpoint their respective rewards and celebrate their achievements. In the context of the Hereafter, the believer will be allowed to mention his good deeds with a sense of pride and celebration.

One can juxtapose this servant's good fortune with the dreadful consequences that the first human questioned on the Day of Judgement will face. As noted in Chapter 11, the latter was heedless of Allah ﷻ and neglectful of his religious obligations. Allah will ask him: "Did you not ever come to the realisation that you will be meeting Me?" Because this person failed to be cognisant of Allah and His commandments, he will be placed in Hellfire. But this God-conscious and spiritually

---

[53] *Al-Ḥāqqah*, 19–20.

awake servant never forgot his Lord and prepared himself for the Day of Judgement. This is why he will say: "I surely knew I would meet my reckoning." Thus, the Muslim must adequately prepare himself for this momentous gathering so that he may celebrate his admission into the eternal abode of bliss and share his success story with his friends and loved ones.

فَأَمَّا مَن ثَقُلَتْ مَوَٰزِينُهُۥ فَهُوَ فِي عِيشَةٍ رَّاضِيَةٍ

"So as for those whose scales are heavy with good deeds, they will be in a life of bliss."

AL-QĀRIʿAH, 6–7

21

Heavy Words on One's Scale

Salvation does not actually lie in the quantity of one's deeds. Instead, the real yardstick of success lies in whether one undertakes righteous actions with a sincere heart. This explains why Allah ﷻ said:

الَّذِي خَلَقَ الْمَوْتَ وَالْحَيَاةَ لِيَبْلُوَكُمْ أَيُّكُمْ أَحْسَنُ عَمَلًا.

"[He is the One] Who created death and life in order to test which of you is best in deeds."[54]

One notes that this verse states "best in deeds", not "most in deeds", which confirms that virtuousness of deeds is the moral standard set by Allah ﷻ. On the Day of Judgement, it is not the abundance of works that will save one from the punishment of Hellfire. Instead, the servants who had sincerity in their conduct and performed deeds for the sake of Allah alone will be showered with His mercy. One of the most feasible ways

---

54 *Al-Mulk*, 2

to instil sincerity in one's heart is to consistently perform the effortless and easy acts of goodness that have been prescribed in the religion. Such actions have been gifted to us by Allah as a means to raise our moral rank and obtain Paradise with relative ease. Indeed, it is difficult for one to assert that one is sincere to Allah and His religion if one consistently fails to undertake the simplest of good deeds. The wise Muslim is the one who performs his works with due diligence and orients his outlook towards the Hereafter. Allah ﷻ reminds us of the just procedures and standards that will be used in the Hereafter:

وَنَضَعُ ٱلْمَوَٰزِينَ ٱلْقِسْطَ لِيَوْمِ ٱلْقِيَٰمَةِ فَلَا تُظْلَمُ نَفْسٌ شَيْـًٔا.

"We will set up the scales of justice on the Day of Judgement, so no soul will be wronged in the least."[55]

The noble Companion Salmān al-Fārisī رضي الله عنه once made the following insightful remark:

يُؤْتَى بِالمِيزَانِ يَوْمَ القِيَامَةِ، فَلَوْ وُضِعَتْ فِي كَفَّتِهِ السَّمَوَاتُ وَالأَرْضُ وَمَنْ فِيهِنَّ لَوَسِعَتْهُ.

"The Scales (Mīzān) will be brought on the Day of Judgement. Were the Heavens, the Earth and everything in them were placed on them, it would encompass them."

55 *Al-Anbiyā'*, 47.

In another narration, Salmān is reported to have mentioned the following apodosis instead at the end of his report: “It would be able to weigh them accurately.” Upon witnessing the stationing of the *Mīzān*, the angels will turn to Allah ﷻ and ask:

يَا رَبَّنَا مَنْ تَزِنُ بِهَذَا.

“O Lord, who will You be weighing with this?”

In response to their query, Allah ﷻ will state:

مَنْ شِئْتُ مِنْ خَلْقِي

“Whomever I wish from among My creation.”

What makes this exchange fascinating and worthy of examination is the fact that the angels are protected from sin; they are beings of light whose sole purpose is to serve and worship Allah. Subsequently, they will not be subject to any form of trial on the Day of Judgement, since by their intrinsic nature they cannot disobey Allah in any way whatsoever. Yet, once they receive this latter response from Allah ﷻ, they will feel so overawed that they will end up making the following admission:

سُبْحَانَكَ رَبَّنَا مَا عَبَدْنَاكَ حَقَّ عِبَادَتِكَ.

“Glory be to You! Our Lord, we did not worship You as You deserved to be worshipped.”

By this statement, the angels are alluding to the gross injustice of failing to appreciate Allah's uncontested supremacy and right to be worshipped alone:

وَمَا قَدَرُوا اللَّهَ حَقَّ قَدْرِهِ.

"They have not shown Allah His proper reverence."[56]

What makes this story so powerful is the fact that the angels are infallible worshippers of Allah ﷻ. Despite their constant glorification of Allah, they nevertheless acknowledge that Allah can never be worshipped in a manner which befits His majesty and grandeur. Even if a person accumulates a lifetime's worth of good deeds and has them placed on the *Mīzān*, they can never match up the degree of reverence and worship that the Lord of the worlds deserves.

In an important report, the great Successor al-Ḥasan al-Baṣrī رحمه الله provided a vivid description of the *Mīzān*. He mentioned that it possesses a tongue, which means that, just like other objects and beings on the Day of Judgement, it will have the ability to speak. Moreover, he mentioned that it has two weighing pans that will precisely measure the mass of any deed that is placed on it. In fact, its weighing capabilities will be so error-free that it will determine that the virtues and vices of some people are equal in measure. Such people who have an equal share of virtuous and immoral deeds are known as *aṣḥāb al-aʿrāf.* Had they registered even one more righteous deed in their account, the scales would have tilted in their favour, whereby they would

---

[56] *Al-Zumar, 67.*

be immediately among the inhabitants of Paradise. In order to attain eternal bliss, they will have to obtain Allah's mercy and favour. Taking such a category of people into account, one will realise that no good deed should be underestimated.

It is now worthwhile to explore some of the uncomplicated supplications and words of remembrance (*dhikr*) that one can recite on a daily basis to fill one's scale with good deeds. In a notable narration, the Prophet ﷺ said:

الطُّهُورُ شطْرُ الإِيمَانِ والحَمْدُ للهِ تَمْلَأُ المِيزَانَ وَسُبْحَانَ اللهِ والحَمْدُ للهِ تَمْلَآنِ مَا بَيْنَ السَّمَاءِ وَالأَرْضِ.

"Purity is half of faith, and saying alḥamdulillāh (all praise is due to Allah) fills the Mīzān, while saying subḥānallāh (glory be to Allah) and alḥamdulillāh fills what is between the Heavens and the Earth."

The words of remembrance prescribed in this report consist of two essential elements: *tasbīḥ* (glorification of Allah) and *taḥmīd* (praising of Allah). The former stresses the sublimity of Allah ﷻ, which is implicitly contrasted with one's own fallibility and weakness. The *taḥmīd* indicates one's gratitude and thankfulness to Allah for every blessing He has granted one in this world, while also recognising that one can never praise Him sufficiently. Because of the powerful denotations and connotations of these two expressions, it is no surprise to find that, on the Day of Judgement, they will spiritually assist the one who says them regularly. While each of these two expressions has its own benefits and implications, and when they are repeated in congregation, the virtues and rewards they

On the Day of Judgement, it is not the abundance of works that will save one from the punishment of Hellfire. Instead, the servants who had sincerity in their conduct and performed deeds for the sake of Allah alone will be showered with His mercy.

bring forth are even greater. This latter point is underscored in the following narration:

كَلِمَتَانِ خَفِيفَتَانِ عَلَى اللِّسَانِ، ثَقِيلَتَانِ فِي المِيزَانِ، حَبِيبَتَانِ إِلَى الرَّحْمَنِ:
سُبْحَانَ اللهِ وَبِحَمْدِهِ، سُبْحَانَ اللهِ العَظِيمِ.

"There are two phrases that are dear to the All-Merciful (al-Raḥmān), light on the tongue, but extremely heavy on the Scale (Mīzān): subḥānallāh wa bi-hamdih (how perfect is Allah the Most Praiseworthy), and subḥānallāh al-ʿaẓīm (how perfect is Allah the Almighty)."

The scholars have provided a number of explanations for why these two formulas of *dhikr* hold such immense blessings and virtues. Perhaps one of the simplest explanations is that each of these two phrases is an expression of veneration of Allah ﷻ which uses two words of praise. They point to how the first fuses the elements of *tasbīḥ* and *taḥmīd*, whereby the servant glorifies Allah's name and praises Him for his countless blessings. The second combines the notions of *tasbīḥ* and *taʿẓīm* (affirming the greatness of Allah), such that one proclaims the splendour and magnificence of one's Creator. It comes therefore as no surprise that these expressions of supplication will have a considerable weight on the *Mīzān*.

There are other *ḥadīths* which further underscore the importance of reciting these compound phrases. In one beautiful narration, the Prophet said ﷺ:

مَنْ قَالَ: حِينَ يُصْبِحُ وَحِينَ يُمْسِي: سُبْحَانَ اللهِ وَبِحَمْدِهِ، مِائَةَ مَرَّةٍ، لَمْ يَأْتِ أَحَدٌ يَوْمَ الْقِيَامَةِ، بِأَفْضَلَ مِمَّا جَاءَ بِهِ، إِلَّا أَحَدٌ قَالَ مِثْلَ مَا قَالَ أَوْ زَادَ عَلَيْهِ.

"Whoever says subḥānallāh wa bi-hamdih one hundred times each in the morning and evening, then no one else will be come on the Day of Judgement with better than what he comes with, except for someone who says the same as him or even more than what he says."

In another report, the Prophet ﷺ is reported to have said:

مَنْ قَالَ سُبْحَانَ اللهِ وَبِحَمْدِهِ، غُرِسَتْ لَهُ نَخْلَةٌ فِي الجَنَّةِ.

"Whoever says subḥānallāh wa bihamdih a palm tree shall be planted for them in Paradise."

One should carefully reflect on the gravity of these reports and ensure that one recites these formulas of *dhikr* daily. One can plant an entire field of trees for oneself in Paradise simply by reciting these few words which take only a few minutes. Furthermore, by reading these basic formulas, one is able to efface one's sins and replace them with virtuous deeds, thereby making one's *Mīzān* heavy with good works. One should also attempt to embrace the practices of the *Salaf* (pious predecessors) as a model for one's acts of remembrance. For instance, the noble Companion Abū Hurayrah ؓ mentioned that his daily regular practice (*wird*) consisted of 12,000 iterations of *tasbīḥ*. One then can only surmise how weighty his *Mīzān* will be on the Day of Judgement.

The Prophet ﷺ taught his nation a simple but effective cluster of litanies that one can recite after every single daily prayer. In this narration, the Prophet ﷺ said:

خَصْلَتَانِ لَا يُحْصِيهِمَا رَجُلٌ مُسْلِمٌ إِلَّا دَخَلَ الْجَنَّةَ، وَهُمَا يَسِيرٌ، وَمَنْ يَعْمَلُ بِهِمَا قَلِيلٌ: يُسَبِّحُ اللَّهَ دُبُرَ كُلِّ صَلَاةٍ عَشْرًا، وَيُكَبِّرُهُ عَشْرًا، وَيَحْمَدُهُ عَشْرًا".

"No Muslim acquires two qualities except that he will enter Paradise. They are quite easy, yet those who do them are very few: glorifying Allah after every prayer ten times, praising Him after every prayer ten times, and declaring His greatness (saying Allah Akbar) after every prayer ten times."

ʿAbdullāh ibn ʿAmr ﷺ—who was the narrator of the aforementioned report—also related that the Prophet used his fingers to count the number of these expressions. He then went on to add that the Prophet ﷺ said:

فَتِلْكَ خَمْسُونَ وَمِائَةٌ بِاللِّسَانِ وَأَلْفٌ وَخَمْسُمِائَةٍ فِي الْمِيزَانِ وَإِذَا أَخَذْتَ مَضْجَعَكَ تُسَبِّحُهُ وَتُكَبِّرُهُ وَتَحْمَدُهُ مِائَةً فَتِلْكَ مِائَةٌ بِاللِّسَانِ وَأَلْفٌ فِي الْمِيزَانِ فَأَيُّكُمْ يَعْمَلُ فِي الْيَوْمِ وَاللَّيْلَةِ أَلْفَيْنِ وَخَمْسَمِائَةِ سَيِّئَةٍ.

"If one does that, then it will add up to 150 formulas with the tongue and 1500 deeds on the Mīzān. And when one goes to one's bed, one should say subḥānallāh thirty-three times, alḥamdulillāh thirty-three times, and Allāhu akbar thirty-four times. That will add up to one-hundred formulas with the tongue and one thousand deeds on the Mīzān. Now, who among you commits 2500 sins per day?"

The Companions responded to this query by stating: "How could we not consistently observe such a practice?" The Prophet ﷺ then explained to them how the *Shayṭān* is able to divert them from reciting such simple words of remembrance by stating:

يَأْتِي أَحَدَكُمُ الشَّيْطَانُ وَهُوَ فِي صَلاَتِهِ فَيَقُولُ: اذْكُرْ كَذَا، اذْكُرْ كَذَا حتى يَنْفَتِلَ، وَلَعَلَهُ لا يَعْقِل، ويَأْتِيهِ وَهُوَ فِي مَضْجَعِهِ فَلاَ يَزَالُ يُنَوِّمهُ حَتَّى يَنامَ.

"The Shayṭān appears while one of you is praying, and says, 'Remember to do this,' and 'Remember to do that,' until finishes his prayer, he rushes to do those errands and most likely does not do them. Likewise, when he goes to bed, the Shayṭān lulls them to sleep until they fall to sleep."

Unfortunately, the state of affairs described in the aforementioned *ḥadīth* applies to numerous Muslims. This ultimately means that many of us fail to capitalise on this golden opportunity to add 2500 deeds on our *Mīzān* for every day that passes. The *Shayṭān* is acutely aware of this fact, which explains why he expends innumerable efforts to distract the Muslim population from engaging in *dhikr* in their daily lives. In order to remedy this state of affairs, one should habitually say these virtuous formulas and engage in simple deeds of good so that one develops a character that is attuned to righteousness.

22

The Weight of One's Character

Although they may have been physically bulky and prominent, in terms of faith and character both Abū Jahl and Abū Lahab were insignificant in their spiritual constitution. This is akin to how some people enjoy the gift of eyesight but lack any spiritual foresight and vision due to the blindness of their hearts. Thus, the truly insignificant and small person is not the one who is limited in his physical constitution, but rather the one who is devoid of character and morals. People who lack such inward attributes oftentimes resort to making their physical appearances, expressions, and interpersonal interactions more prominent, which often causes them to become even more obnoxious in nature. All the scales and measures of this world focus on the physical dimension of human beings, with the key targeted attributes being weight, height, muscle density, and other physical variables. Yet, in this world, one cannot find any scale—regardless of its level of sophistication—that can measure the nature of one's character. Such a scale only exists in the Hereafter.

In terms of his character and contributions to the religion of Islam, ʿAbdullāh ibn Masʿūd ﵁ was undoubtedly a towering figure who carved a legacy for himself in Islamic history. For instance, he bravely volunteered to be the first public reciter of the Qur'ān in the hostile Makkan environment. Secondly, the Prophet ﷺ himself praised his mode of recitation by stating: "Whoever would like to know how to recite the Qur'ān properly as it was originally revealed should listen to the recitation of Ibn Umm ʿAbd (i.e., Ibn Masʿūd)." The Prophet ﷺ used to be so touched by Ibn Masʿūd's recitation that he sometimes shed tears. Lastly, Ibn Masʿūd was such a prolific narrator of *ḥadīths* that the mere mention of the name ʿAbdullāh at the end of the chain is a reference to his identity.

In terms of physical size and social stature, one cannot compare Ibn Masʿūd with Abū Jahl, since the latter was a towering figure, while the former was known to be one of the shortest amongst the Prophet's Companions. In fact, in some accounts and narrations, Abū Jahl is compared with ʿUmar ibn al-Khaṭṭāb ﵁, since both of them were known for their physical strength and endurance. However, one crucial difference between these two figures is that ʿUmar recognised the vast knowledge and lofty character of Ibn Masʿūd and benefitted from his knowledge. On the other hand, Abū Jahl obstinately refused to accept Islam. In fact, when Ibn Masʿūd volunteered to read *Sūrah al-Raḥmān* in public, he received a hostile reception that almost culminated in his death; the main polytheist who struck and injured him on that day was none other than Abū Jahl himself. Because of Abū Jahl's crimes and transgressions against the nascent

Muslim community, the Prophet ﷺ called him the Firʿawn of this Ummah.

In a moving manifestation of His divine justice, Allah caused the tide to turn in favour of the Muslims at the Battle of Badr. While fighting between the two camps was raging, Abū Jahl was severely wounded and fell to the ground. but despite his serious injuries, he was still alive. While lying down in this humiliating state, the leader of the Quraysh was approached by Ibn Masʿūd and then placed one of his feet on Abū Jahl's chest. The latter could not believe that he was being subjected to this form of humiliation at the hands of the same person he used to persecute in Makkah. In a fit of rage, he addressed Ibn Masʿūd by stating:

لَقَدْ اِرْتَقَيْتَ مُرْتَقًى صَعْبًا يَا رُوَيْعِي الغَنَمِ.

"You have climbed a difficult mountain, O tiny shepherd!"

Ibn Masʿūd reminded Abū Jahl that it was Allah ﷻ Who granted the believers this momentous triumph over the stubborn and impenitent polytheists. Before delivering the decisive *coup de grâce*, Ibn Masʿūd said: "Victory belongs to Allah, the Messenger, and the believers."

Throughout his life, the Prophet ﷺ delivered a number of reminders and lessons to ensure that his Companions understood that true power and strength lie in one's faith, not in physical prowess. On one occasion, Ibn Masʿūd was attempting to hand-pick a twig from a tree so that he may use it as a tooth-stick (*siwāk*). At this very moment, a severe air current swept Ibn Masʿūd towards the tree and uncovered his legs in the process. The Companions began to laugh at this sight, and when the Prophet ﷺ asked why they were laughing, they pointed to how thin and slim Ibn Masʿūd's legs were. Instead of rebuking them, the Prophet made the following declaration:

وَالَّذِي نَفْسِي بِيَدِهِ لَهُمَا أَثْقَلُ فِي المِيزَانِ مِنْ أُحُدٍ.

"By Him in Whose Hand is my soul, those two legs will be heavier than Uḥud when placed on the Mīzān."

This report indicates that Ibn Masʿūd will appear on the Day of Judgement with prominent and bulky legs that will exceed the size of Mount Uḥud. His colossal form will reflect his virtuous character and standing as one of the best Companions of the Prophet ﷺ. His immense weight will then be taken into account when he is placed on the *Mīzān*, and then all of humanity will be able to witness his virtuous status. Contrary to popular belief, the *Mīzān* will not just weigh one's deeds and actions, but it will also measure every physical body as well, whose otherworldly mass will be exclusively determined by the character of its possessor. This explains the shocking implications found in the following *ḥadīth* in which the Prophet ﷺ said:

إنَّه لَيَأْتِي الرَّجُلُ العَظِيمُ السَّمِينُ يَومَ القِيامَةِ، لا يَزِنُ عِنْدَ اللهِ جَناحَ بَعُوضَةٍ

"On the Day of Judgement, a huge and stout man will be brought forth, but he will weigh no more than the wing of a mosquito in the sight of Allah."

One's actions, motives, and intentions will be recorded in one's register of deeds. Whoever performs even a minuscule act of good in this temporal world will reap its fruits in the Hereafter. Such a promise reflects the infinite mercy and justice of Allah عزّ وجلّ*.*

The Prophet ﷺ then proceeded to recite the following verse:

فَلَا نُقِيمُ لَهُمْ يَوْمَ الْقِيَامَةِ وَزْنًا.

"So We will not give their deeds any weight on Judgement Day."[57]

These aforementioned reports clearly indicate that a person's weight and leverage on the Day of Judgement will be exclusively based on his inward character and temperament. This was explicitly noted by the Prophet ﷺ himself in the following *ḥadīth*:

مَا مِنْ شَيْءٍ أَثْقَلُ فِي مِيزَانِ المُؤْمِنِ يَوْمَ القِيَامَةِ مِنْ حُسْنِ الخُلُقِ.

"Nothing is heavier on the scale than good character."

Good character ensures that one's conduct is honourable and upright, just as sincerity causes one's faith (*īmān*) to be incorruptible. To ensure that one's deeds and overall form are weighty on the Day of Judgement, one must develop a character that is sincere and oriented towards the Hereafter, for that is the true yardstick of success. In a notable report, the prominent Companion ʿAlī ibn Abī Ṭālib رضي الله عنه vividly illustrated the mechanics of the weighing process on the Day of Judgement:

مَنْ كَانَ ظَاهِرُهُ أَرْجَحَ مِنْ بَاطِنِهِ خَفَّ مِيزَانُهُ يَوْمَ القِيَامَة. وَمَنْ كَانَ بَاطِنُهُ أَرْجَحَ مِنْ ظَاهِرِهِ ثَقُلَ مِيزَانُهُ يَوْمَ القِيَامَة.

"Whoever's outward is preponderant than his inward, his scale shall be light on the Day of Judgement. And whoever's inward

---

[57] *Al-Kahf*, 105.

is preponderant than his outward, his scale shall be heavy on the Day of Judgement."

One's actions, motives, and intentions will be recorded in one's register of deeds. In fact, even the abstract, mental, and intangible thoughts and intentions will be taken into consideration. Allah ﷻ states in the Qur'ān:

إِنَّا نَحْنُ نُحْيِي الْمَوْتَىٰ وَنَكْتُبُ مَا قَدَّمُوا وَآثَارَهُمْ ۚ وَكُلَّ شَيْءٍ أَحْصَيْنَاهُ فِي إِمَامٍ مُّبِينٍ.

"It is certainly We Who resurrect the dead, and write what they send forth and what they leave behind. Everything is listed by Us in a perfect Record."[58]

Even the works that are deemed to be negligible or minute in this world will be fully considered and weighed in the *Mīzān*. There are several religious texts which confirm that whoever performs even a minuscule act of good in this temporal world will reap its fruits in the Hereafter. Such a promise reflects the infinite mercy and justice of Allah ﷻ. In an authentic narration, the Prophet ﷺ is reported to have said:

مَنْ اِحْتَبَسَ فَرَسًا فِي سَبِيلِ اللهِ، إِيمَانًا بِاللهِ وَتَصْدِيقًا بِوَعْدِهِ فَإِنَّ شِبَعَهُ وَرِيَّهُ وَرَوْثَهُ وَبَوْلَهُ فِي مِيزَانِهِ يَوْمَ القِيَامَةِ.

"Whoever looks after a horse for the sake of Allah while also exercising faith in Him and believing in His promise, the horse's fodder, drink, droppings, and urine will all be positively reflected in his balance on the Day of Judgement."

---

[58] *Yā-Sīn*, 12.

Similarly, Anas ibn Mālik رضي الله عنه related that the Prophet ﷺ once said:

مَنْ رَاحَ رَوْحَةً فِي سَبِيلِ اللهِ كَانَ لَهُ بِمِثْلِ مَا أَصَابَهُ مِنَ الغُبَارِ مِسْكًا يَوْمَ القِيَامَةِ.

"Whoever goes forth in the cause of Allah, any dust which strikes him in his journey will appear as musk on the Day of Judgement."

These reports clearly indicate that Allah عز وجل will measure every single deed that is performed in this world, regardless of its size or significance. In fact, in addition to deeds, the whole body will be inspected as well. Thus, one can never doubt or question the fact that our registers of deeds will accurately reflect our personality, character, and moral fabric.

فَأَمَّا مَن ثَقُلَتْ مَوَٰزِينُهُۥ فَهُوَ فِى عِيشَةٍ رَّاضِيَةٍ

"So as for those whose scales are heavy with good deeds, they will be in a life of bliss."

AL-QĀRIʿAH, 6–7

23

The Deeds Worth Seven-Hundred and More

In an inspirational and thought-provoking verse, Allah ﷻ states to us:

مَّثَلُ ٱلَّذِينَ يُنفِقُونَ أَمْوَٰلَهُمْ فِى سَبِيلِ ٱللَّهِ كَمَثَلِ حَبَّةٍ أَنۢبَتَتْ سَبْعَ سَنَابِلَ فِى كُلِّ سُنۢبُلَةٍ مِّا۟ئَةُ حَبَّةٍ ۗ وَٱللَّهُ يُضَٰعِفُ لِمَن يَشَآءُ ۗ وَٱللَّهُ وَٰسِعٌ عَلِيمٌ.

"The example of those who spend their wealth in the cause of Allah is that of a grain that sprouts into seven ears, each bearing one hundred grains. And Allah multiplies to whoever He wills. For Allah is All-Bountiful, All-Knowing."[59]

After reading and reflecting on this verse, one's priority should be to undertake the kind of works that will help multiply one's virtues and rewards in the Hereafter. By fostering a mode of behaviour that is based on the values of spiritual purification (*tazkiyah*), one will be able to grow spiritually and reach certain spiritual stations (*maqām*). By adopting these measures,

[59] *Al-Baqarah*, 261.

one will become accustomed to performing acts of goodness on a regular basis, thereby multiplying the rewards preserved in one's register of deeds.

Allah's mercy is so expansive that He multiplies the rewards for each single good deed, while He only records a single demerit for each sin committed. In other words, while Allah ﷻ may give a servant numerous rewards for a single act of good, He will never multiply the penalties for a sin. In a beautiful *ḥadīth* which neatly outlines this distinction, the Prophet ﷺ said:

إنَّ اللَّهَ كَتَبَ الحَسَناتِ والسَّيِّئاتِ ثُمَّ بَيَّنَ ذَلِكَ، فمَن هَمَّ بحَسَنَةٍ فَلَمْ يَعْمَلْها، كَتَبَها اللَّهُ لَهُ
عِنْدَهُ حَسَنَةً كامِلَةً، فَإِنْ هُوَ هَمَّ بِهَا فَعَمِلَها، كَتَبَها اللَّهُ لَهُ عِنْدَهُ عَشْرَ حَسَناتٍ،
إلَى سَبْعِ مِائَةِ ضِعْفٍ، إلَى أضْعافٍ كَثِيرَةٍ، ومَن هَمَّ بسَيِّئَةٍ فَلَمْ يَعْمَلْها، كَتَبَها اللَّهُ لَهُ
عِنْدَهُ حَسَنَةً كامِلَةً، فَإِنْ هُوَ هَمَّ بِهَا فَعَمِلَهَا، كَتَبَهَا اللَّهُ لَهُ سَيِّئَةً واحِدَةً.

"Indeed Allah has ordained good and evil deeds, while also making their nature clear. So whoever intends to do a good deed but does not perform it, Allah will record it as one good deed. If he intends to do it and performs it as well, then Allah will record it as ten good deeds up to seven hundred times, or even a figure greater than that. If he intends to perform a bad deed but does not do so, then Allah will record for him one complete good deed. But if he does intend to perform it and does end up doing it, then Allah will write against him one bad deed."

Upon perusing this *ḥadīth*, one is left absolutely amazed at the mercy and generosity of Allah ﷻ. Perhaps the most intriguing segment of this narration is the attestation that a good deed can have its reward multiplied exponentially at a figure even greater than 700. The key question that one may naturally ask as a result is how one can activate and accrue this multiplicity of rewards in one's own daily actions. First and foremost, sincerity is a key element that must be inwardly present whenever one undertakes a righteous action. Secondly, one must exert oneself to the utmost by performing virtuous deeds in their complete and ideal form. For instance, one may greet one's fellow brother or sister in faith by simply saying *as-salāmu 'alaykum* (may peace be upon you). However, should one wish to, one may give a better greeting by stating *as-salāmu 'alaykum wa raḥmatullāh* (may the peace and mercy of Allah be upon you). Although the two phrases may seem more or less equal in their purpose and content, using the latter will be awarded with ten additional deeds. In fact, the one who uses the most complete form of the greeting—namely *as-salāmu 'alaykum wa raḥmatullāh wa barakātuh* (may the peace, mercy, and blessings of Allah be upon you) will earn ten rewards more than the former. In an authentic *ḥadīth*, it is reported that a person came to the Prophet ﷺ and greeted him by saying *as-salāmu 'alaykum*. The Prophet ﷺ responded to him and then said:

عَشْرَ

"[This person has received] ten rewards."

A second individual then entered in upon the Prophet ﷺ and issued the relatively longer greeting of *as-salāmu 'alaykum wa raḥmatullāh*. The Prophet ﷺ responded to him and then said:

عِشْرُونَ

"[This person has received] twenty rewards."

Then a third person approached the Prophet ﷺ and issued the most complete greeting of peace, specifically *as-salāmu ʿalaykum wa raḥmatullāh wa barakātuh*. After responding to this latter person, the Prophet ﷺ said:

ثَلَاثُونَ

"[This person has received] thirty rewards."

While all three individuals correctly began their respective interactions with the Islamic greeting, the third person earned the most rewards since he opted to use the complete formula of greeting. One can implement these same guidelines for other acts of worship as well. For instance, the Prophet ﷺ informed his Ummah that one will receive ten rewards for every single letter (*ḥarf*) of the Qur'ān that one reads. Such a guaranteed rate of return should prompt every Muslim to increase the number of Qur'ānic verses that he or she reads on a daily basis. Ideally, one should set a minimum number of pages, *Sūrahs*, or sections to be recited for each day. No matter what one's daily minimum amount is, one should always be cognisant that one will add ten rewards in one's account for every additional letter of the Qur'ān one recites.

If one carefully reads the verse and *ḥadīth* mentioned in the beginning of this chapter, one will find that 700 is always mentioned to indicate the number of multiplied rewards. This naturally leads to the question of whether this number possesses a specific purpose or wisdom, literally or metaphorically. An examination of the Sunnah allows one to make a number of tentative conclusions towards answering this question. The key inference that one can make in this regard is that the Prophet ﷺ used 700 to indicate the rewards that some individuals reap due to undertaking difficult works or making great sacrifices for the sake of Allah's religion. It is this sincere assumption of adversity which causes a single good deed to exponentially multiply into 700 fold. The specific mention of grain in the verse is doubly significant insofar as it indicates that what is done or given for the sake of Allah ﷻ does not have to be of great value. It may be something of a moderate or even relatively low value. The symbolic use of grain in the verse immensely pleased the Companions, since the overwhelming majority of them were financially disadvantaged. In actual fact, what causes an act to be blessed and accrue continuous and increasing rewards is expending something that one loves with a sincere heart. This type of moral integrity and probity can be witnessed in a beautiful *ḥadīth* reported by the Companion Abū Masʿūd al-Anṣārī ؓ. In this report, he mentioned that a man gave a single haltered she-camel to the Prophet ﷺ and then said:

هَذِهِ فِي سَبِيلِ اللهِ.

"This is offered in the cause of Allah (fī sabīl Allāh)."

The Prophet ﷺ responded to the man by stating:

لَكَ بِهَا يَوْمَ القِيَامَةِ سَبْعُ مِائَةَ نَاقَةٍ كُلُّهَا مَخْطُومَةٌ.

"On the Day of Judgement you will have 700 she-camels, with every single one of them haltered."

Allah's mercy is so expansive that He multiplies the rewards for each single good deed, while He only records a single demerit for each sin committed. While Allah ﷻ may give a servant numerous rewards for a single act of good, He will never multiply the penalties for a sin.

The eminent Companion and celebrated Qur'ānic exegete Ibn 'Abbās ﵄ said that the reward indicated in the passage "a grain that sprouts into seven ears, each bearing one hundred grains" applies to all forms of alms expended *fī sabīl Allāh*, even the wealth given to help one perform *Ḥajj*. He also explicitly noted that every coin that one spends for the sake of Allah will be multiplied 700 times on the Day of Judgement.

There is one particular act of worship whose virtues are so eminent that Allah will provide for it even more than seven-hundred rewards. Of course, Allah can multiply the rewards for any deed—regardless of how big or small it is—by any number He wishes. But what makes this particular ritual so special is that Allah emphasised its virtues and promised an astronomically high reward for it. That act of worship is none other than fasting. In a beautiful report, the Prophet ﷺ said:

لِلصَّائِمِ فَرْحَتَانِ: فَرْحَةٌ حِينَ يُفْطِرُ وَفَرْحَةٌ حِينَ يَلْقَى رَبَّهُ.

"The fasting person has two moments of joy: he experiences delight when he breaks his fast, and when he meets his Lord he will be overjoyed that he fasted during his life."

In another noteworthy report, the Prophet ﷺ said:

كُلُّ عَمَلِ ابْنِ آدَمَ يُضَاعَفُ الْحَسَنَةُ عَشْرُ أَمْثَالِهَا إِلَى سَبْعِمِائَةِ ضِعْفٍ قَالَ اللهُ عَزَّ وَجَلَّ:
إِلَّا الصَّوْمَ فَإِنَّهُ لِي وَأَنَا أَجْزِي بِهِ.

"Every good deed of the son of Adam will be multiplied between ten and seven hundred times. However, Allah has said: 'This is with the exception of fasting, for that is for Me, and I shall reward it exclusively.'"

In other words, Allah ﷻ has promised His sincere servants that He will reward their fasting in a manner which is unlike the reward of any other act of worship or good deed. The exact figure or number of rewards assigned to fasting has been left undetermined by the Creator. Muslim scholars and commentators note that the eminent status of fasting rests on two key factors: (1) it is a private act of worship which only Allah is aware of, and (2) due to its relative difficulty, its observance requires patience (*ṣabr*) on the part of the believers. There are numerous scriptural proofs which indicate that Allah ﷻ supports the patient ones and gives them an unrestricted rate of reward. It is also important to note that these aforementioned virtues of fasting are not simply restricted to the month of Ramadan; rather, they are applicable to any day of the year when one abstains from food and drink. Thus, if one wishes to have a joyful and momentous standing on the Day of Judgement, one should consistently observe fasting, since it represents the epitome of *ṣabr*. Any person who doubts this prescription should look no further than the following verse, which promises the best of rewards for those who exercise patience:

إِنَّمَا يُوَفَّى الصَّابِرُونَ أَجْرَهُمْ بِغَيْرِ حِسَابٍ.

"Only those who endure patiently will be given their reward without limit."[60]

[60] *Al-Zumar*, 10.

24

The *Shahādah* Card

There is nothing in this temporal world or in the Hereafter that can rival the magnificence and greatness of Allah's name. After all, the whole purpose of one's existence in this world is to read and actualise the testimony of faith (*shahādah*), namely by saying *lā ilāha illā Allāh* (there is no God but Allah). If one sincerely adopts this testimony of faith as one's motto in life and lives by its values during one's time in this world, one will acquire an unshakeable moral compass that is geared towards preparing one for the Hereafter. However, if the general human population fails to abide by this testimony's directives and implications through forgetting the rights of Allah ﷻ, immorality will become rampant and the world will decay spiritually and become a purposeless realm.

The vision and ethos of a good life was clearly established in the following *ḥadīth* of the Prophet ﷺ:

أَصْدَقُ كَلِمَةٍ قَالَهَا شَاعِرٌ كَلِمَةُ لَبِيدٍ: أَلَا كُلُّ شَيْءٍ مَا خَلَا اللهَ بَاطِلُ.

"The most truthful words uttered by any poet are the words of Labīd, who said: 'Everything besides Allah is void.'"

Regardless of whether one is a sincere believer or an individual struggling to maintain his faith (*īmān*), one must never take one's *shahādah* for granted. This is because *īmān* is subject to serious fluctuations and variations throughout the vicissitudes of life. In fact, a key tenet articulated in works of Muslim creed is the following:

الإِيمَانُ يَزِيدُ وَيَنْقُصُ.

"Īmān increases and decreases."

Once this crucial point is grasped, one can understand why a number of Companions used to occasionally inform the Prophet ﷺ that they were experiencing changes in their level of *īmān*. The Prophet ﷺ not only confirmed that such spiritual shifts are possible, but he also warned them that during the later stages of history, there will be individuals who find themselves believers in the morning but, comes the night, they turn into disbelievers, and *vice-versa*. In other words, one will go to sleep in one state and wake up in another. What makes this narration shocking is that a person will alternate between the states of belief and disbelief in a mere 24-hour cycle. This report clearly indicates that one cannot treat *īmān* as a passive concept; instead, it must be actively nurtured.

It is important to note that one's *shahādah* is not simply manifested through one's deeds, but it is also spiritually safeguarded through outward actions. Put in another way, the more one actualises the values of the *shahādah* in one's outward conduct, the more likely it is to settle and establish itself firmly in one's heart. But if one is heedless and fails to perform the rituals and acts of worship mandated in the religion, one may actually miss the golden opportunity of uttering the *shahādah* on one's deathbed. As a *ḥadīth* indicates, one who utters these words before passing away will be raised on the Day of Judgement while continuously professing the oneness of Allah ﷻ:

مَنْ قَالَ: لَا إِلَهَ إِلَّا اللهُ مُوقِنًا دَخَلَ الجَنَّةَ.

"Whoever says lā ilāha illā Allāh with conviction will enter Paradise."

In another version of the narration, the apodosis that is issued as the resulting effect is the following:

حَرَّمَ اللهُ عَلَيْهِ النَّارَ.

"Allah will make it unlawful for the Hellfire to touch him."

Intuitively speaking, it is impossible for one to utter the testimony of faith with conviction without actually exerting any physical efforts to gain Allah's pleasure. Thus, the only way for one to demonstrate one's genuine belief in the oneness of Allah is to consistently perform acts of goodness for His sake.

Chapter 21 of this work outlined the spiritual benefits and rewards that are added for one on the Scale (*Mīzān*) when one makes *tasbīḥ* (glorification of Allah) and praises Allah (*taḥmīd*). One may add further insights into that discussion by examining a noteworthy connection that al-Ḥāfiẓ Ibn Rajab al-Ḥanbalī ﷺ drew between the notions of *taḥmīd* and *tahlīl* (professing the oneness of Allah). In this noteworthy passage, he states: "As for every blessing, you pay for it by saying and living *alḥamdulillāh* (all praise is due to Allah). As for Paradise, you pay for it by saying and living *lā ilāha illā Allāh*." Ibn Rajab's astute observation is in fact confirmed by the following *ḥadīth*:

أَفْضَلُ الذِّكْرِ لَا إِلَهَ إِلَّا اللهُ وَأَفْضَلُ الدُّعَاءِ الحَمْدُ لله.

"The best form of remembrance (dhikr) is saying lā ilāha illā Allāh, while the best form of supplication (duʿā') is saying alḥamdulillāh."

On the Day of Judgement, the *Mīzān* will be prominently erected, and thereafter the works of people will be assessed in it. One noteworthy *ḥadīth* outlines how this weighing process will be carried out while also vividly illustrating the infinite justice of Allah ﷻ. In this report, the Prophet ﷺ describes a man in the Hereafter whose good deeds will be placed on one pan of the *Mīzān* while his vices and sins are gathered on the other one. His vices and wrongdoings will outweigh his virtues, and for that reason, it will said:

أَلْقِهْ فِي النَّارِ.

"Throw him into Hellfire."

He will be subsequently removed from the *Mīzān* so that he may be thrown into Hellfire. But just as he is about to meet such a devastating end, one of the divinely appointed assessors near Allah ﷻ Himself will intervene and state:

لَا تَعْجَلْ.

"Do not be so hasty."

With the man's fate now hanging in the balance due to this apparent impasse, Allah ﷻ will directly judge the case of the man. After enumerating the man's numerous sins, He will address him by stating:

أَتُنْكِرُ مِنْ هَذَا شَيْئًا؟

"Do you challenge or deny the commission of any of these sins?"

The man will say:

لَا، يَا رَبِّ.

"No, O Lord."

Allah ﷻ will continue interrogating him by asking:

أَظَلَمَكَ كَتَبَتِي الحَافِظُونَ.

"Did My angels recording your deeds treat you unjustly?"

The man will once again reply in the negative by stating:

لَا، يَا رَبِّ.

"No, O Lord."

Then Allah ﷻ will pose the following question:

أَلَكَ عُذْرٌ؟ أَلَكَ حَسَنَةٌ؟

"Do you have any valid excuse or good deeds that may improve your account?"

Upon hearing this question, the man will be petrified, since he will be aware of his abysmal catalogue of deeds. Because of what he observed earlier during the weighing process, he will inform Allah ﷻ that he does not have any exculpating or mitigating factors that may improve his record. However, Allah will surprise this man by stating:

بَلَى، إِنَّ لَكَ عِنْدَنَا حَسَنَاتٍ وَإِنَّهُ لَا ظُلْمَ عَلَيْكَ الْيَوْمَ.

"In actual fact, you do have some good deeds in Our records. Today, you shall not be judged in an unjust manner."

A small card (*biṭāqah*) will be brought forth on which is inscribed the man's utterance of the testimony of faith:

أَشْهَدُ أَنْ لَا إِلَٰهَ إِلَّا اللّٰهُ وَأَنَّ مُحَمَّدًا عَبْدُهُ وَرَسُولُهُ.

"I bear witness that there is no deity except Allah, and that Muhammad is His servant and Messenger."

The man will be unimpressed by this single act of good, and will even ask Allah ﷻ how it can counterweigh his evil deeds: "O Lord, how can this *biṭāqah* be compared to all these scrolls which enumerate my evil deeds?" After all, the man had just recently witnessed how overwhelming and weighty his vices and sins were upon being measured. But Allah ﷻ will reassure this man that He will take into account this act of good and determine whether it outweighs his sins by stating:

إِنَّكَ لَا تُظْلَمُ.

"You will not be treated unjustly."

As a result, all the scrolls enumerating the man's evil deeds will be placed on one pan of the *Mīzān*, while his declaration of faith will be placed on the other. The rest of the report then dramatically describes the upshot of this weighing process:

فَتُوضَعُ السِجِلَّاتُ فِي كَفَّةٍ وَالبِطَاقَةُ فِي كَفَّةٍ، فَطَاشَتِ السِجِلَّاتُ وَثَقُلَتِ البِطَاقَةُ.

"The scrolls will be placed on one side of the balance while the biṭāqah will be placed on the other. The pan holding the scrolls will shoot up into the air while the biṭāqah will cause its pan to firmly settle down."

This *ḥadīth* serves as an important lesson for all Muslims, especially those currently struggling with their faith. Regardless of one's sins and shortcomings, one must always cling tightly to one's *shahādah* and maintain one's faith in Allah and His Messenger. The *Shayṭān* is aware of the momentous weight of this *biṭāqah* and, as a result, he will try to convince people suffering with weak *īmān* to renounce Islam. Anyone subjected to such doubts should reflect on Allah's proclamation: "You will not be treated unjustly." This promise reflects Allah's infinite mercy and how He will treat each one of His servants with absolute justice; salvation is always within reach when a forgiving Lord presides over one's case. The person who fails to realise this truth and turns away from the Lord will only wrong himself and get exposed to eternal punishment. For as Allah ﷻ says:

وَمَا ظَلَمَهُمُ اللَّهُ وَلَٰكِن كَانُوا أَنفُسَهُمْ يَظْلِمُونَ.

"And Allah never wronged them, but it was they who wronged themselves."[61]

"So as for those whose scales are heavy with good deeds, they will be in a life of bliss."

AL-QĀRIʿAH, 6–7

---

[61] *Al-Naḥl*, 33.

25

Sincerity Shines and Hypocrisy Blinds

Maintaining and upholding the teachings of the religion (*dīn*) is a perpetual spiritual struggle which requires vigilance and scrupulousness. The Prophet ﷺ described the difficult conditions that will be found at the end of times by stating that the vigilant believer who attempts to uphold his religion will be like someone who holds a burning piece of coal in his hand. He also stated that the person who exerts himself and implements the teachings of the *dīn* in such difficult conditions will have his rewards multiplied by 50 times, as opposed to the standard rate of reward given to those who came before them. When this vigilant believer ascends on the Day of Judgement, his hand—once metaphorically burning due to the struggle of maintaining his faith—will be beaming with a shining light, in recognition of his prioritisation of the *dīn* over this temporal world (*dunyā*). But the individuals who misappropriates the *dīn* in order to gain material benefits or status in this *dunyā* will be humiliated in the Hereafter and receive no honourable reception from Allah ﷻ and His angels.

This is because all the outward acts of righteousness that he did in this world were not performed for the sake of Allah ﷻ.

A beautiful *ḥadīth* mentions that, on the Day of Judgement, the polytheists will be resurrected along with their idols; upon being reunited with their false gods, the followers and associates of false faiths will realise the dreadful destination that awaits them. As for the Muslims, they will be approached by Allah ﷻ Himself, Who will then ask them:

مَنْ تَنْظُرُونَ؟

"Who are you waiting for?"

At this point, the Muslim servants will not realise that their Creator is actually addressing them, since He will be speaking to them with His divine presence concealed. Subsequently, they will say:

نَنْظُرُ رَبَّنَا.

"We are waiting for our Lord."

Allah ﷻ will then reveal His identity to the believers by stating:

أَنَا رَبُّكُمْ.

"I am your Lord."

The person who exerts himself and implements the teachings of Islam in difficult conditions will have his rewards multiplied by 50 times. When this vigilant believer ascends on the Day of Judgement, his hand will be beaming with a shining light, in recognition of his efforts.

In a clear manifestation of their loyalty and love for their Creator, the Muslims will state:

هَذَا مَكَانُنَا حَتَّى يَأْتِينَا رَبُّنَا، فَإِذَا جَاءَ رَبُّنَا عَرَفْنَاهُ.

"We will remain put in this location until our Lord comes to us. When He does come, we will recognise Him."

Such is the ethos of the believers: as they witness the polytheists and disbelievers face their plight with their false gods, they will patiently listen and long for the appearance of their Lord ﷻ. This form of virtuous behaviour is a marvellous illustration of the deferential motto *samiʿnā wa aṭaʿnā* (we hear and obey). In other words, the believers will not move or shift from their location until they become certain that their interlocutor is Allah. This cautious and scrupulous stance of the Muslims is confirmed through their statement:

حَتَّى نَنْظُرَ إِلَيْكَ.

"Until we see You [we will not move]."

Allah ﷻ will positively respond to their request and show Himself to His obedient servants:

فَيَتَجَلَّى لَهُمْ يَضْحَكُ فَيَنْطَلِقُ بِهِمْ وَيَتَّبِعُونَهُ.

"He will then manifest Himself while smiling towards them. Then He will take them with Him, and they will closely follow Him."

The *ḥadīth* then mentions that, at this juncture, every individual from the Muslim community—whether he is a genuine believer or a hypocrite—will be given a light in order to see through the path to the Bridge-over-Hell (*Ṣirāṭ*). During this ordeal over the *Ṣirāṭ*, the true nature and faith of every individual will become clear, and the hypocrites will not be able to cross the Bridge. Regarding this sifting process, the Companion Abū Saʿīd al-Khudrī ؓ narrated that he heard the Prophet ﷺ state that Allah ﷻ will reveal His glory and majesty (*sāq*)—before all of humanity on the Day of Judgement. Upon viewing this awe-inspiring sight, all the believers will immediately make prostration (*sujūd*) to the Lord of the worlds. As for the hypocrites who insincerely performed acts of worship in this world out of ostentation or in order to achieve nefarious ends, they will be unable to prostrate. In fact, the Prophet ﷺ described their state on that day by saying: "Their backs will be as stiff as rods." Although the hypocrites were able to delude many people in this world by creating a false image of righteousness, on the Day of Judgement their deep-rooted state of disbelief will be blatantly exposed:

يَوْمَ يُكْشَفُ عَن سَاقٍ وَيُدْعَوْنَ إِلَى ٱلسُّجُودِ فَلَا يَسْتَطِيعُونَ.

"The Day the Shin will be bared, and the wicked will be asked to prostrate, but they will not be able to do so."[62]

Furthermore, the scholars and jurists who used to enjoin the good in public but commit evil acts in private will also be subjected to humiliation on the Day of Judgement.

---

[62] *Al-Qalam*, 42.

In a chilling report, the Prophet ﷺ mentioned that these once highly-touted religious authorities will be wandering with their intestines and internal organs hanging from the sides of their bodies. The onlookers will be shocked by this sight and will ask one of the scholars they identify: "Were you not the one who used to order us not to perform such-and-such acts when you taught us?" He will reply: "Yes, but I would then do the exact opposite of what I taught you." As this narration informs us, one of the key signs of the hypocrite is that he will propagate virtuous works in the public sphere, but he will then indulge in evil actions and vices in his private dwellings, thereby contravening his own teachings. Such are the individuals who use religion as an instrument to gain fame and prestige among people. Allah ﷻ will humiliate them all on the Day of Judgement by issuing them the following address:

اِذْهَبُوا إِلَى الَّذِينَ كُنْتُمْ تُرَاؤُونَ فِي الدُّنْيَا، فَانْظُرُوا هَلْ تَجِدُونَ عِنْدَهُمْ جَزَاءً؟

"Go to those who you used to show off to in this world, and see if they have any reward (jazā') to offer to you."

It is thus imperative to comprehend that the painful chastisement of Hellfire is not simply designated for the disbelievers and idol-worshippers. It will also be the destination of those who feigned religiosity in order to make a small profit in this world. This latter class believed that they could deceive everyone with their artificial display of religiosity, but on the Day of Judgement Allah ﷻ will reveal the inward condition of their hearts. He will also reveal to them the futility of their long-term efforts to impress others with their actions, since none save Allah will be able to provide them deliverance on that day.

Within the context of this discussion, it is also important to note that, on the Day of Judgement, the entire setup of the universe will be radically transformed. In a notable *ḥadīth*, the Prophet ﷺ mentioned that both the Heavens and earth will be folded up, thereby they cease to exist. Only the *Ṣirāṭ*, Hellfire, and the Heavens will continue to exist. All of humanity will be made to first stand over a flat and stretched-out plane, where they will be judged one by one. Then they will be required to cross the *Ṣirāṭ*, which in several respects marks the climax of the proceedings. It is crucial to note that one will not be able to safely pass these obstacles without having a sufficient amount of light—which is commensurate to one's righteousness and good works. As for the hypocrites, they will be deprived of any such guiding light, and will ultimately meet their impending doom. This latter point has been beautifully elaborated in the following Qur'ānic parable:

مَثَلُهُمْ كَمَثَلِ ٱلَّذِي ٱسْتَوْقَدَ نَارًا فَلَمَّآ أَضَآءَتْ مَا حَوْلَهُۥ ذَهَبَ ٱللَّهُ بِنُورِهِمْ وَتَرَكَهُمْ فِي ظُلُمَٰتٍ لَّا يُبْصِرُونَ.

"Their example is that of someone who kindles a fire, but when it lights up all around him, Allah takes away their light, leaving them in complete darkness—unable to see."[63]

In his thoughtful and analytical study of this parable, Imām Ibn Qayyim al-Jawziyyah ﵀ pointed out that while the fire of the hypocrites remains burning, their works are bereft of any light (*ḍaw'*). In other words, while they are devoid of the light of faith, they must still bear the repercussions of professing Islam.

---

[63] *Al-Baqarah*, 17.

As for the believers, they will be rewarded with glimmering lights as a result of their genuine observance of the religion in this temporal world, despite experiencing the pain of holding burning pieces of coal in their bare hands. The pleasant state of the believers is beautifully depicted in the following verse in *Sūrah al-Ḥadīd*:

يَوْمَ تَرَى ٱلْمُؤْمِنِينَ وَٱلْمُؤْمِنَٰتِ يَسْعَىٰ نُورُهُم بَيْنَ أَيْدِيهِمْ وَبِأَيْمَٰنِهِم بُشْرَىٰكُمُ ٱلْيَوْمَ جَنَّٰتٌ تَجْرِى مِن تَحْتِهَا ٱلْأَنْهَٰرُ خَٰلِدِينَ فِيهَا ۚ ذَٰلِكَ هُوَ ٱلْفَوْزُ ٱلْعَظِيمُ.

"On that Day you will see believing men and women with their light shining ahead of them and on their right. [They will be told:] 'Today you have good news of Gardens, under which rivers flow, to stay in forever. This is the ultimate triumph.'" [64]

In his commentary of this verse, the great Companion Ibn Masʿūd ﷺ said:

يُؤْتَوْنَ نُورَهُمْ عَلَى قَدْرِ أَعْمَالِهِمْ.

"They will be given their light in accordance with their deeds."

In many respects, this is analogous to how a person's shade during the opening proceedings on the Day of Judgement will be based on the sincerity and form of his deeds. But as people begin to trek the path leading to the *Ṣirāṭ*, the entire setting around them will become pitch-black. The only thing which will be able to illuminate their surroundings is the good deeds they performed. Just like how one's acts of charity can generate useful shade and protect one from the heat of the Last Day, they will also brighten

---

[64] *Al-Ḥadīd*, 12.

one's path for one to be able to see. Regarding the various sizes and forms that this light assumes, Ibn Masʿūd said:

مِنْهُمْ مَنْ نُوره مِثْل الْجَبَل وَمِنْهُمْ مَنْ نُوره مِثْل النَّخْلَة وَمِنْهُمْ مَنْ نُوره مِثْل الرَّجُل الْقَائِم.

"There will be some people whose light will be as huge as a mountain. For others it will be like the size of a tree. And for others, the light will be equivalent to the dimensions of a standing man."

Moreover, the right hands of the believers will also be brimming with light. This is because they will enjoy the blessing of receiving their record of deeds in their right hands. Throughout this process, they will carefully cling on to their respective books in order to have an additional source of light at their disposal. As the believers advance and move forward, the hypocrites will soon come to the realisation that they do not have any spiritual light; without the believers on their side anymore, they will not be able to discern their surroundings or progress forward. The plight of the hypocrites in this regard has been dramatically described in the following verse:

يَوْمَ يَقُولُ الْمُنَافِقُونَ وَالْمُنَافِقَاتُ لِلَّذِينَ آمَنُوا انظُرُونَا نَقْتَبِسْ مِن نُّورِكُمْ قِيلَ ارْجِعُوا وَرَاءَكُمْ فَالْتَمِسُوا نُورًا فَضُرِبَ بَيْنَهُم بِسُورٍ لَّهُ بَابٌ بَاطِنُهُ فِيهِ الرَّحْمَةُ وَظَاهِرُهُ مِن قِبَلِهِ الْعَذَابُ.

"On that Day hypocrite men and women will beg the believers, 'Wait for us so that we may have some of your light.' It will be said, 'Go back and seek a light!' Then a wall with a gate will be erected between them. On the near side will be grace and on the far side will be torment."[65]

---

[65] *Al-Ḥadīd*, 13.

All of humanity will be made to first stand over a flat and stretched-out plane, and judged one by one before having to cross the Ṣirāṭ. One will not be able to safely pass these obstacles without having sufficient light—which is commensurate to one's righteousness and good works.

At this point, the hypocrites will be alarmed and apprehensive of the predicament they find themselves in. They will try to convince the departing Muslims that they are part of their community:

يُنَادُونَهُمْ أَلَمْ نَكُن مَّعَكُمْ.

"The tormented will cry out to those graced, 'Were we not with you?'"[66]

This plea of the hypocrites is not incidental, but carefully formulated. As the Qur'ān confirms in another verse, in this world the hypocrites used to make false pretences to faith by going to the Muslims and reiterating their fealty of allegiance to them by saying: "We are with you." However, they would then privately meet with the disbelievers and say:

وَإِذَا خَلَوْا إِلَىٰ شَيَاطِينِهِمْ قَالُوا إِنَّا مَعَكُمْ إِنَّمَا نَحْنُ مُسْتَهْزِئُونَ.

"But when alone with their evil associates they say, 'We are definitely with you; we were only mocking.'"[67]

Though their deception and trickery were effective in this temporal world, their ruse will be useless in the Hereafter. For this reason, when the hypocrites claim that they were followers of the Islamic faith, the believers will effectively silence them by issuing the following response:

قَالُوا بَلَىٰ وَلَٰكِنَّكُمْ فَتَنتُمْ أَنفُسَكُمْ وَتَرَبَّصْتُمْ وَارْتَبْتُمْ وَغَرَّتْكُمُ الْأَمَانِيُّ حَتَّىٰ جَاءَ أَمْرُ اللَّهِ وَغَرَّكُم بِاللَّهِ الْغَرُورُ.

---

66 *Al-Ḥadīd*, 14.

67 *Al-Baqarah*, 14.

"Yes, but you chose to be tempted, awaited [our demise], doubted [the truth], and were deluded by false hopes until Allah's decree came to pass. And the Chief Deceiver deceived you about Allah."[68]

At this point, not only will the hypocrites be submerged in darkness, but they will also begin to receive their chastisement from the Lord of the worlds and His angels. A barrier will then be propped up which will come between them and the sincere Muslims. The believers will continue to progress ahead until they finally reach the *Ṣirāṭ*. Then they will call out to their Lord ﷻ with the following supplication:

رَبَّنَا أَتْمِمْ لَنَا نُورَنَا وَاغْفِرْ لَنَا إِنَّكَ عَلَىٰ كُلِّ شَيْءٍ قَدِيرٌ.

"Our Lord! Perfect our light for us, and forgive us. You are truly Most Capable of everything."[69]

They will then advance headlong while receiving guidance with the various forms of light that have been granted to them. They will continue to pray and supplicate to their Lord ﷻ by asking Him to make their journey towards the *Ṣirāṭ* trouble-free and painless.

---

68 *Al-Ḥadīd*, 14.

69 *Al-Taḥrīm*, 8.

26

The Many Blessings of *Wuḍū'*

Upon completing the Fajr prayer on one occasion, the Prophet ﷺ approached the noble Companion Bilāl رضي الله عنه and said:

يَا بِلَالُ حَدِّثْنِي بِأَرْجَى عَمَل عَمِلْتَهُ فِي الإِسْلَامِ، فَإِنِّي سمِعْتُ دَفَّ نَعْلَيْكَ بيْنَ يَدَيَّ فِي الجَنَّة

"O Bilāl, tell me about the most hopeful deed that you have ever performed since entering Islam, for I heard the sound of your footsteps in Paradise."

In response, Bilāl said:

مَا عَمِلْتُ عَمَلاً أَرْجَى عنْدِي مِنْ أَنِّي لَمَ أَتَطَهَّرْ طُهُوراً فِي سَاعَةٍ مِنْ لَيْلٍ أَوْ نَهارٍ إِلاَّ صَلَّيْتُ بِذلكَ الطُّهورِ مَا كُتِبَ لِي أَنْ أُصَلِّيَ.

"I have not done any deed more hopeful than the fact that whenever I perform minor ritual ablution (wuḍū') at night or in the day except that I immediately pray after that wuḍū' whatever it has been ordained for me to pray."

Of course, while the virtue and spiritual station outlined in the aforementioned *ḥadīth* is specific to Bilāl, there is a general reward granted to any person who prays immediately after completing his *wuḍū'*. This is because in another *ḥadīth*, the Prophet ﷺ stated:

مَنْ تَوَضَّأَ نَحْوَ وُضُوئِي هَذَا ثُمَّ صَلَّى رَكْعَتَيْنِ لَا يُحَدِّثُ فِيهِمَا نَفْسَهُ غُفِرَ لَهُ مَا تَقَدَّمَ مِنْ ذَنْبِهِ.رابط

"Whoever performs wuḍū'—like this wuḍū' of mine—and then follows it with two units (rakʿāhs) of prayer, without letting his mind wander in thoughts, then all his previous sins will be forgiven."

The *wuḍū'* is intrinsically virtuous since it is an act of worship. Moreover, its merits are amplified for it is a precondition of the prayer (*ṣalāh*) itself. Moreover, if the purification process is followed with repeating specific formulas of remembrance (*dhikr*), then the rewards accrued shall be multiplied. For instance, in one notable *ḥadīth*, Abū Saʿīd al-Khudrī رضي الله عنه related that he heard the Prophet ﷺ say:

وَمَنْ تَوَضَّأَ ثُمَّ قَالَ سُبْحَانَكَ اللَّهُمَّ وَبِحَمْدِكَ لَا إِلَهَ إِلَّا أَنْتَ أَسْتَغْفِرُكَ وَأَتُوبُ إِلَيْكَ كُتِبَ فِي رِقٍّ ثُمَّ طُبِعَ بِطَابِعٍ فَلَمْ يُكْسَرْ إِلَى يَوْمِ القِيَامَةِ.

"And whoever performs wuḍū' and then follows it by saying, 'Glory to You, O Allah, and all praise belongs to you, I bear witness that there is no god but You, I seek Your forgiveness and repent to You,' his righteous deed will be written on a piece of parchment and tightly sealed. It will not be opened until the Day of Judgement."

Likewise, there is another rigorously authentic narration of the Prophet ﷺ which indicates the virtues of uttering the testimony of faith (*shahādah*) after performing *wuḍū'*. The fact that so many supplications have been prescribed during and after the ablution process implicitly indicates the noble status of the *ṣalāh* itself, which represents a light (*nūr*), proof (*burhān*), and means of salvation (*najāh*) for the praying person. These three virtues of *ṣalāh* have been outlined in a number of Prophetic sayings. For instance, in one narration stressing the otherworldly *light* granted to those who frequent the mosques, the Prophet ﷺ states:

بَشِّرِ الْمَشَّائِينَ فِي الظُّلَمِ إِلَى الْمَسَاجِدِ بِالنُّورِ التَّامِ يَوْمَ الْقِيَامَةِ.

"Give glad tidings to those who walk to the mosques in the dark of a complete light on the Day of Judgement."

The pious believer who attends the mosque will be given this special gift on the Day of Judgement because his heart was sincere, because he spends his time in these blessed places only to gain the pleasure of his Creator ﷻ. Thus, the believer will be provided various forms of light (*nūr)* that will protect and guide him from all directions. The previous chapter explored the type of light that guides one's path. This form of illumination is a product of one's deeds, which *ipso facto* includes attending the mosque and performing the prayer in congregation.

However, there is yet another form of light given to the special believers. This type of light will permeate their own bodies and cause them to brightly glow. In this regard, there is a beautiful narration narrated by Abū Hurayrah that the

Prophet ﷺ once visited the cemetery of al-Baqīʿ and greeted its inhabitants by saying:

السَّلَامُ عَلَيْكُمْ دَارَ قَوْمٍ مُؤْمِنِينَ، وَإِنَّا إِنْ شَاءَ اللهُ بِكُمْ لَاحِقُونَ.

Peace be onto you, O believers of this abode. And Allah willing we shall join you all soon."

After supplicating for the deceased believing men and women in the graveyard, the Prophet ﷺ suddenly made the following remark:

وَدِدْتُ أَنَّا قَدْ رَأَيْنَا إِخْوَانَنَا.

"I would have wished to see our brothers."

The people who were present there thought that the Prophet was either referring to his departed loved ones or his living Companions. So quite naturally, the Companions posed the following question to the Prophet:

أَوَلَسْنَا إِخْوَانَكَ يَا رَسُولَ اللهِ.

"Are we not your brothers, O Messenger of Allah?"

In response, the Prophet ﷺ said:

أَنْتُمْ أَصْحَابِي وَإِخْوَانُنَا الَّذِينَ لَمْ يَأْتُوا بَعْدُ.

"You are my Companions. Our brothers are those who are yet to be born."

Upon hearing this reply, the Companions intuitively posed a follow-up question immediately thereafter:

كَيْفَ تَعْرِفُ مَنْ لَمْ يَأْتِ بَعْدُ مِنْ أُمَّتِكَ يَا رَسُولَ اللهِ؟

"How are you going to identify those of your Ummah who are yet to be born, O Messenger of Allah?"

The Prophet ﷺ illustrated to them the possibility of such recognition by giving them an example:

أرَأَيْتَ لو أنَّ رَجُلًا له خَيْلٌ غُرٌّ مُحَجَّلَةٌ بيْنَ ظَهْرَيْ خَيْلٍ دُهْمٍ بُهْمٍ ألا يَعْرِفُ خَيْلَهُ؟

"Tell me: were a man to have black horses that have some white streaks and patches on their limbs and foreheads amidst other jet-black horses, would he not be able to distinguish his horses?"

The Companions said, "Yes of course, O Messenger of Allah." Subsequently, the Prophet ﷺ proclaimed:

فإنَّهُمْ يَأْتُونَ غُرًّا مُحَجَّلِينَ مِنَ الوُضُوءِ، وأنا فَرَطُهُمْ علَى الحَوْضِ.

"[You should know therefore that] they will come on the Day of Judgement with marks of radiating light on their forelocks and arms (ghurr muḥajjalīn) and I shall be patiently waiting for them at the Pool (Ḥawḍ)."

Thus, one's *wuḍū'* will manifest itself as a bright light on the Day of Judgement which illuminates one's limbs and body parts that were washed on a daily basis. In another authentic report narrated by Abū Hurayrah, the Prophet ﷺ said:

إِنَّ أُمَّتِي يَأْتُونَ يَوْمَ القِيَامَةِ غُرًّا مُحَجَّلِينَ مِنْ آثَارِ الوُضُوءِ ، فَمَنْ اسْتَطَاعَ مِنْكُمْ أَنْ يُطِيلَ غُرَّتَهُ فَلْيَفْعَلْ.

"Indeed, on the Day of Resurrection, [the members of] my Ummah will appear ghurr muḥajjalīn as a result of the spiritual effects of their wuḍū'. So whoever can increase the area of his radiance, let him do so."

The most correct and stronger interpretation of this *ḥadīth* is that one should not wash more than the prescribed areas outlined for *wuḍū'*. Instead, the report highlights the need to thoroughly, judiciously, and consistently saturate one's limbs with water during the ablution process. To attain the virtues and rewards outlined in the above *ḥadīth*, one must ensure that one does not miss any areas or spots of the four main limbs being cleansed. This is because the Prophet ﷺ said in another narration:

تَبْلُغُ الحِلْيَةُ مِنَ المُؤْمِنِ حَيْثُ يَبْلُغُ الوُضُوءُ.

"On the Day of Judgement, the believer's adornment will reach and encompass all the areas saturated with the water of his wuḍū'."

One can even find a beautiful and comprehensive *ḥadīth* which neatly integrates the virtues found in performing *wuḍū'*, performing *ṣalāh*, and visiting the mosque. In this narration, the Prophet ﷺ said:

أَلَا أَدُلُّكُمْ عَلَى مَا يَمْحُو اللَّهُ بِهِ الذُّنُوبَ وَيَرْفَعُ الدَّرَجَاتِ؟

"Shall I not inform you of that through which Allah forgives sins and raises [people's] ranks?"

The Companions immediately responded: "Of course, O Messenger of Allah." The Prophet ﷺ then listed three different concrete actions:

إِسْبَاغُ الوُضُوءِ عَلَى المَكَارِهِ وَكَثْرَةُ الخُطَا إِلَى المَسْجِدِ وَانْتِظَارُ الصَّلَاةِ بَعْدَ الصَّلَاةِ فَذَلِكَ الرِّبَاطُ.

"Performing wuḍū' despite the presence of difficulties [such as extreme cold or illness], taking numerous steps to walk to the mosque, and waiting for one prayer after the other. Such actions are like guarding fortresses situated at Muslims' frontiers."

If one consistently undertakes these three actions, one will have a spiritually complete life that shall provide one with the brightest and most magnificent form of light (*nūr*) on the Day of Judgement. Ritual ablution (*wuḍū'*) is a mighty cleanser and extinguisher of sins. In one beautiful *ḥadīth*, the Prophet ﷺ is reported to have said:

إِذَا تَوَضَّأَ العَبْدُ المُسْلِمُ، أَوِ المُؤْمِنُ، فَغَسَلَ وَجْهَهُ خَرَجَ مِنْ وَجْهِهِ كُلُّ خَطِيئَةٍ نَظَرَ إِلَيْهَا بِعَيْنِهِ مَعَ المَاءِ، أَوْ مَعَ آخِرِ قَطْرِ المَاءِ، فَإِذَا غَسَلَ يَدَيْهِ خَرَجَ مِنْ يَدَيْهِ كُلُّ خَطِيئَةٍ كَانَ بَطَشَتْهَا يَدَاهُ مع المَاءِ، أَوْ مَعَ آخِرِ قَطْرِ المَاءِ، فَإِذَا غَسَلَ رِجْلَيْهِ خَرَجَتْ كُلُّ خَطِيئَةٍ مَشَتْهَا رِجْلَاهُ مَعَ المَاءِ، أَوْ مَعَ آخِرِ قَطْرِ المَاءِ، حَتَّى يَخْرُجَ نَقِيًّا مِنَ الذُّنُوبِ.

"When the Muslim servant or believer performs wuḍū' and begins by washing his face, every single sin that he committed with his eyes will be washed away with the water he uses or its last drop. When he washes his hands, every sin that he committed with his hands will be washed away with the water he uses or its last drop. And when he washes his feet, every sin that he committed with his feet will be washed away with the water he uses or its last drop to the extent that he emerges completely purified from sins."

In fact, in another similarly worded report, the Prophet ﷺ mentioned that the sins of the performer of ablution will all depart from his body, including the vices that are found under his nails. The key conclusion that one can derive from these reports is that *wuḍū'* functions like the process of repentance for it removes the darkness of sins, it ultimately allows the heart and the rest of the body to be illuminated with the light of faith. This light will prove to be crucial in ensuring one's safe navigation of the challenging dark routes on the Day of Judgement.

27

Crossing the *Ṣirāṭ*

In this world, it is difficult to adopt a way of life that allows one to remain on the straight path (*al-ṣirāṭ al-mustaqīm*). For this reason, one asks Allah ﷻ to keep one on this unswerving and spiritually balanced path whenever one recites *Sūrah al-Fātiḥah*. Until the last day of one's life, one must resist the temptation of falling into the evil paths that are promoted by the *shayāṭīn* (devils) around them. And in order to maintain a positive record with Allah ﷻ, one must avoid falling into major and minor sins, for every lapse either blemishes or blots one's record. The only way for one to pass the different spiritual trials and vicissitudes of life is to be constantly conscious of Allah's divine call and spiritually navigate oneself toward Him.

By exercising perseverance, fulfilling Allah's commandments, and remaining morally upright in this world, one will be able to obtain the Paradise of Certainty (*Jannat al-Yaqīn*) in the Afterlife. Such a successful spiritual path can only be treaded if one avoids falling into the paths of sin and disobedience that surround it. Similarly, if crossed successfully, the Bridge-over-Hell (*Ṣirāṭ*) of the Hereafter shall lead one to Paradise. As noted in some reports, this Bridge is thinner than a hair strand, serrated like a sword, and surrounded by giant threatening hooks that will torment the disbelievers and wrongdoers. And as Hellfire is situated directly under it, any person who falls off of it will face a devastating end. Regarding this structure, Abū Hurayrah ﵁ related that the Prophet ﷺ said:

فَأَكُونُ أَوَّلَ مَنْ يُجِيزُ وَدُعَاءُ الرُّسُلِ يَوْمَئِذٍ: اللَّهُمَّ سَلِّمْ سَلِّمْ.

"I will be the first to cross it, and the supplication (duʿā') of the messengers on that day will be: 'O Allah, keep us safe, keep us safe.'"

Due to the immense horrors of that day, the only individuals who will be able to speak and supplicate to Allah ﷻ will be the messengers. The *Ṣirāṭ* will be a terrifying sight indeed, since it will be surrounded by massive hooks and pincers bearing thorns that will rival the size of the thorns of al-Saʿdān, which were relatively large in size. But in any case, the true dimensions of these hooks and pincers are only known to Allah ﷻ, as anything mentioned in these reports is only an approximation. While the rest of humanity will be struggling to cross the *Ṣirāṭ*, all the prophets and messengers—with our beloved Prophet Muhammad ﷺ leading the way—will cross with ease, while constantly chanting, "O Allah, keep us safe, keep us safe".

The Prophet ﷺ then issued a moving reminder to his Companions by saying:

خُذُوا جُنَّتَكُمْ.

"Take up your shields."

The Companions reacted to this imperative by stating: "O Messenger of Allah, are you referring to an enemy who is present?" The Prophet ﷺ then gently indicated that their intuitive understanding of his imperative was in fact mistaken:

بَلْ جُنَّتُكُمْ مِنَ النَّارِ قَوْلُ: سُبْحَانَ اللهِ والحَمْدُ للهِ وَلاَ إِلَهَ إِلاَّ اللهُ وَاللهُ أَكْبَرُ، فَإِنَّهُنَّ يَأْتِينَ يَوْمَ القِيَامَةِ مُقَدِّمَاتٍ وَمُعَقِّبَاتٍ وَمُجَنِّبَاتٍ وَهُنَّ الْبَاقِيَاتُ الصَّالِحَاتُ.

"No, rather your shield from the Hellfire consists of saying: subḥānallāh (glory be to Allah), alḥamdulillāh (all praise is due to Allah), lā ilāha illā Allāh (there is no God but Allah), and Allāhu akbar (Allah is great). For they [i.e. these expressions] will appear on the Day of Judgement as saviours, guardian angels, and virtuous deeds. They are the everlasting good deeds (al-bāqiyāt al-ṣāliḥāt)."

Thus, the words of remembrance (*dhikr*) recited in this world through invocations will constitute a crucial form of spiritual protection for the person crossing the *Ṣirāṭ*. Through these preventative measures, one will be protected from the dangers that surround one while also enabling one to walk at a rapid pace. An examination of the prophetic Sunnah reveals that any sincere acts of voluntary charity (*ṣadaqah*) will also guard one from the horrors of this ordeal. In a well-known narration related by the Mother of the Believers 'Ā'ishah ﵂, the Prophet ﷺ issued the following imperative:

اِتَّقُوا النَّارَ وَلَوْ بِشِقِّ تَمْرَةٍ.

"Guard yourselves against Hellfire, even if it be by means of half a date."

But perhaps one of the greatest forms of protection from Hellfire and the *Ṣirāṭ* erected above it can be achieved by protecting one's fellow Muslims' honour by repelling the words of slander hurled against them. Regarding the person who guards the reputation and standing of his brothers and sisters in this world, the Prophet ﷺ said:

مَنْ حَمَى مُؤْمِنًا مِنْ مُنَافِقٍ بَعَثَ اللَّهُ مَلَكًا يَحْمِي لَحْمَهُ يَوْمَ الْقِيَامَةِ مِنْ نَارِ جَهَنَّمَ.

"Whoever protects a believer from a hypocrite, Allah will send an Angel who will protect his flesh on the Day of Judgement from the fire of Jahannam."

On the other hand, the same narration notes that the person who attempts to damage the reputation of his fellow Muslims will face a terrifying fate on the Last Day:

وَمَنْ رَمَى مُسْلِمًا بِشَيْءٍ يُرِيدُ شَيْنَهُ بِهِ حَبَسَهُ اللَّهُ عَلَى جِسْرِ جَهَنَّمَ حَتَّى يَخْرُجَ مِمَّا قَالَ.

"And whoever accuses another fellow Muslim [with something], intending thereby to harm his reputation, Allah will keep him stuck over the Bridge of Jahannam until he is acquitted of everything that he said."

Every Muslim must deeply internalise within his heart having a good opinion (ḥusn al-ẓann) of Allah عزّ وجلّ and His judgement. Besides preparing for the Day of Judgement through good deeds, one must also think well of Allah عزّ وجلّ, that He will deal with His Muslim servants with kindness and generosity.

The antithesis of harming others is helping them; while the commission of the former will expose one to punishment in the otherworld, the latter will allow one to ascend to a lofty and enviable station. Regarding the virtues and rewards of helping one's fellow believers, the Prophet ﷺ says:

وَمَنْ مَشَى مَعَ أَخِيهِ فِي حَاجَةٍ حَتَّى أَثْبَتَهَا لَهُ، أَثْبَتَ اللهُ عَزَّ وَجَلَّ قَدَمَهُ
عَلَى الصِّرَاطِ يَوْمَ تَزِلُّ فِيهِ الأَقْدَامُ.

"Whoever goes with his fellow brother to help him in one of his needs until he gets it done for him, Allah will make his feet firm on the Ṣirāṭ when feet of countless others shall slip."

Furthermore, there are other deeds which will protect one from the trials of that day. The Prophet ﷺ mentioned that truthfulness (*ṣidq*) and keeping one's ties of kinship (*ṣilat al-raḥim*) will appear on the Day of Judgement; they will preside on the two sides of the *Ṣirāṭ* and ensure that had the three abovementioned qualities in this world will advance smoothly to the end. Regarding the crossing of the *Ṣirāṭ*, the Prophet ﷺ mentioned that the elite class of believers will cross as fast as lightning. Upon hearing this, one of the Companions said: "May my mother and father be sacrificed for your sake, O Messenger of Allah! What does crossing like the speed of lightning entail?" The Prophet addressed this Companion's query by saying: "Have you not noticed how lightning becomes apparent and then instantly disappears in the blink of an eye?" By advancing this rhetorical answer, he demonstrated that their pace will be so astonishingly fast that it will not be possible to measure it. Then the Prophet ﷺ

mentioned that a second group of believers will cross it with the speed of the wind. A third group will cross it with the speed of a flock of flying birds. Fourthly, a group will gallop through it like a herd of horses. But there will be a group of believers who will struggle immensely; they will be forced to crawl throughout the length of the *Ṣirāṭ*. The variations found in the pacing and speed of these various groups has been adequately explained in the following *ḥadīth*:

فَيَمُرُّونَ عَلَى قَدْرِ أَعْمَالِهِمْ.

"The speed with which they cross [it] shall be according to their deeds."

While some of the believers struggle to pass, the Prophet ﷺ will eagerly wait for their successful passage and pray, "O Allah, save us, O Allah, save us." At this critical juncture, the deeds of some Muslims will prove insufficient to help them reach the end of the *Ṣirāṭ*. As they attempt to crawl and creep through the Bridge, some of them will be captured, restrained, and injured by the dangerous hooks that surround them. Through Allah's mercy, some of these individuals will be released from their grip and will ultimately be saved, while others will be thrown into Hellfire for a period of time until Allah ﷻ orders that they be freed.

There is another elite group of believers whom Allah ﷻ will honour immensely on the Day of Judgement by calling them His own neighbours (*jīrān*). An important *ḥadīth* outlines the distinguishing characteristics of this group of believers:

الْمَسْجِدُ بَيْتُ كُلِّ تَقِيٍّ وَتَكَفَّلَ اللهُ لِمَنْ كَانَ الْمَسْجِدُ بَيْتَهُ بِالرُّوحِ وَالرَّحْمَةِ وَالْجَوَازِ عَلَى الصِّرَاطِ إِلَى رِضْوَانِ اللهِ إِلَى الْجَنَّةِ.

"The mosque is the home of every God-fearing person. And Allah has guaranteed for whomever the mosque is his home blessings, mercy, and safe passage over the Sirat towards the good pleasure of Allah in Jannah."

The mosque has an eminent status because it is the primary place for the worship of Allah ﷻ and observance of congregational prayer (*ṣalāh*). In fact, the very word mosque in Arabic (*masjid*) is a noun of place (*ism makān*) which is derived from the word *sujūd* (prostration). In other words, the term *masjid* is literally translated as "the place of prostration". This should indicate the importance of performing the prayer by consistently bowing and prostrating to Allah ﷻ. In another *ḥadīth*, the Prophet ﷺ mentioned that Allah ﷻ will order His angels to free from Hellfire any individuals who had an iota of faith (*īmān*) in their hearts. Interestingly, the identifying marker of their *īmān* will be the sign of *sujūd* on their foreheads. Unlike the rest of the body, the foreheads of the disobedient Muslims will not be burned in Hellfire, since it is that the part that directly touches the ground when one prostrates. After they are removed from Hellfire, Allah ﷻ will submerge them in a special reservoir which contains the miraculous Water of Life (*Mā' al-Ḥayāt*), from which they will emerge with fully repaired bodies.

When preparing for the Day of Judgement, there is an important point which every Muslim must deeply internalise within his heart, which is none other than having a good opinion (*ḥusn al-ẓann*) of Allah ﷻ and His judgement. In other words, besides preparing for one's standing on the Day of Judgement through the performance of good deeds, one must also think well of Allah ﷻ, i.e. that He will deal with His Muslim servants with kindness and generosity. For instance, in a beautiful narration, the Prophet ﷺ said:

وَرَأَيْتُ رَجُلًا مِنْ أُمَّتِي قَائِمًا عَلَى الصِّرَاطِ يَرْعَدُ كَمَا يَرْعَدُ السَّعَفُ فِي رِيحٍ عَاصِفٍ،
فَجَاءَهُ حُسْنُ ظَنِّهِ بِاللَّهِ فَسَكَنَتْ رَعْدَتُهُ، وَمَضَى.

"I saw a man from my Ummah standing and shaking over the Ṣirāṭ shaking like a branch of a palm tree upon a turbulent wind. But then his ḥusn al-ẓann of Allah came to him and his fear was pacified, allowing him to continue his march."

The Prophet ﷺ will be standing on the other side of the *Ṣirāṭ* and awaiting the arrival of his followers by saying, "O Allah, save us, O Allah, save us." Just as the Prophet ﷺ will be concerned about the state of his followers on that occasion, the Muslim should also continuously concentrate and reflect on the Prophet by reciting salutations and blessings (*ṣalawāt*) on him. The Messenger ﷺ gave glad tidings to the one who constantly remembers him by stating:

وَرَأَيْتُ رَجُلًا مِنْ أُمَّتِي يَزْحَفُ عَلَى الصِّرَاطِ وَيَحْبُو أَحْيَانًا وَيَتَعَلَّقُ أَحْيَانًا فَجَاءَتْهُ صَلَاتُهُ
عَلَيَّ فَأَنْقَذَتْهُ وَأَقَامَتْهُ عَلَى قَدَمَيْهِ.

"I saw a man from my Ummah creep the Ṣirāṭ, sometimes crawl on it and sometimes hanging on it until his salutations and blessings on me came, made him stand on his feet, and saved him."

At that point, one would have successfully traversed the last major trial of the Day of Judgement, and will then be greeted by the Prophet ﷺ. Thereafter, one will enjoy the blessed opportunity to drink from the blessed hands of the Messenger of Allah, which will be the subject of the next chapter.

فَأَمَّا مَن ثَقُلَتْ مَوَازِينُهُ فَهُوَ فِي عِيشَةٍ رَّاضِيَةٍ

"So as for those whose scales are heavy with good deeds, they will be in a life of bliss."

AL-QĀRIʿAH, 6–7

28

Drinking from the Prophet's ﷺ Hands

Guidance (*Hidāyah*) can be appreciated through the simile of watering a plant; just as a tree dies unless it is watered, one's spiritual vitality will be threatened if it is bereft of the teachings of the Prophet ﷺ. To push the analogy further, water is deemed to be most precious when one suffers from extreme thirst. Likewise, religious guidance is considered to be most valuable when it is retrieved immediately when one is suffering from nihilism or hyper-scepticism vis-à-vis religious truths. The sweetness of perceiving the divine in absolute terms is most appreciated when one has already experienced the darkness of doubts regarding religion. However, such religious certainty and guidance can only be obtained when one observes the religious instructions of the Prophet ﷺ, which function as a nourishing fountainhead of wisdom.

After passing the trials of the Bridge-over-Hell (*Ṣirāṭ*) and the Scales (*Mīzān*), the final stage of the Day of Judgement will be none other than the Pool (*Ḥawḍ*), where the sincere

Muslim believers will be blessed with a drink provided by the Prophet ﷺ himself. In a famous report related by Anas ibn Mālik, the Prophet ﷺ said that, on the Day of Judgement, he could be found in three different places. After he mentioned the *Ṣirāṭ* and the *Mīzān* as the initial points of liability on the Last Day, he finally alluded to the *Ḥawḍ*. The *Ḥawḍ* is very significant in Islamic theology due to its inimitable features, for once one partakes of its water, one shall never experience thirst for all eternity.

There are a number of narrations which provide crucial details of the *Ḥawḍ*'s nature and dimensions. The massive reservoir derives its water from two straits that are directly connected to al-Kawthar, a blessed river in Paradise that was gifted to the Prophet ﷺ. In a notable *ḥadīth*, the Prophet ﷺ said that the *Ḥawḍ*'s water is unique and totally unlike the liquid found in this world; this reservoir's water is not just whiter than milk and sweeter than honey, it also bears the aromatic scent of the musk of Paradise. As for the two straits connected to Paradise, one will be made of pure gold, while the other will consist of pure silver. In sum, the *Ḥawḍ* is a remarkable blessed repository of water that earnestly awaits the believers who will be graced by drinking from it. In fact, after successfully overcoming the trials of the *Ṣirāṭ*, the sight of the *Ḥawḍ* itself will immensely please the Muslims; upon seeing it, they will know that all the major trials are left behind and there is only one last stage remaining.

In terms of dimension, the *Ḥawḍ* is colossal. While one narration states that its distance spans from Madinah to

'Ammān al-Balqā' (a medieval city in the Levant), another states that its full extent approximates the distance between the cities of Aylah (a medieval coastal city on the Red Sea) and Sanaa. In fact, the Prophet ﷺ mentioned in another narration that a rider would have to continuously travel for a month to cross it. As for the blessed nature of the water itself, the Prophet ﷺ said:

مَنْ شَرِبَ مِنْهُ لَمْ يَظْمَأْ بَعْدَهَا أَبَدًا.

"Whoever drinks from it will never become thirsty again."

One must avoid the actions and heretical beliefs that may prevent one from accessing the *Ḥawḍ* of the Prophet ﷺ. The Prophetic Sunnah has elaborately outlined the actions which may prevent one from the eminent privilege of drinking from this blessed fountain. In one authentic narration, the Prophet ﷺ stated:

وَلَيُرْفَعَنَّ مَعِي رِجَالٌ مِنْكُمْ ثُمَّ لَيُخْتَلَجُنَّ دُونِي، فَأَقُولُ: يَا رَبِّ أَصْحَابِي، فَيُقَالُ: إِنَّكَ لَا تَدْرِي مَا أَحْدَثُوا بَعْدَكَ.

"Some men from amongst you [i.e. his companions] will come to me, but then suddenly they will be taken away from me. I will then say, 'O Lord, My companions!' But it will be said: 'You do not know what they innovated after your demise.'"

In another version of the report, the Prophet ﷺ receives the following response from the angels:

إِنَّكَ لَا تَدْرِي مَا بَدَّلُوا بَعْدَكَ.

"You do not know what they have changed after you."

Commentators have noted that this *ḥadīth* is a serious warning against inventing and promoting blameworthy innovations in the religion. Other scholars interpret the report more narrowly by arguing that it refers to the individuals who became apostates after the death of the Prophet ﷺ and rebelled against Abū Bakr al-Ṣiddīq ؓ. In any case, the *ḥadīth* serves as a strong reminder that anyone who aspires to drink from the *Ḥawḍ* must wholeheartedly embrace the prophetic Sunnah. Without emulating the prophetic model, one cannot expect to be among the fortunate ones who shall drink from his fountain.

Another topic which is worthy of analysis is determining the various classes of believers who will reach the *Ḥawḍ* and their hierarchy in terms of merit. On this topic, one can cite the famous incident of the pious Umayyad Caliph ʿUmar ibn ʿAbd al-ʿAzīz who summoned the *Ḥadīth* narrator Abū Sallām al-Ḥabashī ؒ for an urgent matter. To undertake his journey, the latter only managed to find a mule while he had to set off in haste and travel in difficult conditions. Upon reaching the Caliph, Abū Sallām al-Ḥabashī complained about the difficulties he had to endure during his hastily arranged trip, and the Caliph apologised to him. Then, ʿUmar revealed the reason for this surprise summon: he was aware that al-Ḥabashī had heard a *ḥadīth* from the Companion

Thawbān ﷺ regarding the *Ḥawḍ* and he wanted to hear it directly from him. Abū Sallām obliged and related that Thawbān ﷺ informed him that the Prophet ﷺ said:

حَوْضِي مِنْ عَدَنٍ إِلَى عَمَّانَ البَلْقَاءِ مَاؤُهُ أَشَدُّ بَيَاضًا مِنَ اللَّبَنِ وَأَحْلَى مِنَ العَسَلِ وَأَكْوَابُهُ عَدَدُ نُجُومِ السَّمَاءِ، مَنْ يَشْرَبُ مِنْهُ شَرْبَةً لَمْ يَظْمَأْ بَعْدَهَا أَبَدًا، أَوَّلُ النَّاسِ وُرُودًا عَلَيْهِ فُقَرَاءُ المُهَاجِرِينَ: الشُّعْثُ رُؤُوسًا، الدُّنْسُ ثِيَابًا، الَّذِينَ لَا يَنْكِحُونَ الْمُتَنَعِّمَاتِ وَلَا تُفْتَحُ لَهُمُ السُّدَدُ.

"My Ḥawḍ stretches as far as the distance between Aden and ʿAmmān al-Balqāʾ. Its water is whiter than milk and sweeter than honey, and its cups as many as the number of stars in the sky. Whoever drinks from it one sip will never experience thirst again. The first group of people to reach it are the poor among the Emigrants (Muhājirūn), those whose hairs are dishevelled, wear dirty clothes, are denied marriage to women of high status and are not let in people's homes."

While these individuals were shunned and considered to be lowly in this temporal world, they will enjoy the highest rank and will be the first to drink from the Prophet's *Ḥawḍ*. This report deeply affected ʿUmar ibn ʿAbd al-ʿAzīz and caused him to reflect on his own social status. He mentioned the following to Abū Sallam:

لَكِنِّي نَكَحْتُ الْمُتَنَعِّمَاتِ وَفُتِحَ لِي السُّدَدُ وَنَكَحْتُ فَاطِمَةَ بِنْتَ عَبْدِ الْمَلِكِ لَا جَرَمَ أَنِّي لَا أَغْسِلُ رَأْسِي حَتَّى يَشْعَثَ وَلَا أَغْسِلُ ثَوْبِي الَّذِي يَلِي جَسَدِي حَتَّى يَتَّسِخَ.

"But I married women of prestige, the doors of others are opened for me and I also married Fāṭimah bint ʿAbd al-Malik. There is no harm, from this point forward, that I refrain from washing my hair until it becomes dishevelled, and leave my unwashed clothes until they become dirty."

ʿUmar ibn ʿAbd al-ʿAzīz adopted these drastic measures in order to ensure that he would be among the select group of believers who first reach the *Ḥawḍ*. However, in actual fact, the true nature of this elite class does not lie in their clothes or outer appearance. Instead, it strictly relates to their inner state of humility and meekness towards the Almighty ﷻ and His Messenger ﷺ. This was the very ethos that the Companions championed throughout their lives. Despite the bouts of poverty and subjugation that they faced, their faith in Allah ﷻ was never shaken. Because of their immense sacrifices in this temporal world, they will be handsomely recompensed in the Hereafter. In fact, in one notable narration, the Prophet ﷺ said:

اِبْغُونِي الضُّعَفَاءَ فَإِنَّمَا تُنْصَرُونَ وَتُرْزَقُونَ بِضُعَفَائِكُمْ.

"Find for me the downtrodden ones, for it is only through them that you receive sustenance and divine aid."

On the other hand, the antithesis of the aforementioned class consists of the corrupt elites who willingly serve and support the tyrants. While the former group firmly rejects any offers of power or influence from the oppressive authorities, the corrupt elites aid and abet their superiors in terms of spreading harm in their respective societies. Regarding this crucial matter, Kaʿb ibn ʿUjrah ؓ related that the Prophet ﷺ once approached him and nine other Companions, four of whom were non-Arabs while the rest were members of Arabian tribes. In other words, the Prophet ﷺ ensured that the message he was imparting would be received by a heterogeneous group of Companions. After he ensured that they were carefully listening to him, he delivered a stern warning that consisted of the following words:

اِسْمَعُوا، هَلْ سَمِعْتُمْ أَنَّهُ سَيَكُونُ بَعْدِي أُمَرَاءُ؟ فَمَنْ دَخَلَ عَلَيْهِمْ فَصَدَّقَهُمْ بِكَذِبِهِمْ وَأَعَانَهُمْ عَلَى ظُلْمِهِمْ فَلَيْسَ مِنِّي وَلَسْتُ مِنْهُ وَلَيْسَ بِوَارِدٍ عَلَيَّ الحَوْضَ، وَمَنْ لَمْ يَدْخُلْ عَلَيْهِمْ وَلَمْ يُعِنْهُمْ عَلَى ظُلْمِهِمْ وَلَمْ يُصَدِّقْهُمْ بِكَذِبِهِمْ فَهُوَ مِنِّي وَأَنَا مِنْهُ وَهُوَ وَارِدٌ عَلَيَّ الحَوْضَ.

"Listen attentively! Have you heard that after me a number of tyrants shall appear? Whoever enters in on them, condones their lies, and supports them in their oppression is not of me, I am not of them and he shall not reach the Ḥawḍ. As for the one who does not enter in on them, does not aid them in their oppression, and does not condone their lies, he is of me and I am of him and he shall have access to the Ḥawḍ."

Thus, one who aids or assists an oppressor in this world will be barred from drinking from the blessed hand of the Messenger of Allah ﷺ. There are in fact other narrations which further underscore the moral-immoral dichotomy existing in the humble and oppressing classes respectively. In one beautiful *ḥadīth*, Usayd ibn Huḍayr related that a man from the Helpers (*Anṣār*) approached the Prophet ﷺ and asked to be appointed in a position of political authority. In response, the Prophet ﷺ said:

إِنَّكُمْ سَتَلقَوْنَ بَعْدِي أَثَرَةً فَاصْبِرُوا حَتَّى تَلقَوْنِي عَلَى الحَوْضِ.

"After me, you will encounter selfishness and partisan treatment. So be patient until you meet me at the Ḥawḍ."

In other words, the Prophet ﷺ gently advised this man to forego being appointed in any position of political privilege in this world, since the greatest of benefits will be accrued the moment he will meet him at the *Ḥawḍ*. Instead of potentially slipping and falling victim to the trappings of this temporal world, one should persistently cling to the prophetic Sunnah, exercise humbleness, and prepare oneself for the golden opportunity of drinking from the Prophet's own blessed hands. With the sole exceptions of entering Paradise itself and the beatific vision, nothing can match such a blissful moment.

فَأَمَّا مَن ثَقُلَتْ مَوَٰزِينُهُۥ فَهُوَ فِى عِيشَةٍ رَّاضِيَةٍ

"So as for those whose scales are heavy with good deeds, they will be in a life of bliss."

AL-QĀRIʿAH, 6–7

29

Waiting at the Gates of Heaven

Just as there is a subtle distinction between blameworthy hastiness and praiseworthy efficiency, there is also a translucent line that separates self-confidence from hubris. The same level of ambiguity can be found in differentiating proactiveness from obstructive behaviour. These points are relevant since one can observe some individuals who have a religious awakening and suddenly become committed to the religion (*dīn*). Oftentimes, they perceive themselves to be inferior to their fellow peers and colleagues, and ultimately feel the need to undertake all the religious obligations and recommendations at once. Yet, it is imperative to note that such outward manifestations of religiosity are not intrinsically virtuous, since the true yardstick of success is sincerity in one's heart.

As a thought experiment, let one picture oneself staring at Paradise, with its gates only a few footsteps away. One can only imagine how much one's heart would long to open those gates and immediately enter eternal bliss. However, before such a transition can occur, one's heart must be fully purified from all spiritual maladies. Of the greatest inner sicknesses which must be treated are the outstanding disputes and grievances that one may have with one's fellow Muslim brothers and sisters. Unless a mutual agreement is reached, one will not be able to advance towards Paradise. The Prophet ﷺ spoke of this very scenario in a notable *ḥadīth*. He mentioned that after the believers successfully cross the Bridge-over-Hell (*Ṣirāṭ*) and are protected from the Hellfire, they will be required to successfully cross yet another bridge known as the Overpass (*Qanṭarah*). This test does not involve or lead to any possible punishments but, without fulfilling its requirements, one will delay one's entry to Paradise. On this Overpass, Allah ﷻ will request the Muslims to amicably settle any lingering forms of dispute or disgruntlement between them, since such feelings of resentment cannot exist within the confines of Paradise.

In his book *al-Mustadrak*, the famous *Ḥadīth* master al-Ḥākim narrates and authenticates a fascinating report regarding the trial of the *Qanṭarah*. At the same time, however, it should be noted that other scholars disagreed with his verdict and deemed the report to be weak. In this report, the Prophet ﷺ relates how two men belonging to his Ummah will stand before Allah ﷻ and level their complaints against each other before Him while they are at the *Qanṭarah*. One of the men will complain to Allah about his opponent's injustice towards him; he will demand compensation by asking for the other man's good deeds or having his sinful burdens transferred to him.

Instead of positively responding to his request, Allah ﷻ will say:

ارْفَعْ رَأْسَكَ فَانْظُرْ فِي الجِنَانِ.

"Raise your head and look at Paradise ahead."

The man will look up as instructed, and he will be able to observe the beautiful palaces and other marvellous sights that await him. Unable to hide his excitement, he will say:

يَا رَبِّ أَرَى مَدَائِنَ مِنْ ذَهَبٍ وَقُصُورًا مِنْ ذَهَبٍ مُكَلَّلَةً بِاللُّؤْلُؤِ، لِأَيِّ نَبِيٍّ هَذَا أَوْ لِأَيِّ صِدِّيقٍ هَذَا أَوْ لِأَيِّ شَهِيدٍ هَذَا؟

"O my Lord, I see conurbations made of gold, as well as palaces that are constructed with gold and adorned with pearls. Which Prophet does all this belong? Or which veridic one (ṣiddīq) does all this belong? Or which martyr (shahīd) does all this belong?"

Allah ﷻ will surprise him with the following answer: "This will all be yours if you forgive your brother today." The man will ultimately pardon his brother in faith, and then walk together with him towards their final abode. The Prophet ﷺ ended this narration by issuing the following statement:

اِتَّقُوا اللهَ وَأَصْلِحُوا ذَاتَ بَيْنِكُمْ فَإِنَّ اللهَ يُصْلِحُ بَيْنَ المُسْلِمِينَ.

"Fear Allah and make peace between yourselves, for even Allah will make peace between the believers."

One who lives
a life of impoverishment
will be far off from
the trappings and
temptations of this world;
and because one would
have experienced a life
of austerity, one will
ultimately be saved from
most of the trials and
tests of the Hereafter.

In the last part of this statement, the Prophet ﷺ was alluding to the Qur'ānic verse:

وَنَزَعْنَا مَا فِي صُدُورِهِم مِّنْ غِلٍّ إِخْوَانًا عَلَىٰ سُرُرٍ مُّتَقَابِلِينَ.

"While We shall have plucked out of their breasts any trace of rancour towards one another, true brethren on blissful raised couches facing each other."[70]

On one occasion, a close friend of mine requested me to serve as a mediator in an outstanding dispute he had with a fellow Muslim brother. This friend specifically noted that he would prefer to resolve their differences in this world rather than unnecessarily delay it to the moment of standing at the *Qanṭarah*. No Muslim will want to delay his or her entrance into Paradise on the Last Day, as it may lead to greater complications. For instance, if one fails to amicably eliminate tensions with one's Muslim brethren, this may in fact lead to a downgrading of one's rank in the otherworld.

In an important *ḥadīth*, Abū Hurayrah ؓ narrated that the Prophet ﷺ said: "The poor Muslims will enter Paradise before the rich Muslims by half a day [of the days of the afterlife], the length of which is 500 years." This is the case since the Last Day will be temporally equivalent to one thousand worldly years. A person who reads this narration might *prima facie* presume that material affluence is intrinsically blameworthy, while poverty is praiseworthy in absolute terms. However, such an understanding is in fact incorrect; instead, this *ḥadīth*

---

70 *Al-Ḥijr*, 47.

must be read in the same manner as other reports regarding the Day of Judgement, such as the narration regarding the *Ḥawḍ*. While the narrations concerning the latter mention that the first people to reach it will be the poor members of the Emigrants (*Muhājirūn*), this obviously does not preclude the senior Companion Abū Bakr ﵁, since a *ḥadīth* mentions that he will be the first person after the Prophet ﷺ to enter Paradise. In fact, when looked at holistically, the teachings of the Prophet indicate that in terms of virtue and rank, the rich but grateful person (*ghanī shākir*) has the same spiritual rank as the poor but patient person (*faqīr ṣābir*). This also explains the *ḥadīth* which mentions that envy is permissible in the case of two individuals: (1) the person who sincerely disseminates the knowledge that Allah ﷻ has gifted him, and (2) the person who sincerely spends the wealth that Allah ﷻ blessed him with. But in empirical terms, the majority of the inhabitants of Paradise will be from among the impoverished and financially disadvantaged people. This is because the state of poverty is instrumentally valuable insofar as it diverts one from the material pleasures of this world. One who lives a life of impoverishment will be far off from the trappings and temptations of this world; and because one would have experienced a life of austerity, one will ultimately be saved from most of the trials and tests of the Hereafter.

Abū Hurayrah ﵁ narrated that on one occasion the Prophet ﷺ addressed Abū Bakr ﵁ and a number of senior Companions by stating:

مَنْ أَنْفَقَ زَوْجَيْنِ فِي سَبِيلِ اللَّهِ نُودِيَ فِي الْجَنَّةِ: يَا عَبْدَ اللهِ هذَا خَيْرٌ، فَمَنْ كَانَ مِنْ أَهْلِ الصَّلاَةِ، دُعِيَ مِنْ بَابِ الصَّلاَةِ. وَمَنْ كَانَ مِنْ أَهْلِ الْجِهَادِ، دُعِيَ مِنْ بَابِ الْجِهَادِ، وَمَنْ كَانَ مِنْ أَهْلِ الصَّدَقَةِ، دُعِيَ مِنْ بَابِ الصَّدَقَةِ، وَمَنْ كَانَ مِنْ أَهْلِ الصِّيَامِ، دُعِيَ مِنْ بَابِ الرَّيَّانِ.

"Whoever spends a pair of things for the sake of Allah, then he will receive a call from the gates of Paradise: 'O servant of Allah, this is good.' Whoever was of the people of prayer (ṣalāh) shall be called from its gate; whoever was of the people of jihad shall be called from its gate. As for the people of fasting (ṣiyām), they shall be called from a special gate known as al-Rayyān. Finally, those who are among the people of voluntary charity (ṣadaqah) shall be called from its gate."

Upon hearing this beautiful proclamation, Abū Bakr started to wonder whether a person could possibly be called from all the gates of Paradise. He subsequently asked the Prophet: "Will there be anyone who will be called from all these gates?" There is no doubt that being called from any one of these doors entails a level of goodness that is beyond quantification. However, Abū Bakr aspired to raise his standing on the Day of Judgement to the highest degree possible, such that he would be called by the angels standing by the eight doors of Paradise. In response to his question, the Prophet ﷺ said:

نَعَمْ، وَأَرْجُو أَنْ تَكُونَ مِنْهُمْ.

"Yes, it is possible. And I hope that you will be amongst them."

Another notable *ḥadīth* provides a useful formula which opens the gates of Paradise for its reciter. In this beautiful narration, the Prophet ﷺ said:

مَا مِنْكُمْ مِنْ أَحَدٍ يَتَوَضَّأُ فَيُبْلِغُ أَوْ فَيُسْبِغُ الْوَضُوءَ ثُمَّ يَقُولُ : أَشْهَدُ أَنْ لَا إِلَهَ إِلَّا اللَّهُ وَأَنَّ مُحَمَّدًا عَبْدُ اللَّهِ وَرَسُولُهُ إِلَّا فُتِحَتْ لَهُ أَبْوَابُ الْجَنَّةِ الثَّمَانِيَةُ يَدْخُلُ مِنْ أَيِّهَا شَاءَ.

"None of you performs ritual ablution (wuḍū') by carefully washing his limbs one by one and then says, 'I testify that there is no God except Allah, alone without any partners, and I testify that Muhammad is His servant and Messenger' except that the eight gates of Paradise will be opened for him such that he can enter from whichever one he wishes."

A version of this report adds the following request at the end of the aforementioned supplication:

اللَّهُمَّ اجْعَلْنِي مِنَ التَّوَّابِينَ وَاجْعَلْنِي مِنَ الْمُتَطَهِّرِينَ.

"O Allah, make me from among the repentant and make me from amongst those who purify themselves."

One cannot imagine the beauty of such a scene, namely when all eight gates of Paradise are opened before one, with angels near each entrance loudly calling out one's name. But the one who will be honoured with the blessing of entering Paradise first will be none other than the Messenger of Allah ﷺ. In one *ḥadīth*, the Prophet ﷺ mentioned that upon approaching the gate of Paradise on the Day of Judgement, he will request that it be opened. Just like in the case of the

One cannot imagine the beauty of a scene, in which all eight gates of Paradise are opened before one, with angels near each entrance loudly calling out one's name. But the one who will be honoured with the blessing of entering Paradise first will be the Messenger of Allah ﷺ.

miraculous night journey of *al-Isrāʾ wa al-Miʿrāj*, an angel will appear and ask:

مَنْ أَنْتَ؟

"Who are you?"

In response to the angel, the Prophet ﷺ will simply mention his name: "Muhammad."

The angel—who is gatekeeping of Paradise—will then say:

بِكَ أُمِرْتُ أَلَّا أَفْتَحَ لِأَحَدٍ قَبْلَكَ.

"I have been ordered not to open for anyone before you."

Upon hearing this proclamation, the Prophet ﷺ will proceed ahead and ultimately enter Paradise. The remaining prophets and messengers ﷷ will closely follow his lead and step inside the blessed abode as well. Other virtuous groups and classes of people will then be permitted to advance forward, such as the Companions, the blessed household of the Prophet ﷺ, the martyrs, the people of truth and justice, as well as the individuals who are protected under the shade of Allah's Throne. From that moment onwards one will never experience or suffer from grief, sadness, or depression, as Paradise shall be the abode of eternal bliss and happiness.

30

One's Eternal Home

Despite possessing a high rank in objective terms, the position of second place is always deemed to be suboptimal; quite naturally, one always wishes to be the first place winner. Such a psychological reaction is deeply-rooted in human nature. But a feeling like this *prima facie* poses as a problem for the lower-ranking members of Paradise, since one may naturally ask: will one feel jealous of the sincerely pious believers who get higher stations than one? The response to this question is that due to the infinite mercy of Allah ﷻ, the lower members (*masākīn*) of Paradise will not feel any grievances or feelings of resentment, as they will realise that they have been granted the highest degree of benefits. In other words, the hearts and minds of all the inhabitants of Paradise will be fully content and satisfied. But of course, according to the Islamic ethos, one must always seek the best station possible.

The Prophet ﷺ said:

إِذَا سَأَلْتُمُ اللهَ الجَنَّةَ فَاسْأَلُوهُ الفِرْدَوْسَ الأَعْلَى.

"When you ask Allah for Paradise, then ensure that you ask Him for the Highest Garden (al-Firdaws al-Aʿlā)."

From this *ḥadīth*, one learns that one should aspire to attain the highest rank available and exert the necessary efforts to achieve it; one should not be content with the bare minimum. In any case, there are Prophetic sayings which explicitly indicate that the last group of individuals to enter Paradise are former inhabitants of Hellfire; they will be asked to enter beautiful and magnificent residences that have their names engraved on them. The previously existing dwellers of Paradise will eagerly await their arrival, and will even playfully coin for them a term alluding to their original abode: "the ex-inhabitants of *Jahannam*" (*al-Jahannamiyyūn*). In a striking and thought-provoking narration, the Prophet ﷺ said:

وَرَأَيْتُ رَجُلاً مِنْ أُمَّتِي انْتَهَى إِلَى أَبْوَابِ الْجَنَّةِ فَغُلِّقَتِ الأَبْوَابُ دُونَهُ، فَجَاءَتْهُ شَهَادَةُ أَنْ لاَ إِلَهَ إِلاَّ اللَّهُ، فَفَتَحَتِ الأَبْوَابَ وَأَدْخَلَتْهُ الْجَنَّةَ.

"I saw a man from my Ummah who came to the gates of Paradise, and the gates were shut in his face. But then his testimony of faith (shahādah) of lā ilāha illā Allāh (there is no God but Allah) came to him, took him by his hand, and entered him into Paradise."

In another oft-cited report, the Prophet ﷺ shared this remarkable vision:

إِنِّي لَأَعْلَمُ آخِرَ أَهْلِ النَّارِ خُرُوجًا مِنْهَا وَآخِرُ أَهْلِ الجَنَّةِ دُخُولًا الجَنَّةَ.

"Indeed I know the very last person who will come out of Hellfire as well as the last dweller of Paradise to enter Paradise."

One should pause and reflect on the ramifications of this *ḥadīth*. Undoubtedly, this low-ranking person must have committed sins of the greatest magnitude during his life. Furthermore, his faith (*īmān*) was likely wavering and flickering throughout his lifetime, with his belief in Allah ﷻ and His Messenger ﷺ having a negligible impact on his life and conduct. Despite the minuteness of his *īmān* and the severity of his sins and faults, Allah ﷻ will still shower him with His mercy and allow him to come out of Hellfire. The Prophet ﷺ dramatically described this man's departure from the Hellfire as follows:

يَمْشِي مَرَّةً، وَيَكْبُو مَرَّةً، وَتَسْفَعُهُ النَّارُ مَرَّةً ، فَإِذَا مَا جَاوَزَهَا الْتَفَتَ إِلَيْهَا، فَقَالَ: تَبَارَكَ الَّذِي نَجَّانِي مِنْكِ ، لَقَدْ أَعْطَانِي اللهُ شَيْئًا مَا أَعْطَاهُ أَحَدًا مِنَ الْأَوَّلِينَ وَالْآخِرِينَ.

"He will momentarily walk, then stumble on other occasions, and even be scorched by Hellfire as he proceeds to come out of it. Once he is past it, he will turn around towards it and say: 'Glory be to the One Who has saved me from you. Allah has granted that which He has not granted anyone of old or of late.'"

While this person praises his Lord for His deliverance, Allah ﷻ will arouse his interest by causing a tree to sprout and grow before his very eyes. After observing the tree momentarily, he will call upon Allah and say:

أَيْ رَبِّ ، أَدْنِنِي مِنْ هَذِهِ الشَّجَرَةِ فَلِأَسْتَظِلَّ بِظِلِّهَا ، وَأَشْرَبَ مِنْ مَائِهَا.

"O my Lord, draw me closer to this tree so that I may take shelter under its shade and drink of its water."

In other words, the man will wish to have the tree in his possession so that he may take advantage of its beneficial properties. Allah ﷻ will respond to his plea by stating:

يَا ابْنَ آدَمَ ، لَعَلِّي إِنْ أَعْطَيْتُكَهَا سَأَلْتَنِي غَيْرَهَا.

"O son of Adam, it may be the case that if I give it to you, you will then ask for more."

The man will promptly state, "No, my Lord," thereby promising that he will not request anything else. Consequently, his request will be granted. Shortly thereafter, Allah ﷻ will cause yet another tree to sprout, but this tree is much bigger than the first one. It will thus provide a larger area of shade and store a larger volume of water in its perimeter. After laying his eyes on this second tree, the man will supplicate to his Lord and say:

أَيْ رَبِّ، أَدْنِنِي مِنْ هَذِهِ لِأَشْرَبَ مِنْ مَائِهَا وَأَسْتَظِلَّ بِظِلِّهَا، لَا أَسْأَلُكَ غَيْرَهَا.

"O my Lord, draw me closer to this one, so that I may take shelter under its shade and drink of its water. I promise that I will not ask for anything else besides it."

Allah ﷻ will remind His servant of the previous promise that he made, namely that he would not ask for anything else after being granted the first tree. But the servant will amend his earlier pledge by stating that this second tree will be the final thing he will ask for. Allah ﷻ will accept his request and will thereby allow him to benefit from the second tree. However, a short time later, Allah will cause a third tree to sprout adjacent to the entrance of Paradise. Due to its proximity to the blessed abode, it will be even more luscious and beautiful than the last tree. In fact, the water stored under it will be sweet and refreshing. After he sees the third tree, the man will immediately say:

أَيْ رَبِّ، أَدْنِنِي مِنْ هَذِهِ لِأَشْرَبَ مِنْ مَائِهَا وَأَسْتَظِلَّ بِظِلِّهَا، لَا أَسْأَلُكَ غَيْرَهَا.

"O my Lord, draw me closer to this third one, so that I may take shelter under its shade and drink of its water. I promise that I will not ask for anything else besides it."

Allah ﷻ will remind His servant of his second modified promise, but the man will reiterate his assurances that this will be his third and final request. Subsequently, Allah will grant the man his wish and allow him to be in close proximity to the third tree. But at this point, the man will be near the entrance of Paradise, and as a result he will be able to see the pleasures and marvels that lie therein. Moreover, the *ḥadīth* also adds the following point:

فَإِذَا أَدْنَاهُ مِنْهَا فَيَسْمَعُ أَصْوَاتَ أَهْلِ الْجَنَّةِ.

"When He brings him close to the third tree he will hear the voices of the people of Paradise."

From his vantage point, the man will be able to directly observe the happy state of the inhabitants of Paradise. Such a sight will affect him a great deal, and he will immediately turn to Allah and supplicate:

أَيْ رَبِّ، أَدْخِلْنِيهَا.

"O my Lord, make me enter it."

After receiving this fourth request, Allah ﷻ will reply with His own set of questions:

يَا ابْنَ آدَمَ مَا يَصْرِينِي مِنْكَ؟ أَيُرْضِيكَ أَنْ أُعْطِيَكَ الدُّنْيَا وَمِثْلَهَا مَعَهَا؟

"O son of Adam, what will cause you to cease making all these requests? Will it please you if I were to give you the entire world and its equivalent along with it?"

The Muslim servant will respond to this offer by stating:

يَا رَبِّ، أَتَسْتَهْزِئُ مِنِّي وَأَنْتَ رَبُّ الْعَالَمِينَ؟

"O Lord, are You mocking me when You are the Lord of the worlds?"

Ibn Masʿūd رضي الله عنه—who was the narrator of the *ḥadīth*—began to laugh while relating this statement. The listeners were puzzled by this spectacle, and they sought clarification for this sudden and seemingly unexplainable turn. Ibn Masʿūd explained that the Prophet ﷺ also laughed when he related this dialogue between the servant and Allah ﷻ. The Prophet ﷺ explained his action by noting that Allah Himself laughed after the servant asked Him whether He was mocking him.

According to the *ḥadīth*, Allah's response will ultimately be:

إِنِّي لَا أَسْتَهْزِئُ مِنْكَ وَلَكِنِّي عَلَى مَا أَشَاءُ قَادِرٌ.

"I am not mocking you, but I am capable of doing whatever I will."

Then in His infinite grace, Allah ﷻ will admit this man into the lowest level of Paradise, which will be better than the current universe by ten times. Despite his relatively low rank, the man will still believe that he is the most fortunate and prosperous individual in the entire cosmos.

Paradise will be an eternal abode of bliss and happiness for the believers. Every one of its inhabitants will know his palace even better than his dwelling in this temporal world. No one will experience any difficulties in finding or receiving what he or she wishes for. While the Muslim is indulging in the pleasures found in this blissful abode, he or she will rejoice and praise Allah ﷻ for facilitating his or her entry to Paradise. For example, upon seeing the luscious gardens of Paradise, the believers will say:

ٱلْحَمْدُ لِلَّهِ ٱلَّذِي صَدَقَنَا وَعْدَهُۥ وَأَوْرَثَنَا ٱلْأَرْضَ نَتَبَوَّأُ مِنَ ٱلْجَنَّةِ حَيْثُ نَشَآءُ.

"Praise be to Allah Who has fulfilled His promise to us, and made us inherit the land to settle in Paradise wherever we please."[71]

---

71 *Al-Zumar*, 74.

They will also be fully aware that their guidance and righteousness were exclusively due to Allah:

الْحَمْدُ لِلَّهِ الَّذِي هَدَانَا لِهَٰذَا وَمَا كُنَّا لِنَهْتَدِيَ لَوْلَا أَنْ هَدَانَا اللَّهُ.

"Praise be to Allah for guiding us to this. We would have never been guided if Allah had not guided us."[72]

Thus, the believers will profusely articulate their gratefulness and thanks to the Lord ﷻ for every blessed moment they savour in Paradise. In fact, they will recall how Allah showered them with His mercy by instilling in them the propensity to perform acts of good consistently in the temporal world. However, despite reflecting on the Creator's generosity and magnificence, the believers will be reminded that they are worthy of this blessed station due to their own virtuous beliefs and actions. They will be told that they are the rightful inheritors of the eternal abode of Paradise as a result of their belief in Allah and their observance of good conduct:

وَتِلْكَ ٱلْجَنَّةُ ٱلَّتِيٓ أُورِثْتُمُوهَا بِمَا كُنتُمْ تَعْمَلُونَ.

"That is the Paradise which you will be awarded for what you used to do."[73]

---

[72] *Al-Aʿrāf*, 43.

[73] *Al-Zukhruf*, 72

Another Qur'ānic verse indicates that the angels will frequently enter in upon the believers from every entrance or walkway of their palace and warmly congratulate them by saying:

سَلَامٌ عَلَيْكُم بِمَا صَبَرْتُمْ فَنِعْمَ عُقْبَى الدَّارِ.

"Peace be upon you for your perseverance. How excellent is the ultimate abode!"[74]

Consequently, the believers will find themselves in a joyous atmosphere; they will constantly have the comfort of embracing their family members, loved ones, and the prophets around them. There is no greater blessing than to be surrounded by the prophets and the righteous for all eternity. This fortuitous trend officially commences on the Last Day's closing session, when Allah ﷻ will honour the people of Paradise by requesting them to come forward. Besides giving them the glad tidings of the blissful abode, He will further cheer their hearts by destroying their locations in Hellfire and then informing them that the trials of the Day of Judgement have formally come to a close. Allah ﷻ will then inform them that death itself has been destroyed, which ultimately means that they will reside in Paradise forever and be in a state of happiness endlessly. Furthermore, in one *ḥadīth* the Prophet ﷺ mentioned that, for the people of Paradise, the entire duration of the Day of Judgement will feel like the short interval between the Ẓuhr and ʿAsr prayers. In other words, all the aforementioned trials and tests will not feel burdensome for the believers. Upon being placed in

[74] *Al-Raʿd*, 24.

the eternal abode of bliss, Allah ﷻ will honour the believers by summoning them with the following vocative expression:

يَا أَهْلَ الجَنَّةِ

"O people of Paradise!"

The inhabitants of Paradise will at once respond to their Lord by stating: "Here we are, O Allah, and pleased to respond to You." Allah ﷻ will then ask the following question:

هَلْ رَضِيتُمْ

"Are you pleased with your current state of affairs?"

The believers will be surprised to receive such a question, and will subsequently state:

وَمَا لَنَا لَا نَرْضَى وَقَدْ أَعْطَيْتَنَا مَا لَمْ تُعْطِ أَحَدًا مِن خَلْقِكَ.

"Why should we not be pleased when You have given us what You have not given to any other of Your created beings?"

In another version of this report, the believers will also enumerate the grand blessings granted to them by their Lord ﷻ:

أَلَمْ تُبَيِّضْ وُجُوهَنَا وَتُزَحْزِحْنَا عَنِ النَّارِ، وَتُدْخِلْنَا الْجَنَّةَ؟

"Did You not already illuminate our faces, protect us from Hellfire, and allow us to enter Paradise?"

In other words, they will be fully content and satisfied with their state, such that it does not occur to them to ask for any further material or spiritual benefits. Yet, Allah ﷻ will still say:

أَلَا أُعْطِيكُمْ أَفْضَلَ مِنْ ذَلِكَ؟

"Shall I not give you all something better than that?"

In amazement, the believers will respond:

وَأَيُّ شَيْءٍ أَفْضَلُ مِنْ ذَلِكَ؟

"And what could possibly be better than all of the above?"

Allah ﷻ will gracefully grant them the following blessing:

أُحِلُّ عَلَيْكُمْ رِضْوَانِي فَلَا أَسْخَطُ عَلَيْكُمْ بَعْدَهُ أَبَدًا.

"I overspread you with My good pleasure such that I will never be angry with you."

This divine declaration constitutes a corroboration of the following Qur'ānic verse:

رَضِيَ اللَّهُ عَنْهُمْ وَرَضُوا عَنْهُ.

"Allah is pleased with them and they are pleased with Him."[75]

For the Muslims, there is nothing more reassuring and comforting than hearing their Creator ﷻ proclaim His infinite love and satisfaction with them. What further amplifies such

[75] *Al-Mā'idah*, 119.

a proclamation is His assurance that nothing will ever cause Him to become angry with them. Receiving such an absolute and eternal declaration of love from the Lord of the worlds ﷻ is even greater than Paradise itself; such a tremendous reward makes worthwhile every sacrifice and trouble endured in this temporal world. But in His infinite grace, Allah will shower the believers with a blessing that is even greater than all the aforementioned assurances. This special divine gift has been indirectly mentioned to in the following verse:

لِلَّذِينَ أَحۡسَنُواْ ٱلۡحُسۡنَىٰ وَزِيَادَةٌ.

"Those who do good will have the finest reward and more."[76]

The exegetes of the Qur'ān note that the statement "and more" is an allusion to seeing Allah in the Hereafter. This view is supported by a notable *ḥadīth* in which the Companions asked the Prophet ﷺ regarding the meaning of this verse. The Prophet ﷺ ultimately said:

فَيَكْشِفُ الْحِجَابَ، فَمَا أُعْطُوا شَيْئًا أَحَبَّ إِلَيْهِمْ مِنَ النَّظَرِ إِلَى رَبِّهِمْ عَزَّ وَجَلَّ.

"Allah will lift the veil [between Him and them], and nothing will be more beloved to them than seeing their Almighty Lord."

Seeing Allah ﷻ in the blissful abode of Paradise will be unlike His perception on the Day of Judgement, for in the former case their Creator will be pleased and smile towards them. Upon noticing that the divine gaze is coupled with love and affection, the believers will experience an unprecedented

---

[76] *Yūnus*, 26.

level of happiness and joy. For as the Prophet ﷺ indicated in a *ḥadīth*, none of the bounties and luxuries of Paradise—such as its mansions, gardens, and rivers—can match the pleasure of the beatific vision. In fact, none of the bounties and luxuries of the entire universe can match the knowledge that Allah is pleased with one, even if it is not possible to see Him.

We ask Allah ﷻ to make us all inheritors of the blissful abode of Paradise. We also ask Him to provide us with the physical and spiritual means to perform the righteous deeds necessary to enter into the eternal abode of happiness. O Allah, we believe in You, Your Prophet, and Your religion and we are fully content with You as our Lord, Islam as our religion, and the Prophet Muhammad ﷺ as the final Messenger. O Allah, we are Your humble servants, so be content with us, provide our hearts with sincerity, and facilitate our spiritual guidance. O Allah, give us the strength and determination to undertake acts of good and to avoid all sins and vices, and grant us all admission to Paradise so that we may be blessed with the beatific vision and the everlasting company of Your Prophet. *Āmīn*.